A **WESTERN HORSEMAN**®

Raise Your Hand
IF YOU LOVE HORSES

Pat Parelli's Journey from Zero to Hero

By Pat Parelli
With Kathy Swan

Edited by Cathy Martindale and Kate Riordan

Raise Your Hand

IF YOU LOVE HORSES

Published by
WESTERN HORSEMAN® magazine

3850 North Nevada Ave.
Box 7980
Colorado Springs, CO 80933-7980

www.westernhorseman.com

Design, Typography, and Production
Western Horseman
Fort Worth, Texas

Front and Back Cover Photos By
Co Co

Printing
Branch Smith
Fort Worth, Texas

©2004 by Western Horseman
a registered trademark of
Morris Communications Corporation
725 Broad Street
Augusta, GA 30901

First Printing: December 2004

ISBN 0-911647-75-9

CONTENTS

DEDICATION &
ACKNOWLEDGEMENTS

I dedicate this book to all the horses and mules who've put up with my inadequacies and still offered me so much, and to all the exceptional humans who've really believed in me. I also dedicate this book to your future. May you be as good with horses at half my age.

Kelly	Double Trouble
Jesse	Sparky
Bridget	Scamp
Mayday	Liberty
Salty	Magic
Thumper	Casper

And the other 12,000-plus horses I've touched.

Doris Parelli	Tom Dorrance
Jack Parelli	Ray Hunt
Caton Parelli	Dr. Bob Miller
Marlene (Parelli) Delanini	Tony Ernst
Linda Parelli	Neil Pye
Mark Weiler	Yvonne Wilcox
Ronnie Willis	

Please look on the Acknowledgements page in my first book,
Natural Horse-Man-Ship, for the dozens of other special people
I deem important in my life.

FOREWORD

Over the years it's been rewarding to watch my son, Pat, develop his God-given talents and natural abilities into the person he has become – a master horseman, great entertainer and a very loving, generous and caring man.

As a baby, Pat loved to entertain; as a little boy, he was very curious and asked hundreds of questions; and, as a young man, he cultivated his great love of people and animals.

It's gratifying to see him intertwine his love for horses and his sense of humor into a program that has helped so many people with their love of horses.

As his mother, I'm very proud of him, not only for what he has accomplished, but for the person he is.

Doris Parelli

PHOTO BY COCO

Pat and his mom Doris.

PREFACE

Before I started co-writing his first book almost 15 years ago, Pat Parelli asked me why I wanted to write it. I explained, "Because I think it's going to be a very important book." I didn't know Pat or his program all that well back then, but after attending only one clinic, my instincts were on full alert and a little voice inside me said, "Pay attention here." Indeed, my prediction came true. *Natural Horse-Man-Ship* has become *Western Horseman's* all-time best-seller, and knowing the equine book industry, I daresay it's probably one of the most popular horsemanship titles ever.

I can't count the number of people who've thanked me over the years for writing it. Many have said it was their first exposure to natural horsemanship, and that it changed the way they approached horses forever. From a writer's perspective, when a book has that kind of impact, it does the writer's heart good.

One of my most indelible memories of Pat happened at the first Savvy Conference in 1997. All of the attendees were standing by a round corral waiting for Pat to make his entrance. Did he ever make one! Pat came flying in at a high lope on Scamp – bareback and bridleless. When he got to the corral, he turned right and charged up a fair-sized hill, stopped at the top, spun around and roared back down. He came back through the crowd and performed a fancy sliding stop in front of the corral. Then, he and his horse took their bow. He riveted everyone's attention, mine included. That kind of partnership and communication between man and horse is what all of us who love horses are seeking. Pat's mission in life is to raise the level of horsemanship worldwide. I believe he's doing it.

In my long journalism career, I've been fortunate to have chronicled the best the horse industry has to offer. I've covered many prestigious equine events and competitions and interviewed and written about hundreds of horsemen and women. Maybe that's my mission in life, and for that this writer and horse lover is grateful.

It is my opinion, however, that through all my travels and in all my experiences, I know of no one who has had a more positive and far-reaching influence on horses and horse people than Pat Parelli.

Dr. Robert Miller, in his "People's Perspectives on Pat" in Chapter 12, said that he thought Pat's name would be remembered a century from now. I'd like to go one better. I believe Pat Parelli will go down in history as one of the greatest horsemen the world has ever known. I feel privileged to have played even a small part in helping the world come to know Pat and his philosophy. The impetus for this second book sprang from my desire to continue that same journey.

Many of you are familiar with Pat's 45 P's, and, if not, please read them in the back of this book. They state: "Pat Parelli proudly presents his provocative and progressive program…" and so on.

In *Raise Your Hand if You Love Horses*, I proudly present Pat Parelli and his provocative and progressive life.

Kathy Swan

PROLOGUE

I t's all my parents' fault. Both my dad and I are passionate about our careers. Neither of us thinks of our work as a job; it's who we are. He's Jack Parelli, the world's best furniture rep. I'm Pat Parelli, whose mission in life is to advance the cause of horsemanship worldwide, and I'm doing it. Actually, my father has a bigger fan club than I have. People really love him, and his good friends have been his loyal friends forever. I find that to be my case, as well.

My mom, Doris, has always been proud of me. I think she knew I had something special, not pulling me but pushing me from behind. Maybe it was spiritual, I don't know. She's sensed that about me and has always been supportive of anything I do.

In my estimation, we live in 12-year cycles. From age 1 to 12, you're a child. From 13 to 24 you're a young adult. By the time you're 36, you're a mature adult and have probably decided which career suits you best. At age 48, you probably either made it in your life's work or you didn't. By that time, it seems as if you've lived through four seasons; in other words, a lifetime. Then, you enter a second life cycle. Now that I've lived one full life cycle, and so have my parents, I find that we have more to talk about than ever before. I'm not just a kid anymore; I've experienced a full generation of life, as have my parents.

Dad is in his early 70s and mom in her late 60s as of the printing of this book. Now, more than ever, my parents and I are closer. Their permanent home is in California, but they purchased property in Ocala, Florida, on a golf course, just a few miles from where our new facility is. Linda, Caton and I will be able to spend a lot more time with them during the winter.

I think, in the end, all children really do want to please their parents. That's universal. I regard myself as a product of both my parents – tough like my dad, but gentle like my mom. Using my parents as a model, I came up with the Love, Language, Leadership concept that I use in my seminars, for my parents gave me all three as I was growing up.

A lot of people say their parents abused them or their misfortune in life is their parents' fault. I absolutely think that my solid foundation and success are my parents' fault. I give them the credit for a great beginning in life.

Jack and Doris Parelli.

SOUL MATES

How do I begin to talk about one of the most extraordinary beings I've ever met? Throughout my life doors have opened and I've fallen through them because I was prepared to accept the choices life offered me, and I knew there was always choice.

My teachers of education and sales and marketing had me mentally prepared. My teachers of philosophy had me emotionally prepared. My teachers of riding (my horses and instructors) and my sheer athleticism and bravado had me physically prepared. What I wasn't prepared for was my total life change.

When I first met Pat, I didn't realize we were soul mates. I didn't know what meeting your soul mate felt like, and it was really only in reflection that I understood.

Many of my teachers (mentioned in this book) are some of the most progressive and influential in the world, even if their names are not well known. At a seminar I attended, one of them said, "Some teachers can influence the way you feel; others influence the way you think; and others influence the way you act. It's a very, very rare teacher who can influence all three." When I met Pat, I recognized I'd met one of those.

Years ago, Pat and I had a deeply philosophical talk, and in it he told me, "If I can, I must." I completely understood what he meant. His role in the world and for horse people especially supercedes virtually everything else. Pat will go down in history for what he has done. I truly think that one day people will say, "Horsemanship changed when Parelli started."

Pat is unusual as a teacher, mentor and celebrity, and he always credits the people who've shaped him. He tells his students, "My goal is to have people be better than I am at half my age," and he means it. He doesn't hold back information, but he doesn't give it out at the wrong time in someone's development either. Neither does he give it to doubters or people with the wrong motives when it comes to horses.

I'm so privileged to be part of a revolution in the way horses are treated and people are empowered. What I brought to Pat was an energy to help people realize their dream with horses no matter where they live or how little they could afford. I offered some structure and a bit of business savvy. And over the years we've assimilated a team of people who've advanced that beyond anything I could've done. In turn, it's led me to another evolution I never would have dared dream – that of teaching my passion (horsemanship) and in developing supportive methods to Pat's essential program.

People ask me, "What's it like living with Pat? Don't you have husband-and-wife issues when he tells you what to do with respect to horsemanship?" I tell them, "It's easy because I never forget who the real master is. I ask him for advice all the time."

It's also unusual for a man to push and champion his wife to levels she never dreamed of and to listen to the advances she's made because of his encouragement. That's the kind of man Pat Parelli is, and that's why he's changing the world of horses and horse-people as we know it.

Linda Parelli

INTRODUCTION

I received a letter and a nice bottle of wine from a couple of students who spent two weeks riding with us. The letter said, "Thanks for the time we were at the center. Pat and Linda, you've not started a church, you've started a religion."

That's a deeply moving statement, and one that humbles me. Yet, it speaks to my soul, not because I wanted to start anything that resembles a religion, but because it validates my life and what I've tried to do with it.

I've always had an incurable disease called "share-itis," a burning desire to share a good thing with other people. All my life I've tried to share everything that I thought was worth sharing, and to help other people get there more efficiently and in a more accelerated manner. It shouldn't take a lifetime to learn someone else's lifetime of study. My life has been about horses and horsemanship and helping other people become partners with their horses.

To be good with horses, you don't need to be born with a silver spoon in your mouth or have great horsemen for parents. I certainly didn't. I hope this book inspires you to realize that successful people spell "luck" as "w-o-r-k," defined as when preparation meets opportunity. That's as true in the world of horses as it is anywhere else.

Through passion, focus, discipline and energy, I've tried to raise the level of horsemanship worldwide and make a better place for horses. In this book, I want to share with you how I've lived my journey, from zero to hero.

Part 1 Overview

SEARCH FOR IDENTITY

When we're young, we try to decide what we're going to be when we grow up. That's universal with all of us. Something in our souls searches for an identity.

For me, I found myself gravitating toward horses from the time I was very young. Once I got the chance to be around them, that was it for me. I never had a moment when I looked back and wanted anything else.

I feel I must be one of the luckiest people in the world to be born when I was, where I was, to the parents I had, and then in an environment and in a time that offered an opportunity to see the nation's best in rodeo and horse show competitions.

I had the Salinas and Livermore rodeos and the Grand National Horse Show and Rodeo practically in my back yard. Dr. Billy Linfoot, the famous veterinarian who was a nine-goal polo player and a horse-tamer, was nearby. Within 200 miles of where I was born, there was a giant melting pot of great horsemen and horse activities.

That said, I know lots of people who were born at the same time, had the same experiences and opportunities and didn't take advantage of them.

One of my fondest memories, as a child, was going to the Grand National at the Cow Palace in San Francisco. From the time I was nine years old until I was 18, I went there every night for two weeks. I couldn't get enough of it. The way the performances worked, there'd be a rodeo event alternating with a horse-show event, followed by an entertaining act. I saw the best of everything: rodeo riders, gaited horses, rope horses, fine harness horses, jumpers, stock horses, reiners, cutters, you name it. Plus, I got to see the best cattle and livestock in a multistate area.

The breadth and scope of the horse world that I saw and experienced at the Grand National lit a fire in my soul, and I knew in my heart that I wanted to be around horses all my life.

Here's my story.

1 BIRTH OF A HORSEMAN

*"I was born in Oakland, California,
so I could be near my mother."*

A horseman in the making – Pat, at three years old in 1957, poses on a pony.

A lot of people, including myself, look at other people who're great with horses and assume they were born into it. They often make the assumption that their fathers or mothers must have been great horse people, too.

But that isn't the way it was with me at all. My dad, Jack Parelli, was born in New York. As a young man he was two-times Golden Gloves boxing champion, all-service boxing champion and fought professionally on the West Coast. He also golfed, bowled and played baseball. He's been a wholesale furniture sales rep for many years and still lives in the San Francisco Bay Area with my mother, Doris. As a housewife, mom raised two children, me and my younger sister, Joy, bowled a little and went to church. We were your typical suburban American household. I didn't grow up on a ranch, nor was I born to horse-show folk, nor could I ride before I could walk.

I was born March 17, 1954, in Oak Knoll Naval Hospital, while my dad was stationed at Alameda Naval Air Station in Alameda, California. He wanted to name me Mario, after his favorite singer, Mario Lanza. But my mother nixed that. With me being born on St. Patrick's Day, she wanted to name me something Irish, so my first name is Jack and my second name is Patrick, but everyone called me "Pat."

After my dad got out of the Navy, our family moved to Oakland, California, to a government project neighborhood, full of poor

Jack Parelli, two-time Golden Gloves Champion.

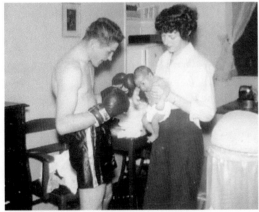

The boxer and his baby. Jack looks on as Doris holds their infant son.

Italians. Our house was on East 14th Street, about as close to Harlem-like as you can get on the West Coast.

My dad was fighting professionally at the time and his manager was a man named Joe Keirsey. Joe was the first horseperson I ever met. In his 70s (as of this book's printing), he still competes in and wins gymkhanas and team pennings.

Joe had only daughters. Our families were really close, and I was the son for both families. Joe was determined to get me into horses.

First Horses

We moved to Newark, California, just south of Oakland, where my dad got a job at a government-subsidized, plastic pipe company. As plant manager, he was given the use of 40 acres that bordered the plant as one of his perks. The plant was right around the corner from the last horse slaughterhouse in the state of California.

The slaughterhouse owner, Jim Augustine, became a family friend. Back then horses were going for three cents a pound, and thousands of mustangs were processed every year.

As a kid, I'd go down to the crowded slaughter pens and look at the hundreds of horses milling around. Watching them really caught my interest. If my parents couldn't find me, they knew where to look – I'd be at those corrals. I didn't learn until years later what the pens were for.

Jim would often go through the corrals and find good, old horses for us kids to ride.

Pat, just a few months old, takes his first look at a horse. He's being held by his Granmother Jennie, and his dad is behind them.

PHOTO BY DORIS PARELLI

A horse for his first Christmas, what else?

So, my first riding horses were actually rescued slaughter horses. My dad and Joe, his ex-manager and still good friend, kept them on the 40 acres surrounding the pipe factory. Joe was the only horseperson in either family, so we relied on him for knowledge about everything from feeding the horses to riding them.

Heroes and Parade Horses

But the slaughterhouse wasn't the only place I ran into horses. I was raised in the era of the Hollywood Western, on television and on the silver screen. My dad's favorite TV shows were "Wyatt Earp," "Have Gun, Will Travel" and "The Rifleman." The only time I got to stay up past my bedtime was to watch one of those shows. I absolutely believe they colored my world and gave me my first heroes – all cowboys. And I wanted to be just like them, and, of course, they all rode horses.

One of the things I enjoyed most growing up in Newark was the annual town parade. We lived one street over from the parade route, and that's where parade participants parked their vehicles and trailers. There were floats, marching bands, baton twirlers, and, of course, mounted units. The horses and riders were decked out in silver saddles and all the parade finery typical of an equestrian unit.

One of my earliest remembrances, as a child of three or four, is the riders painting their horses' hoofs with sparkling glitter hoof polish. They would spray-paint the horses' hoofs on the concrete or sidewalks in the parking area. For months afterward, the hoof prints would still be there, and I was always fascinated with them. In my mind, they were a link to those wondrous creatures in the parade and on TV. I found myself constantly thinking about horses, horses and more horses.

Movin' on up

We found ourselves stepping up in the world. We went from a government-project house to an inexpensive house in Newark, but it was ours. I think it cost my dad about $11,000 back then.

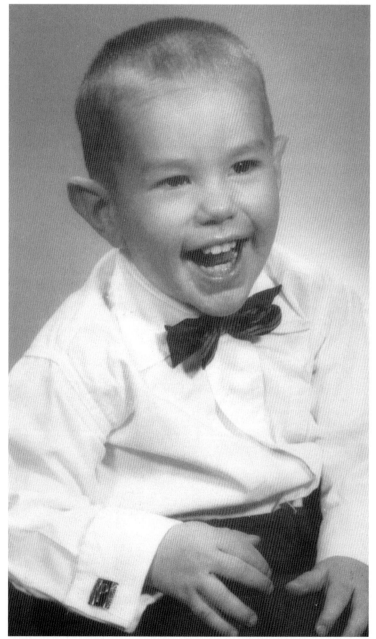

Nine-month-old Pat already had a lot to smile about.

Some years later, we moved to Fremont, and upgraded to a brand new $22,000 tract home, and we thought we'd finally arrived. The tracts of homes were situated in between orchards, farms and the hills outside the East San Francisco Bay Area. Back then, developers chewed up large chunks of farmland to build housing units.

Lucky for me, there were people with small acreages in between the housing tracts, and they owned horses. All I had to do was walk 100 yards, and I'd run into a horse.

At eight years old, I'd definitely be classified as a horse-crazy kid. But all my friends leaned toward minibikes and motorcycles, so I got caught up in that, as well. I was at the age when a young child wants to get on something that moves fast.

Birthday Present

For my ninth birthday, my parents asked me what I wanted. I told them a minibike. Since minibikes were all the rage back then, peer pressure for a bike was strong. When asked if I didn't want a horse instead, I said, "Welllll, I'd like a horse, too." They promptly made the decision for me and took me horse-hunting.

I remember reading the classified ads in the newspaper and, of course, many would read something like, "spirited horse, needs experienced rider." I think those same ads are still running today! But that didn't deter me; I was on track to get a horse.

Naturally, I wanted to buy the first horse we went to look at. But my dad knew better; so we kept searching. Frankly, I really didn't know what I wanted or needed. Anything would do as long as it was a horse.

My dad was now in the business of selling wholesale furniture, which is how we got out of Newark and landed in Fremont. He had connections there with friends who had horses. One of them was a man named Roland Reed, who owned Reed's Auction. On Thursday nights, he sold furniture, used and seconds. The horse auction was on Friday nights, the pig and cow auction on Saturday and on Sunday was the rabbits, chickens and what-not auction.

PHOTO BY DORIS PARELLI

Two-year-old Pat on his tricycle in front of the government housing projects in 1956.

Pat, on a horse, of course, with his mom and Grandma Jennie in 1956.

Always fascinated with animals, two-year-old Pat with his Grandma Margie and her dog.

Pat and his dad in front of their Oakland apartment in 1957.

PHOTO BY DORIS PARELLI

PHOTO BY DORIS PARELLI

My dad asked Roland, an experienced horseman from Oklahoma who had thousands of horses go through his auction, to find a gentle horse for me. Roland found one for $300. Her name was Kelly, a big, buckskin mare who was very laid back.

In those days, every horse came with its own bridle and bit. This one happened to be the cheapest metal bit money could buy. I saw a bunch of them in a tack store not long ago and was surprised to see that they're still being sold.

The day we got Kelly, Roland asked me if I could ride. Of course, I said I could. What else would a kid my age say? I jumped up in the saddle, and my dad said, "Well then, ride her to the stables," which was seven miles away.

My friend and I had already plotted the way. Off we went – he on his bike and me on Kelly.

Even though Kelly was lazy, she was like most horses. Once I got her going, she took off and I couldn't get her stopped. I was riding in tennis shoes and my stirrups were too long. I remember that I looked down and my feet were all the way through the stirrups. Like any other dumb kid, I thought I knew how to ride. As I look back, I don't know how I survived that first ride. I just kicked her to go and pulled back to stop.

I was ecstatic over getting my first horse, but, except for that first ride home, "slow" was Kelly's middle name. I literally had to spank Kelly with a willow switch to get her to trot. There I was at age nine or ten, raring to go. All Kelly would do is slow jog for a few steps and then stop. Of course, my dad was absolutely right – she was perfect as a first horse, but I wanted to go some place faster than a turtle trot.

Growing up to be a Cowboy

From the first moment I got a horse, I knew what I wanted to be when I grew up – a cowboy.

As a kid, I was a *Western Horseman* magazine and *Black Stallion* series fanatic. I started

Just what he wanted for Christmas — a saddle. Pat turned 13 in 1967.

Pat was five when he and his sister, Joy, got their first dog, Lady.

subscribing to the magazine in the early '60s, and I read every book on horses available, but Walter Farley's *Black Stallion* series was my favorite. I read every one of them. I wasn't an avid reader, but they captivated me. In my daydreams those books took me to a place I wanted to go.

The one Farley book that really struck a chord with me was the *The Horse Tamer*. In it, Alec Ramsey's uncle was well known as a horse-whisperer type who traveled the country giving seminars and demonstrations. He had a system for taming horses and traveled around the country showing people what he could do. He'd take on the worst horses that people would bring him. He proved to them that you didn't have to be mean to horses to get through to them, nor did you have to put up with their bad behavior. I remember reading this book and thinking that this would be great work. Little did I know how close to that character I'd become one day.

Auction Go'fer

Because my dad was such good friends with Mr. Reed, I got to work at the auction yard as a go'fer, which I did until I was about 15 or so. I was one of those kids who got on all the auction horses and rode them around the small arena, showing off, while the bidding climbed higher.

On Saturdays, I'd help push the pigs into the auction pen. One day a big sow and her piglets came in. One of the people in the audience asked me to show them a particular pig, so I picked up the cute, little, squealing piglet and went over to the person. The sow saw what I'd done and came for me, and chased me around the pen at least three times. Everyone started laughing as I chucked the piglet, ran for my life and dove through the cables. When I looked up, there were at least 300 people having a good belly laugh. I was the butt of their joke.

Dr. Billy Linfoot

I remember attending my first registered horse auction, put on by Mr. Reed. To attract an audience to the sale, Mr. Reed promoted a demonstration by Dr. Billy Linfoot, who was supposed to get on a wild mustang's back. I was used to watching the mustangs as they came through by the truckloads every Friday night, but no one ever rode a wild one.

Linfoot was the first nine-goal polo player in the United States. As a veterinarian, he was known as an incredible "leg man." As a horseman, he had a reputation as a horse-tamer and was especially good with fixing problem horses.

I sat at ringside and watched as Linfoot did exactly what Alec Ramsey's uncle did in *The*

PHOTO BY DORIS PARELLI

Pat and friend rode in the Newark parade in 1960 on Lady, a rescued slaughter horse.

Horse Tamer. He got on the mustang's back in less than 30 minutes, and he did it in a gentle way. I sat there in awe. That was an enormously significant moment in my life. In my mind, I said, "That guy must be the greatest horseman in the world." I had friends and acquaintances who could ride, but Linfoot could do way more. I said to myself, "That guy is good with horses. I want to be like him."

First Foal

Kelly was getting slower and slower, and I was getting bored with her. She started getting very fat, so we stopped feeding her as much. Finally, someone suggested she might be pregnant. It turns out we must've bought her in that condition and didn't know it. When Kelly was about a month from foaling somebody jokingly commented that since we didn't know who the father was, the foal could possibly be a mule. I was horrified at the thought.

One day in school shortly thereafter, I got a note from my mother saying that Kelly had foaled a male. She didn't know to call it a colt. But I read the writing as "mule," and was devastated. I had to wait the rest of the school day to get home and see the newborn. I was beside myself and not with joy. I wanted a horse, not a mule.

When I got home, I saw that the little bundle was really a colt. Relieved, I named him Thunder. But Thunder didn't have much thunder. He wasn't much of a horse. Later, I traded him as a yearling for $27 and a cheap guitar, since I'd gone guitar-crazy as a pre-teen.

My First Training Project

Now that Kelly was a mom, I no longer had a horse to ride, so my dad took me to another local auction (not Reed's). There, we bought the highest priced horse of the sale – a mare that went for the grand total of $165. Her name was Jesse, a Tennessee Walking Horse/Thoroughbred cross or something unusual like that.

We got her home and put my cheap bit on her. Somebody mentioned something about her being fast and that suited me just fine after slowpoke Kelly.

I rode her around and when it was time to put her up, we put her in our pasture, right on the corner of Mission Boulevard and Highway 680. Once she was in the pasture, I thought I'd cool her out and jumped on her bareback with only a halter. She started walking faster and faster. I pulled back on the halter to try to stop her, which only encouraged her to take off at a gallop. She ran what to me felt like 90 miles an hour straight to the corner. I pulled back as hard as I could, but got no response. I was wearing my first bona fide blue jean jacket. I was so proud of it, and thought I was just like "Stoney Burke," my favorite television character, a rodeo rider played by actor Jack Lord.

Jesse went to the corner, put on the brakes and turned right at the last moment. I was promptly ejected and landed in a 5-strand barbed-wire fence. I didn't get hurt, but I was stuck in the fence, and my jacket was ripped to shreds.

That was my first real feeling of being out of control on a horse. For the first time in my young life, I'd tasted fear. Before that, I had none. Horses to me were something you just got on and rode. Of course, Kelly never went anywhere that fast, so being out of control wasn't a concern.

Jesse, on the other hand, was an impulsive horse, jigged all the time and had lots of issues that got me thinking about horses and their behavior problems. She was my first "training" project.

But, in time, I did get her under control enough to compete on her. She was very fast, and I ran her in barrels and poles in local gymkhanas. I had a double-edged sword in her. She was the fastest horse in my neighborhood, and that thrilled me and my friends, but she was also the most difficult to deal with. I rode the wheels off her anyway. I could put her into a single-foot gait and motor all over the neighborhood.

Down the street from us on Mission Boulevard were several stables, and one of them had a café called Faye and Frank's. It was everyone's favorite watering hole. This joint had a jukebox and sold deli sandwiches, beer and wine, but no hard liquor. The café had a hitching rail out front and riders could tie their horses up with the reins, just like in the movies.

One day, I tied Jesse to the rail, made some sort of knot with my split reins, and went inside to get a soda. Not long after, I heard a huge racket and went outside to see what it was. Jesse had pulled back and ripped out the hitching rail. She was running full bore down Mission Boulevard, dragging a hitching rail that beat her legs with every stride.

Luckily, she didn't get hit by a car. I can remember thinking, "How can I teach a horse never to pull back?"

Jesse was the horse who got me thinking about becoming a horse trainer. I was only about 11 years old at the time. Because of having to deal with all her issues, I spent time daydreaming and theorizing what I'd do with horses in a variety of problem situations. Mentally, that was challenging and fun for me.

At this time I had Kelly's colt, too, so I daydreamed about what I'd do with him. When would I ride Thunder for the first time? When he was six months old, I started leaning over him to get him used to weight

Pat, sparring with his dad, learned to savvy "savvy." His sister Joy is looking on.

on his back. I dreamed about making him a perfect horse. I remember thinking that I wouldn't let Thunder be as impulsive as Jesse. I'd make sure to only walk him on the way home so he wouldn't get barn-sour like Jessie did. I was drawn to the idea of training animals to do things. Interspecies communication was fascinating to me.

Mr. Reed owned (or leased) a half-million-acre ranch in Nevada, and he leased about 20,000 acres around the Bay Area. When I was about 12, I got a job working on Reed's Bay Area ranch.

One summer we gathered about 600 steers off one of the pastures called the Frog Pond pasture. I rode Jesse. One of the steers decided to duck off, and I went after it. Well, instead of heading off the steer, Jesse took off, and I found myself on a full-blown runaway. I pulled back as hard as I could, and I got nothing. The thought occurred to me to run into the frog pond, and I somehow managed to steer her toward it. She ran blindly and never even attempted to stop at the water's edge. She ran headlong into the pond and both of us tumbled over and made a big splash. Neither of us got hurt, but I was one soggy young "cowboy."

Jesse was definitely a big challenge for a little kid. She didn't deter me, however. I was

Pat, 13 years old, with Kelly and her foal Thunder.

PHOTO BY DORIS PARELLI

more determined than ever to find a way to fix behavior problems and deal with the fear, like a cowboy would.

Deadly Gather

I had the chance to work for many of the area's big ranches, where I really got the taste of what it's like to be a working ranch hand.

At one of Reed's ranches, we had to gather the cattle out of a very steep pasture. It was so precipitous that we couldn't get the semi-trucks up to the pasture to truck the cattle out. We had to drive across a couple of properties, including park property. We weren't allowed to push the cattle out on horseback. We had to use a Mack bobtail cattle truck, load up 30 head at a time and drive them six miles down to another set of corrals, where we loaded them in the semi-trailers.

On the very first truckload, I sat on the passenger side as a 16-year-old kid named Danny drove the rig down the steep, dirt road. We'd just come off the steepest part where the drop-off was about 800 feet down. Danny found another low gear and turned around a corner, when a tire blew. The truck veered off the dirt road. Danny fought with the wheel and tried his best to keep

the rig on the road. But the cattle shifted in the trailer and, when they did, the entire rig went with them. Then we were upside down in the middle of nowhere with most of the cattle dead or dying in the back.

Gas was spewing everywhere. Danny scrambled out of the cab and told me to as well, but I couldn't because my arm was stuck in the window, which had been crushed. My arm wasn't hurt, just stuck.

Danny was scared to death, and his adrenaline was flowing. He hustled to my side of the truck, literally pulled the frame of the truck up an inch, grabbed me by the belt and dislodged me from the truck. He threw me over his shoulder (remember, I'm a strapping 12-year-old boy at this time) and started running from the scene.

I'll never forget that day I was wearing a pair of batwing chaps I had bought at the local tack store. They were my prized possession. I had taken them off, folded them neatly and put them on the dashboard before the accident happened.

I jumped off Danny's shoulder and ran back to the truck for my chaps, which were stuck in the window as well. I tried to grab them, but they wouldn't budge. Danny grabbed me a second time and ran as fast as he could, with me over his shoulder again. When he got far enough away, he stopped, we looked back, but the truck never blew up. There were a few dazed cattle walking around, and the rest were dead.

We walked back to the staging area and found Mr. Reed there. He always drove a Cadillac convertible and would smoke great big cigars. He reminded me of Boss Hogg on the television series, "Dukes of Hazard." I remember being surprised that he wasn't angry about what happened to his truck or his cows; he was just concerned about our well-being.

By this time I was getting a really good taste of cowboying. I'd been in runaway situations, in a cattle stampede and survived falling off a steep mountain road. It dawned on me that some people are very good at this sort of thing and I wasn't. I was just young and dumb and rode a flighty horse that ran away at the drop of a hat.

The Kid Who Was Good With Horses

Up and down Mission Boulevard, known for its many stables, I got jobs to start colts and exercise other people's horses for around $20 a month. I even worked with some problem horses, teaching them not to jig, etc. Instead of mowing lawns for extra cash, I was the kid who was good with horses.

Beginning in junior high and until I graduated high school, I worked at Silvera's Feed Store in Fremont. The store sold feed primarily, but carried a few saddles as well. They had a saddle called the Hawaiian Roper, made of latigo leather. It was the first cushion-seat saddle I'd ever seen. I just drooled over it. It was $500 and, at age 13, that was a lot of money for me to come up with. So instead of getting paid, I applied my paycheck toward the saddle.

I used the saddle on a filly I was riding for Jim Kubas, one of the local stable owners. One day I tied the filly to a hitching rail, unbuckled the front and back cinches first, but left the breast collar on. My dog Snoopy, an English Pointer, came tearing around the corner, chasing a cat underneath the hitching rail. The horse pulled back and the saddle whipped off her back and landed around her neck. In her terror, she broke the hitching rail, dragged my saddle until the

breast collar broke, and then ran through a barbed-wire fence. I had to spend $70 to fix my new saddle and around $130 to have the filly stitched up. It took two months for her to heal, and I had to pay for her board at the same time.

This, of course, has taught me why you should take off your saddle by first removing the breast collar and back cinch. That's why now, in my horsemanship program, I teach the correct order of saddling and unsaddling and that whatever snap or buckle you put on last (breast collar or back cinch), you take off first.

As a young kid, I learned valuable lessons in expensive ways.

Oakland, the Beginning

My quote, "I was born in Oakland, California, so I could be near my mother," is a bit of tongue-in-cheek humor, but it has a double meaning. Obviously, I was near my mother, and both my parents were instrumental in my life and career, but the real significance of being born in Oakland is that I was in the midst of a thriving horse and ranching community that fostered my love of and experiences with horses. From the time I was born and throughout the rest of my life, horses have played an enormous role in shaping my destiny and, in turn, that of today's natural horsemanship movement. If I hadn't been born in the San Francisco Bay Area at that time in history, as I will explain in this book, maybe there would be no story to tell.

PHOTO BY DORIS PARELLI

Pat on Jessie and his dad, Jack, on Kelly.

2 HORSEMEN AND MENTORS

"I eventually found out that he was getting more by doing less."

Freddie Feriera, a horseman and government trapper, was Pat's first mentor and the one who introduced him to a natural way of doing things with horses.

I spent my pre-teen and teen years with an eclectic mix of horsemen and mentors who left an indelible impression on my young mind. Horses had become my passion by this time, and I felt blessed to hang around and work with these experienced hands. With their help, I began my long journey toward becoming a horseman.

Four Sacks of Grain

One of the more colorful characters I ran into was an old man named Rufio, whose last name I never knew. He was known as the best horseshoer in our area and also well respected as a noted horsemen. He had a funny accent I couldn't quite place. It didn't sound like the Spanish and Portuguese I had heard spoken. I found out years later he was of Basque descent.

Rufio owned a stallion named Drifting Sen, by Mr. Sen Sen and out of Drifting Sally. This was the first registered Quarter Horse stallion I'd ever seen. At one of the very first horse shows I went to I remember all the young halter horses were sired by Drifting Sen. He was a big deal in our local horse community at that time.

One day my dad and I went to Rufio's home. Rufio kept Drifting Sen in an open shed along one side of a rectangular-shaped pen, approximately 30 feet wide by 40 feet long. Rufio could open or close the shed gate to contain the stallion.

Rufio always liked to offer people this bet: If you'd bring over four sacks of grain and put one in each corner of the pen, he'd lead the stallion around and allow him to eat a little bit of grain out of each of the sacks. He'd then release the horse in the corral and said that the horse would make 10 laps of the corral at a trot, without stopping, going inside the shed or trying to eat more grain. His pitch was that if the stallion did any of those three things, he'd give you a free breeding. The breeding fee was $100 and in those days it seemed like a lot of money. The other side of this bet was that if the stallion did exactly what Rufio said he would do, Rufio would keep the grain. My dad and I got a kick out of bringing over the four sacks of grain just to watch him do it.

Of course, Rufio had his stallion trained at liberty to make those 10 laps, all with quiet cues from his eyes and hands.

One other thing I'll never forget is watching Rufio teach a horse to stop. He tied the horse to a tree with a 45-foot rope. He'd spook the horse and when it was about to hit the end of the rope, Rufio would yell "Whoa!" About the fourth time, the horse would stop when he heard "whoa" and before he hit the end of the rope. As the familiar saying goes: He knew what was going to happen before what happens, happens.

Bridget Bar Dough

Jim Kubas owned a stable on Mission Boulevard and stood a stallion named Cee Bar Satin, by Cee Bars Jr., a son of the famous Three Bars (TB). His stud fee was $25 for unregistered mares and $50 for registered ones. I remember thinking: "Jim's filthy rich because that stallion bred 20 mares a year." I did the math and that meant a lot of money to a young kid.

Jim bred one of his mares to Cee Bar Satin. I was there the day she was bred and the day she foaled a filly with four white socks and a blaze. I thought the filly was the most beautiful horse I'd ever seen. Her registered name is Cissy Bar, but I called her Bridget Bar Dough.

I was probably 13 at the time and had been riding horses for other people. I talked Bev

Hopper, one of the ladies whose horses I rode, into buying Bridget. She let me show her at the 4-H and Quarter Horse shows, where the filly won her share of halter and showmanship classes. This early experience got me interested in the finer aspects of horsemanship. For the first time, I got to see a lot of well-bred horses in one place and could compare them to the horses I'd been exposed to up until that time.

The Hoppers got divorced and decided to sell the mare, but, as usual, I didn't have the money to buy her. So, I did what I'd done before and got someone else to buy her, which I'll explain later.

Freddie Feriera, My First Mentor

My aunt, Donna Garner (now Donna George), became involved with horses long after I did, but it was through her that I met

Freddie Feriera on Patches, the Appaloosa he won many competitive trail rides on.

PHOTO BY DORIS FARELLI

Pat loved riding in parades. Here he is in the 4-H parade on Jesse in 1968.

PHOTO BY DORIS FARELLI

Pat in a bareback equitation class on his Aunt Donna's Morgan named Socks. The show took place at the Livermore Rodeo grounds.

one of the most influential mentors I've ever had, Freddie Feriera. Freddie, of Portuguese descent, was one of the best known horsemen in the east Bay Area, along with Dr. Billy Linfoot, Dr. Frank Santos and Ed Connell. He lived at the old rodeo grounds in Livermore, where he gave lessons, bought and sold horses and had been the Diablo Valley government trapper for 27 years.

Donna took lessons from Freddie, and, after meeting him, I did, too. I spent three summers with Freddie, helping him start about 13 to 15 colts a year. He'd also take me into the mountains when he checked his traps.

As the government trapper, Freddie had the job of trapping and capturing any aberrant animals, such as marauding mountain lions or even a mischievous skunk that trespassed in someone's home.

Freddie had a key ring with dozens of keys on it, one each for all the padlocked fences of the private land he had to cross on his 50-mile range between Mt. Diablo and Mt. Hamilton.

Freddie drove a 1956 Ford stock truck, which would fit four or five horses or that many cows. It had plywood sides and a ramp for loading. I can remember, from time to time, we'd take a few cows in that old truck and kick them out on one place, then two or three more on another place, branding them along the way, never over existing brands, of course.

Many years later my aunt Donna married a man named Buttons George, whom everyone called "The King of the Hill." He lived on Mines Road, near the San Anton junction. This was in the south end of Freddie's range.

Buttons knew how close Donna and Freddie were, so he never made any derogatory remarks in front of her. But at a family reunion, years later, he spilled the beans. As I was talking about all my adventures with Freddie, I explained to Buttons that I remembered going onto his property one time (before he was my uncle). He said, "Yeah, and stealing some of my calves, I suppose."

I asked him what he meant by that remark. He explained, "That damned Freddie Feriera branded more slick calves than anyone in the county." Little did I know back then that I had been a 13-year-old accomplice.

I learned a lot from Freddie, just watching him work. He'd take me back into the mountains for days, with his horses and dogs. He was an amazing man in that he understood the ways of everything natural. He knew about wild animals' habitats and habits. He instinctively knew where they'd be and when. He was equally knowledgeable about horses. When we'd camp, he'd always know which horses to turn loose and which ones he couldn't or they'd turn tail and go home. Some could be let loose during the day and others only at night. He was the last of his breed – a true mountain man, who fathomed all of nature.

Pat and Jesse got a blue ribbon in the barrel race at the 4-H show.

At a parade in Fremont, 15-year-old Pat rode as the "intelligent derriere," aka, "smart ass."

Competitive Trail Riding

Since his horses were always in such good shape from checking traps in the mountains, Freddie would use them to compete in North American Trail Ride Conference (NATRC) competitive rides. My aunt did, as well. On these rides, horse and rider are judged separately. The rider is critiqued on his or her horsemanship, and the horse is evaluated by a veterinarian for soundness, condition, way of going and manners.

Freddie was one of the first champions in NATRC. He had an Appaloosa horse named Patches that won everything. I went on some NATRC rides with him, either riding one of his horses or Jesse, who, as you can imagine from my earlier description, was a going machine.

I don't remember exactly how I did on the competitive rides, but I do remember that the NATRC rides made an impression on me. They burned into my brain that in order to be good enough to win at something, there's a lot more to it than what meets the eyes. Conditioning the horses was a thoughtful and time-consuming job. We didn't just ride from here to there. We practiced interval training, even back then, and were serious about how we went up and down hill. We were judged on everything regarding our horse-handling skills, from the time we unloaded the horses until the end of the ride. There was so much to be aware of. Also, NATRC judges could hide behind trees or rocks, so we knew that there was always someone out there watching.

Also, most horse-show competitions are short events, lasting a few minutes and then they're over. But an NATRC competitive ride takes at least a day and usually two to complete, so you're being judged for a long time. This type of contest gave me a good grounding in competition. Competitive trail riding isn't a flashy sport, no expensive gear, no audience, no money to be won. You traverse all types of terrain, handling natural obstacles properly and safely, which is always stressed.

I felt I learned a lot from this experience — two things specifically: Preparation is key, and in riding horses (and in life in general) there's always someone watching you, no matter where you are or what you're doing.

Riding and Training Naturally

Our regular routine at Freddie's stable was to ride all day, every day. We'd ride the horses from the old Livermore rodeo grounds to the new one, which had an arena and grandstands.

The two rodeo grounds were about a mile apart. We'd string about five horses together and ride them over there. We'd each ride one horse, tie four more together and pony them. Once we got to the grounds, we'd work the horses, then ride them back to the old rodeo grounds.

Freddie showed me how to use a natural obstacle, instead of a fence, to perform fancy rollbacks. On our way to the new rodeo

25

PHOTO BY DORIS PARELLI

Pat with Kelly and his dog Snoopy.

PHOTO BY DORIS PARELLI

Pat got his first pickup when he was 16, in 1970.

grounds, we followed a creek bed with a three-foot drop-off, which naturally frightened the horses. We'd double or turn them toward the creek. They'd lower their heads to look at the steep bank at the same time they'd lighten their front ends and turn on their hindquarters. It was a natural way of getting the horses to perform rollbacks. At a fence, on the other hand, a horse would have to lift his head and turn, and it wasn't as pretty or efficient as the creek-bed turn.

I studied Freddie while he was riding, and it looked like he didn't do anything, but his horses stopped and turned beautifully. I felt like I was "geeing and hawing" (old teamster terms meaning to turn right and left) all over the place, and my horses still couldn't turn in a 40-acre field. This bothered me a lot, and I tried to figure out what Freddie was doing that got his horses so responsive. I eventually found out that he was getting more by doing less. His timing was good, and he understood what he was trying to do. I, on the other hand, was just a young kid trying to get the buck out of the young colts.

Freddie was the first of my mentors to teach me some principles about riding naturally. For example, he showed me how to ride with one rein and double a horse. Basically, we used doubling as a means of lateral flexion to get horses to perform 180-degree turns or rollbacks.

Years later, I discovered this principle again while reading Ed Connell's book titled *Hackamore Reinsman*. Ed was good friends with Freddie; the two men shared similar riding styles and many of the same horsemanship philosophies. As I read the book, I was amazed to find all the stuff Freddie had tried to teach me five years before. This is when the one-rein concept really sunk in. Light bulbs went off in my head, as they say. I'd made the connection.

Velvet Mouth

Every winter when we weren't riding much, Freddie and I would oil all the headstalls, then remove the snaffle bits and put them in a gunnysack. We'd dig a hole, throw the gunnysack in it and cover it with dirt. The next spring we'd dig it up and find all the mouthpieces were rusted; they were made of sweet-iron. Freddie explained that the best thing for colts is a rusty bit; they love the taste. How right he was about that. Most good horsemen today know that sweet-iron is more natural in a horse's mouth than stainless steel.

It was Freddie I talked into buying Bridget Bar Dough, who was then about four years old. He coached me through her first rides. I'll never forget that he said, "She has a velvet mouth, so we're going to ride her in a halter first." The phrase "velvet mouth" has stuck with me over the years, as I think of all the things people do to and put in horses' mouths.

Bridget was the first horse I branded all by myself. Freddie and I held her up next to the barn. I took a piece of wood, about two feet long, and repeatedly pressed it into her shoulder.

After she was used to that feeling, I picked up the Rocking F brand and pressed it into her skin. She never moved. I guess you could say we played the Friendly Game with her, before we played the Porcupine Game. About the time she even thought about moving, it was all over.

Harry Rose

After Freddie, I worked with Harry Rose for about six months in Fremont, at a stable called Barbie's, later called All Seasons. Mr. Barbie, the owner, was in construction and he built a 60-foot wide indoor arena, which was a really big deal in those days. It was the only one around, and I felt lucky to work there. There were around 20 stalls on one side for the jumping horses in training and the other side had Harry's cow horses.

Harry's son, Harry Jr., and I were the same age and good friends, both interested in bucking horses and rodeo.

I was the stall cleaner. I'd get there at 4 o'clock in the morning before school to clean and return after school to clean again and ride colts. At that time, the standard way to break a colt was to hobble and blindfold him, saddle him and get on. We didn't try to make a colt buck, but whatever happened, happened.

When I'd clean the stalls for the jumping-horse owners, they'd pay me 50 cents a week to turn their horses out twice a week. Most were Thoroughbreds or Thoroughbred crosses that got a little wound up after being in a stall 24/7. That extra $10 a week (50 cents x 20 horses) came in handy back then, when $5 would fill a gas tank.

I got the great idea to see how much "play" I could get out of the cooped-up Thoroughbreds. I'd put Harry Sr.'s bareback rigging on one of the horses, and Little Harry would take him over to the indoor arena. I'd get on as Little Harry held the lead rope. He'd say, "Are you ready?" I'd tell him when and he'd unsnap the lead rope from the horse's halter. The free-at-last hunter/jumper would run and buck and jump around to his heart's content as I played at being a rodeo bronc rider. The owners never knew about our rodeo rides on their expensive show horses.

Harry Sr. was a champion reined cow horse and cutting horse trainer, who stood Cal Bar, a famous son of Doc Bar. We rode horses for some very prestigious people. Harry had won bridle and cutting horse contests; he even rode Doc O'Lena's mother, Poco Lena.

In working for Harry, I found myself really interested in western performance and figuring out how to make horses rein well – do sliding stops, fast spins, rollbacks, etc. My exposure to different training methods and philosophies, such as those of Freddie and Harry, added to the scope and depth of my ever-growing knowledge of horsemanship.

End of an Era

Both Freddie and Ed Connell died of heart attacks in the early 1970s. I believe Ed was 77 and Freddie around 70. Ed died while giving a clinic in British Columbia, Canada.

Freddie had a horsehair-twisting machine to make horsehair mecates (ropes). A couple of weeks before he died, he and I were in the barnyard, where I helped him make a mane-hair rope by feeding the horse hair to him as it went into the twisting machine. The mecate, which I still have, starts off black, then runs to black and white, then just white, then brown and white and finally to brown. It's a beautiful piece of work.

Freddie willed some of his belongings to me and my aunt, since we were both serious students of his. Donna inherited Bridget, who was about six or seven years old by that time, and Freddie's old truck. I got the horsehair mecate I mentioned above, a horsehair bosal, a Tree brand pocketknife and a pair of Visalia spurs. They're still my prized possessions today.

As I look back on it, I was born in a place that was the epicenter of an emerging philosophy of horsemanship and at a point in time when new horsemanship ideas were coming to the fore. I was privileged to be surrounded by great horsemen, world champions and mentors who helped shape my future.

3 SCHOOL OF HARD KNOCKS

"Truth is when your opinion matches up with facts."

In junior high and high school, I was active in both Future Farmers of America and 4-H. The five little townships in our district consolidated to create one FFA chapter. It happened to be at Washington High School, where I went after we moved to Fremont, in the township of Centerville. If this consolidation hadn't happened, the kids in Warm Springs, Mission San Jose and the other little towns would've gone elsewhere.

This is significant because all the ranch kids from miles around, if they wanted to be in an ag program, had to go to our school. We had a school farm, a farm shop and several thousand acres of hay crops. I had my own steer at school, and every day I fed the steer and cleaned his pen before classes started.

FOXIE PHOTO

Pat riding Wigwam at the Livermore Rodeo in 1972. The pickup man is Cotton Rosser, of the Flying U Rodeo.

PHOTO BY THOMPSON

From time to time, Pat tried his hand at bull riding. This was at a jackpot at Johnny Hawkins' school. Johnny is in the white shirt by the gate.

My Neighborhood

I was fortunate to be involved with FFA kids and ranch kids. When I'd go to their homes, I didn't go to neighborhoods with sidewalks and streetlights; I went to ranches with cattle and horses, and many had arenas. Most of the ranch kids could really rope, had gone to junior rodeos and had won their share of belt buckles. Since these were my friends, I, too, got the bug to rope and do ranch-type activities.

I found myself being friends with many kids who went on to become either world champions or, at least, exceptionally good at their respective sports, mainly roping. Names like Chris Lybbert, Joe Murray, Doyle Gellerman, Craig Stills and Richie Benbow. And, like my friends, I went to junior rodeos. I think I sat on at least 30 head of stock before I ever stayed on until the whistle blew.

My mom likes to tell the story about the time she waited all day long until it was my turn to ride. We arrived at the rodeo arena at 6 in the morning, thinking I was going to ride at 8 a.m. Unfortunately for us, there were scores of kids wanting to ride steers and cows. I finally rode at 5 p.m. and lasted about two seconds. On top of that, I got my first case of poison oak. It was not a fun day for either my mom or me.

The Bucking Barrel

One of the ranches I visited a lot belonged to the Benbow family. They had five boys, and the three older brothers, Steve, Billy and Ritchie, were very good hands, especially with a rope. Still today, they're competitive ropers.

I was about 15 or 16 at the time, and trying to learn to rope from the older, more experienced boys was difficult for me; I'd never thrown a rope before. But I enjoyed going to the ranch anyway, opening up the roping chutes for them, just doing anything to hang around and be part of it all.

One day the Benbow brothers talked me into riding the bucking barrel they had on the ranch. I was pretty good at gymnastics since my sister and I were quite involved

Pat winning the California State Finals in Folsom, 1974.

with it in school, so this seemed like something I could master.

Once I figured out how to sit on a bucking barrel, it really helped me when I competed in junior rodeos. When you get on a live animal, your adrenaline races so much that you don't have time to figure out technique; consequently, you don't learn anything. You just fall off. But a bucking barrel is a simulator; it helps you work on technique. So when the time comes to mount a live animal, your skills are honed and reactions are quick.

I found that my friends could out-rope me, but they couldn't outride me on the bucking barrel. They could turn it upside down and still not get me off the doggone thing. I was so determined to ride the barrel that I worked through the pain of tearing the skin off my knuckles as I clung to it.

I decided, though, that I needed my own bucking barrel, so I could practice on my own time. At the Mission Boulevard stable where I kept my horses I put one up and come hell or high water, I could really ride that thing.

Cowboy Pride and Tattoos

I was one of the few kids in school to wear a cowboy hat, and I was also a member of Future Farmers of America. There were only about 30 of us who wore the navy blue FFA jackets. So, in a school of about 2,000, we were pretty easy pickings. One day in the cafeteria line, as I was absolutely minding my own business, someone grabbed my hat and taunted me with it. He then threw it across the room, so naturally I punched him. The nice boy in me went away and the son of a Golden Gloves champion came out. I went to get my hat, but the guy who caught it threw it, too. Before long, I was in a big brawl.

The next thing I knew five Mexican boys jumped in to help me, and we cleaned the white kids' clocks. Those five Mexicans were some of the toughest kids in school; they belonged to the Pachucos, a gang famous for guns, knives, the whole nine yards. There was another gang in school called the Cholos, but the Pachucos were the most notorious.

The 1972 California Rodeo Finals Top 15 (two guys are missing). Pat is the second from the left on the top row. He dislocated his shoulder 41 times in competition and did so the night before this picture was taken, Note his arm tucked into his shirt. Also, this was the last time Pat would be seen without a mustache. In the middle row, fourth from the left is Wilson Pate, uncle of well-known clinician Curt Pate. Bottom, first on the right is John Growney of the Growney Brothers Rodeo.

After it was all over and I got my hat back before the principal came, the five guys hustled me over to their little corner of the high school where they hung out. There we were, wiping off blood and combing our hair. They patted me on the back and told me what a tough guy I was, and that I needed to become a Pachuco. I politely declined the offer, but they wouldn't let me wiggle out of it. It crossed my mind that if I didn't come over to their way of thinking, stand in their corner, do what they do, etc., then I'd get in trouble with them, which wasn't a smart thing to do. I certainly didn't want those guys mad at me.

Thinking as fast as I could, I invited them to come to the stable where I had my horses, and I offered to let them ride my bucking barrel. They said, "Oh, wow, yeah man."

Of course, the bucking barrel dumped them on their heads, right and left, although one of the guys actually got to where he could ride it pretty well and went on to have an amateur bull-riding career.

My plan to rid myself of the gang members backfired. Instead of them bucking off into the sunset, never to be seen again, they liked me even more and insisted I get inducted into their gang. Part of the initiation was to get a Pachuco tattoo. I ended up getting one on my left shoulder, which I still have today, but fortunately it's just my initials.

The bucking barrel did do one very important thing for me, though. It distinguished me from the ropers. My friends Ritchie and Craig could see how talented I was on the barrel and encouraged me to consider rodeoing.

Roping Schools

Still, I wanted to learn to rope like my friends. We all went to Ted Ashworth's roping school in Livermore, which was down the street from my grandparents' home. Ashworth, the 1958 RCA world champion in team roping, was the guy who started swinging the heel rope over the left shoulder just as they do today. He taught this to other great world champion ropers, such as Ken Luman, Jim Rodriguez Jr., the Camarillo brothers and later to Walt Woodard. Now everyone does it.

At Johnny Hawkins' rodeo school, Pat rode his first bucking horse, named Martha, for the full eight seconds. He rode in borrowed chaps, boots and spurs.

Livermore used to be called the "Cowboy Capital of the World," and a lot of famous cowboys, including rodeo cowboys, came from that area.

All my friends were fairly accomplished ropers at that time, but not me. After about six weeks, Ashworth took me aside and told me I was the worst roper he'd ever seen. He recommended that I change events. I took his advice and got a little help from him at the same time.

It just so happens that world champions know other world champions. Ashworth introduced me to Johnny Hawkins, who was the 1963 RCA World Champion Bareback Rider and three times runner-up. He ran a rodeo school in Lake Comanche near Clements, and a bunch of us went up there to get our bucks (as opposed to kicks). We paid $5 to get on a horse and $10 to enter the jackpot.

I was pretty cocky since I really knew how to ride the bucking barrel and could even spur it. So, I was really puffed up by the time I went to Johnny's. All of us had tattoos on our arms, smoked cigarettes, chewed tobacco, drank beer and everything else a 16-year-old kid isn't supposed to do. We were tough.

The main reason we wanted to go to rodeo school in the first place was to get bucked off, land in the dirt, show how manly we were and have the cute girls in the grandstands cheer us up. So 10 of us loaded into two pickups, mine and Mike Cohen's, and off to rodeo school we went.

Almost everyone got bucked off that first time. The last one to go, I got on a little mare named Martha. I had had knee surgery a year before, after getting hurt playing soccer. I was really conscious of my knees, which were wrapped in foam and taped.

Lo and behold I rode Martha, spurring her and all. My dream was to get off on the pickup man and I did. Man, did I think I was cool!

The pickup man's name was Mario Cuchi and he said to me, "So, son, how long have you been riding?" I said, "That was my first time." He said, "Naw, tell me how long." And I said, "Truly, that was my first." He immediately took me over to Johnny and told him that that was my first ride ever. Both men saw that I had talent, and from then on they took care of me.

I went to Johnny's regularly and did whatever I could for him. If he needed his lawn mowed or something painted or waxed, I did it. He was my teacher and mentor and I was his top student.

He created a "spur board," sort of a simulator on which I could practice my moves. It was literally "wax on, wax off," as in the "Karate Kid" movies. I didn't buck, as on the bucking barrel, I just practiced my moves for a couple of weeks. Then, Johnny put me on about 10 horses a week. I got stronger and could really use myself. I continued practicing on the spur board two hours a day.

I followed Johnny's program and did everything he told me for about a year. I won the bareback riding at the next three amateur rodeos I went to. I quit trying to get on bulls or rope; I concentrated on bareback riding.

John the Baptist

Johnny's nickname was John the Baptist because he was the first fitness-conscious rodeo cowboy. He worked out, he exercised, he didn't drink or smoke. He was Mr. Health and Fitness. He considered himself a professional athlete and treated his body the same.

Impressed with Johnny's outlook on life, I quit drinking and smoking. When I look back, that was somewhat unusual because that's typically the party time in a young man's life. As a 16-year-old, I'd been smoking, drinking and doing all the stuff you aren't supposed to do behind the barn. But because Johnny was my mentor, I absolutely followed in his tracks.

The only thing I picked up later on was chewing tobacco. It helped keep me awake as I drove the hundreds of miles to the next rodeo. I didn't even drink coffee in those days.

I did all the things Johnny said. I kept up with gymnastics for flexibility, rode a unicycle for balance, jumped on the trampoline, practiced on the spur board and did exercises to increase my "catting ability," which involved ways to land on my feet.

The First Friendly Game

Johnny had a theory about bucking horses. He thought the rider should try to relax his mount in the chutes. Some horses had a reputation of flipping upside down in the chutes, which,

of course, is dangerous. So Johnny showed me some ways to calm my horses, to keep them from becoming overly excited or upset.

The secret was to spend time with the horse before the ride. (Sound familiar?) I'd sit on top of the chute, dangle my feet, rub the horse on his back; basically I played the Friendly Game with the bronc.

Then, when I'd sit on the horse, I'd totally relax, just melt. But when the chute gate opened, I was ready and able to sit the first jump. Other riders would transmit their nervousness to their horses in the chute. That made the horses nervous, and they then would crash and bang around in the chutes, pinning the riders and hurting them before they ever got out.

In my entire rodeo career, I went 14 years without ever breaking a bone. I rode in the Dixon rigging, which had a soft handle. All the riders back then clamored for this type of rigging, made by bronc rider Pete Dixon. The riggings today are hard, and riders can have a difficult time getting out of them. That's why so many of them get hurt.

John Hawkins, Pat's rodeo mentor, was the 1963 RCA World Champion Bareback Rider and three times runner up.

JOHN HAWKINS
Bareback Bronc Rider

TO PAT
KEEP UP THE
GOOD WORK

John Hawkins was one of the first members in the PRCA Hall of Fame. Note his message to Pat to "Keep up the good work." Pat did. His successful rodeo career lasted 14 years. Pat's other "good work" as a horseman and teacher has lasted a lifetime.

At Johnny's, I rode 10 horses every week for practice. At a rodeo, I'd do what Johnny said; I'd get on relaxed and ride well. During the week, I'd practice on the spur board, which helped me ride physically. I got my timing and moves down pat.

But preparing mentally was another thing. At the first rodeo, I was scheduled to ride on Saturday, but by Thursday I was so keyed up I couldn't sleep. Same thing on Friday. By the time Saturday came along, I was exhausted. Even though I was totally physically fit, I discovered I was emotionally unfit. The butterflies in my stomach just went wild.

After the first three rodeos, I was a wreck. I couldn't imagine how I was going to go on with my rodeo career. I saw other guys get nervous, and it didn't help. I'd see guys whose nerves truly got the best of them. Some guys threw up before every ride. They'd worry about their demons — falling off and getting hurt. That got in the way of their riding well.

Butterflies in Formation

I went back to Johnny and asked for help. He explained that I was practicing physically, not mentally. He gave me the two-minute drill. He didn't want me to just physically practice on the spur board; I was to imagine an actual ride and the minutes before, during and after it. That included from the time I sat on the horse in the chute, to the time I completed the ride and got picked up by the pickup man until I, as he said, "touched the chutes."

The first rider I ever saw get killed was at the Salinas Rodeo. The rough-stock rider got off his bucking horse with the help of the pickup men and then nonchalantly started back to the chutes, unbuckling his chaps as he walked. He didn't pay attention to what was happening in the arena. The bucking horse came around, with the pickup men in pursuit, and ran right over the top of the rider. He was killed instantly.

It was Johnny's theory that God would protect you only if you were on the other side of the chutes, so he advised me to get back to the chute and "touch it" with all due haste.

The two-minute drill included from the time I sat on the horse in the chute until I touched the chute again after the ride. I guess another name for this would be mental imagery or visualization. I'd focus my imagination and try to mentally feel every moment of those two minutes. I found my adrenaline pumping even while I practiced on the spur board, because the mind can't tell the difference between imaginary and real.

Johnny also taught me the art of not spurring, which is opposite of what everyone else does. (I use this same kind of philosophy today in many natural horsemanship theories and teaching techniques.) All the other riders would come out spurring. But what Johnny had me do was to set my legs and spurs on the horse's neck as if I were trying to keep him from going forward with my legs.

When the horse took that first bucking jump, it blew my feet outward and set the timing of my spurring. I let the horse help me in my spurring action. Every time the horse would blow out my legs with his jumps, I'd try to set my legs back again. And the horse would repeatedly blow out my legs and I'd repeatedly try to set them. My spurring timing was perfect this way.

The other riders who just came out spurring often got out of sync with their horses. Their legs weren't where they were supposed to be. They'd be out of time, not ride as well and didn't score as well as I did either.

Then, instead of riding the spur board for eight seconds, Johnny had me ride for 10 seconds. He said all the rodeos are won or lost in the last few seconds. Many riders would make it to six seconds and start spurring less and less and then just grab their rigging before they got off.

What I learned to do was spur harder and harder and harder, even beyond the whistle.

In my spur-board practice, I imagined a full eight-second-plus ride, heard the whistle, waited for the pickup man, then ran over and touched the garage door as if it were the chutes.

After I'd practice the two-minute drill for several weeks, I entered my next rodeo. The Thursday and Friday before the rodeo, I was able to sleep. Saturday morning came and I wasn't nervous. Then I'd wonder if I should get nervous because I wasn't getting nervous.

I'd get above my horse in the chutes and still didn't get nervous. I thought to myself, "This is weird." I'd fiddle with the horse in the chute, try to relax him, get on, get off, do the things Johnny taught me. Just before the chute gate opened, my adrenaline hit me like a ton of bricks. But instead of wasting it on Thursday and Friday night and Saturday morning, I had

it when I needed it. My two-minute drill kicked in and I found I had super-strength and super-focus, and I could ride just as I did in my mind during practice.

Johnny told me to teach my butterflies to fly in formation. Use your nervous energy, that adrenaline, to get yourself in the "zone" only in the two minutes prior to an event.

People's Perspectives on Pat

Good Student

Pat was one of the kids at my rodeo schools. The thing I remember most when I first met him was that he talked all the time. I asked him jokingly if he'd been vaccinated with the Victrola needle because he never quit talking. He was insulted for a little bit, but then he started laughing.

Pat was a very good student. He was serious about learning everything I was trying to teach him about bronc riding. His goal was to win.

One thing that separated Pat from my other students was his keen interest in horses. I've always been interested in riding and handling a horse, too, and he and I talked quite a lot about it. Pat learned about horses from everyone, not just one person. He wanted to learn it all.

I still see Pat every once in a while. I love to do anything that has to do with horses, and I've been to several of Pat's clinics. I like to give him a bad time. He gets a kick out of that.

John Hawkins
1963 RCA World Champion Bareback Rider
PRCA Hall of Fame

At the National Finals Rodeo Oldtimers' Reunion in 2004, Pat visited with John Hawkins (left) and all-around, bareback and bull riding champ Harry Thompkins (right).

THE ARGUS
Page 2

Fremont - Newark, California
Saturday, January 31, 1970

They came by mule

Pat and friend Mike Cohen made the cover of The Argus *in January, 1970. The Fremont, California, newspaper showed them riding a donkey to school for Ecology Day, where students were charged to find a way to school by non-motorized means.*

Mentally, Emotionally and Physically Fit

I've learned to use the two-minute drill in everything I do today. I can give the biggest presentation of my life, talk to a huge crowd or demonstrate on wild horses, and I sleep very well the night before. I get up and don't think anything about it. About two minutes before I come out, I bring all my thoughts together, I get my butterflies in formation and I say, "I know what I'm going to do for the day."

Instead of eight-second rides, I now do eight-hour presentations. My seminars are two eight-hour days. I'm on "rodeo-star adrenaline" for eight hours. And at the end of the day, I find I still have more energy.

What I learned from Johnny Hawkins and rodeo was to get mentally, emotionally and physically fit, to teach my butterflies to fly in formation, to get into the zone, to do the opposite and to relax horses. After all, they're athletes, too, and need to be relaxed to perform their best.

About this time, I read a good book titled *Psycho-Cybernetics* by Maxwell Maltz, just like I read Ed Connell's *Hackamore Reinsman* after I'd learned what I learned from Freddie Feriera.

What I found out was that Johnny had already taught me what Maltz had to say in his book. In this original, classic self-help book, Maltz uncovers the body-mind connection, in which a positive attitude, relaxation and visualization play a huge role in how a person views himself, thus affecting the outcome of his life's experiences.

In those days, Gary Leffew was the great bull-riding guru, putting on schools for that event. He, too, recommended his students read Maltz's book. I'd read passages from their copies and say to myself, "That's me. That's what I do, no wonder."

Out of School

To me school was a jail sentence. I hated it throughout grade school and high school. I couldn't wait until 3:00 rolled around. I'd watch the hour hand ticking until the time I could leave school and get to my horses. To me, school was a waste of time.

In our high school, there were too many kids, so the school administrators came up with an early-out program, which had nothing to do with scholastic achievement. The students had to perform certain duties to get out early, which I did, a semester early. By this time, I was winning at a lot of jackpot rodeos and just knew I was going to be a rodeo star someday.

However, all parents want their children to better themselves, and my mother made me promise to try going to college, even for a while. So I enrolled in Modesto Junior College, not only for her, but also because I made the rodeo team, which, of course, made life at school bearable.

What I Learned From My Dad

As a young man about to leave home and enter the big, wide world, I reflected on the things I'd learned to that point. There are three things that I absolutely learned from my dad.

1. Always tell the truth. If you tell the truth,

you never have to be smart enough to remember what you lied about.

2. Whatever you do, do it with excellence. Do it with class. You've got to have class.

3. You have to savvy "savvy."

A thousand times I heard these three things from my dad. My dad has built his reputation and business on those three things. Today, his name is as well known in the furniture world as mine is in the horse world.

My dad always tells the truth. For example, when he sells a furniture store a line of goods, he does the research and says, "I want you to buy this because you're going to sell lots of it. And if you don't sell it, I'll take it back. I'll have it put back on the train and ship it back to wherever it came from. Honest. My opinion will match up with facts. And, if I said that, I'll do that."

My dad always shows class. He always dresses well, drives a good car, buys dinner. Always does all the things that classy people do.

And my dad has savvy. He has an innate understanding of people, sales and everything that his world revolves around. Instead of a formal education, my dad has savvy.

The story I always like to tell about my dad, is when I was growing up, he'd pat me on the back and say, "Son, do you savvy 'savvy?'" I'd say, "Yeah, Dad, I savvy 'savvy.'" Then, he'd whack me on the head and say, "No, you don't."

This went on repeatedly over the years, with always the same result. Evidently I didn't understand what he was saying or what he was trying to teach me.

Then one day when I was about 17, he said as before, "Son, do you savvy 'savvy?'" This time I ducked before I answered and before he could hit me. He said, "Now you do."

The point being that I learned from experience what was going to happen before it happened. Therefore, today I like to say, to be able to savvy "savvy," in other words, know what "savvy" means, you have to know what happens before what happens, happens.

When it was time for me to leave home, I took the three things my dad taught me with me.

I always tell the truth. I try to own classy horses, ride classy saddles, own classy properties. Whatever it is, I want it to be first class.

And one of the main messages that I try to give every dedicated student is: There's a savvy way to do everything. There's a savvy way to put on a halter, a saddle and bridle, to mount, to dismount, to sit in the saddle and ride, to care for horses, you name it.

And if you do it with savvy, two things happen: It's always first class, and it's always truthful. To me, truth is when your opinion matches up with facts.

There's only one untruth that's the most dangerous untruth in the world. That's when people believe their own lies. They truly believe that what they're saying is true and it's not.

Those three things I indelibly learned from my father. He sent me off into the world with that advice to guide me. And every time I didn't do one of them, it's come back to haunt me – every single time.

Pat graduated from high school in 1972.

4 RODEO DAYS

"Through rodeo, I learned the practical application of gambling on myself."

Rodeo became an indelible and important part of my life during my teen and college days, and I was quite good at it. I was the Bareback Rookie of the Year for the West Coast in 1972. I received rodeo scholarships to Modesto Junior College and Fresno State College in California. In those days, a scholarship paid entry fees, travel and food, and you got to keep the winnings. Sometimes,

it'd really pay me to go to two amateur rodeos and a college rodeo in one weekend.

Riding the Tough Ones

I had a lot of success riding animals that were well-known for bucking riders off. For example, at the Livermore Rodeo, I rode 01 High Tide, a famous bareback horse who'd

Pat (standing second from left) and his rodeo buddies at the 1975 College National Finals Rodeo, Bozeman, Montana.

1975 COLLEGE NATIONAL FINALS RODEO Bozeman, Montana

Pat and his rodeo traveling partners, from left, Jim Johnson, Bob Berg, Pat and Harold Cook.

bucked off five-time world champion Joe Alexander the week before I rode him. 01 High Tide was still bucking off riders at the National Finals Rodeo when he was in his early 30s!

The next year at the Clovis Rodeo I won second on Pendleton Rose, a new mare on the circuit that all the top riders were winning on.

The following year I rode Mr. Smith, four-times bareback bucking horse of the year and one of the most phenomenal bucking horses of all time.

Riding the tough ones made me feel 10 feet tall and bulletproof. Sometimes, though, I'd spur so hard, I'd spur myself off the horse instead of getting bucked off. I didn't mean to, but the effect of spurring that hard launched me into the air, and I just kept going. I didn't make the full eight seconds,

but I'd often land on my feet, and that was good.

Rodeo was the first thing in my life I really felt supremely confident doing. For the couple of minutes when I was in the chute before, during and after my ride, I was the most confident, super-human being that I could be. I never thought about anybody or anything else. It was just me and the situation. One thing I could always do is drown out the audience. Whether there was no one in the stands watching, or a million people, the thought never entered my mind.

I knew I was good at riding bucking horses, probably better than 99 percent of the riders out there. My most disappointing times came when I had trouble drawing really good horses. I hated watching great horses buck right in front of or behind me. I'd get so frustrated. I just knew I could ride them, or I'd

Pat and his rodeo buddies traveled in style in their "Rodeomobile," a 1962 Cadillac funeral car. From left, Dave Quinn, Dave Ericson, Bob Berg, Jim Ericson, Pat ad Dave Carlson.

damn near die trying.

Rodeo gave me my first real taste of success. When I'd ride the really tough ones, like 01 High Tide or Mr. Smith, I felt as if I were one of the best in the world, because not too many people could do it. I was a little cocky about it, to be sure. Years later, at a seminar I was giving, I ran into a college friend who remembered me. After a short conversation, he patted me on the back and said, "You're not the same Pat Parelli you used to be." I said, "Thank you." He meant it as a compliment, because I was pretty arrogant when I was young, as a lot of 19- and 20-year-old rodeo cowboys are.

Got My Permit

After I rode Mr. Smith, Johnny Hawkins, Joe Alexander and Jack Roddy (all Professional Rodeo Cowboys Association world champions) wrote a letter to the PRCA recommending that I forego the standard procedure of getting a PRCA permit and automatically get my card, based on the ability I'd shown in the arena.

As far as I know, I'm one of the last rodeo riders to receive his card that way. Back then, if riders got three cardholders to write a letter of recommendation for them, they might get the PRCA to issue them a card, but that doesn't

happen anymore. In the permit system today, the rider has to earn his card by winning $2,500 in minor rodeos before he can compete in major PRCA-sanctioned events, like Salinas, Cheyenne or the Cow Palace.

Birds of a Feather

I met many interesting people through my association with rodeo. One in particular is Bob Berg, the renowned silversmith, whom I'd met in a roundabout way, and who later become one of my rodeo traveling buddies. He was an Australian rodeo rider and talented saddlemaker and leather-tooler who wanted to ride rodeo in America. I often refer to him as the Larry Mahan of Australia because he won the all-around title there several times.

Bob's friend, John Stanton, was big on campdrafting (the Aussie version of working cow horse) and was the first person to bring Ray Hunt over to the land down under. Through one of Stanton's friends, Johnny Clements from Sacramento, Bob found out about my rodeo school at Don Gates' roping arena (See Chapter 5). He came over to the States, and we hit it off immediately. But only two weeks after he arrived, he broke his leg while riding bulls. All that winter he and I worked and tinkered in Jess Tharp's saddle shop. (I was in college at the time.) Jess used to be a saddletree

Pat is so proud of this winning ride in Pine Mountain, California, in 1974, that he still wears the belt buckle today.

maker, and he taught us to make our own bronc saddles. Bob even completely tooled his.

The next winter I worked for Farmer's Warehouse, a wholesale feed mill in Modesto, for $2.00 an hour. I worked during the week and put in 12-hour shifts on weekends. Grain came in on a train, would be dropped down a chute and carried to the mill, where we'd mill the grain and bag it for delivery to local feed stores. There was also a small retail section, and I'd greet people who came in the door and offer to help ladies take the feed sacks out to their trucks.

I'd worked there for about four to five months when the owner took me aside and asked me to come into his office. He told me I had real talent, and he offered me a raise to $2.10/hour. He told me not to tell anyone because he said no one had ever earned that big of a raise in such a short time. Needless to say, I was under-whelmed.

The next weekend Bob, who by now was my rodeo partner, and I went to a rodeo and came away with about $1,800 in winnings between us. The difference between earning $2.10/hour and $1,800 for eight seconds' work really left an impression on me. I never went back to the feed mill again.

Bob and I roomed together, each paying $25 a month to rent a small room above a water tower on the Turner family farm. The family was poor with five growing boys to feed, and their father, George, was the only income-earner. In fact, he made only $500 a month as a veterinarian's assistant. Their house was so meager that when the wind blew, it literally would rattle through the walls. The family ate lots of potatoes in those days. They'd buy them in 100-pound sacks and go through a couple of bags a month.

After one of our winning rodeos, Bob and I laid $1,000 cash on the family kitchen table one day. We wanted to help them out, and this was the best way we knew how. Years later, when I moved to Clements, one of the family's boys, Billy, turned out to be the UPS driver whose route included our ranch. I invited him in for a cup of coffee one day. He told me about his dad having passed away about four years earlier. He said his father never forgot our generous gift.

Over the years, I've found that our altruism was typical of rodeo folk. Many are considerate and thoughtful people, who often lend a helping hand to those in need — inside the arena and out.

A side note about Bob: He eventually learned to engrave silver and formed his own highly regarded silver buckle and jewelry com-

*Pat riding
Arizona Strip,
California
Bucking Horse of
the Year in Wells,
Nevada, 1974.*

pany. Bob has an innovative and distinctive engraving style, and his buckles and other sterling silver pieces and jewelry are considered works of art.

They say birds of a feather flock together, and I think that's very true. Besides Bob, my other rodeo partner was Dave Carlson, from Davis, California, who has become a very well-known horseshoer, always on the leading edge of farriery. He dedicated his life to becoming a progressive shoer.

In my young and formative years, I was surrounded by people, including rodeo people like Bob and Dave, who thought outside the box. I think that helped influence my line of thinking, which is also outside the box.

What Rodeo Taught Me

I rodeoed hard for about seven years and then slowed down to intermittent rodeos as I began training horses more. All told, I rodeoed for 14 years. I rode 98 percent of my horses and went seven years without ever getting bucked off. I traveled everywhere, from one coast to the other. Riding in Madison Square Garden was as far East as I ventured.

After a seven-year hiatus from rodeo, just for kicks I went to Salinas (California) Rodeo and Wyoming's Cheyenne Frontier Days (my last rodeo) in 1992. I liked my last horse and the ride he gave me so much that I bought him. There was a 66 brand on his hips. I called him "Route 66" and used to say that I got my kicks on Route 66, just like the song by the same name. I donated him to the West Hills Community College rodeo team in Coalinga, California.

Rodeoing taught me a lot of important things I still use today in my clinics, demonstrations, business and in dealing with people in general.

Through the sport I learned a lot about people and relationships. I'd see people in a variety of situations; sometimes their worst would come out and sometimes their best. I saw sportsmanship and the generosity of human spirit. I saw the good, the bad and the ugly.

Rodeo attracts all kinds of people, from health nuts to those taking drugs, from religious zealots to those with criminal tendencies. Every sort of person in the world shows up at a rodeo at some point.

During my rodeo days I started sorting out the type of people I wanted to be around: those who are positive, progressive and natural.

I also learned about team-manship. The three of us — Dave Carlson, Bob Berg and I — were like the Three Musketeers. We had a synergism that caused all of us to ride better than we were probably supposed to. We did a lot for each other's mental and emotional states. We wouldn't critique each other, but instead tell one another what we did well. We didn't criticize either; we only complimented one another. It'd be up to the fellow who was the subject of the conversation to tell us what he thought he could do to improve. It was a very positive experience. I'd traveled to rodeos with guys who'd do everything they could to defeat me mentally. Instead, our little trio built up each other mentally and emotionally.

Through rodeo, I learned how to travel and how to organize traveling logistics. In all those years, I was late for only one rodeo, and that's because I made a logistical mistake. I thought I was up on Sunday, and I was supposed to ride on Saturday.

You've heard of "going with the flow." Well, in bareback riding, I learned how to flow with the horse's go, which, of course, helped me immensely years later in my horsemanship career. Even with saddle broncs, the rider has a saddle in between the horse and his body and in some ways that impedes him. But on bareback horses, you have to go with the horse, not pull against him.

Pat won the College Rodeo in Merced, California, in 1975.

43

Pendleton Rose was a horse all the top riders were winning on. Pat won second on her at the Clovis Rodeo.

Pat riding #12 Classic Velvet at the Clovis Rodeo.

Through rodeo, I learned the practical application of gambling on myself. I rarely ever go to Las Vegas. To me that's betting on the stars and the moon to line up. I learned to bet on my own probabilities. I knew what my abilities were, and the only luck of the draw was the horse. I found that even if I didn't draw the best horse to ride, if I did my job the best I could, I could still get in the money.

I also learned that in competition there are only two people who're happy – the one who wins first and the one who wins fourth. Because the guy who wins second thinks he should've won first and the guy who wins third thinks he should've won second. The guy who got fourth is just glad he snuck in. So, I figured that if you had 30 people in an event, you have 28 unhappy people and two happy ones.

Since then, in my horsemanship program, I've thought about how I can create a situation where it's win-win for everyone. I try to think of things from everyone's perspective, including the horse's.

Pat won the 1975
Clovis Rodeo
on Mr. Smith,
four-time bareback
bucking horse of
the year.

PHOTO BY HUBBELL

"Pat's last rodeo was
Cheyenne Frontier
Days in Wyoming,
1992. He entered "just
for kicks," and liked the
horse so much he
bought him and named
him "Route 66."
People asked, "Who's
that old guy in the
short chaps?"

45

5 ANYTHING FOR A BUCK

"I thought I was in heaven because I was around somebody I considered to be really good with horses...."

While at Modesto Junior College, besides being active in rodeo, I worked for Don Gates, who, at the time, had to be one of the world's biggest horse traders. He'd run 10,000 horses a year through his stable in Ceres, California, a small town outside of Modesto.

World's Best Horse Trader

Don was a real interesting horse trader. He had pens of horses separated by price. There was a $500 horse pen, one for $700 horses and one for $900 and up. He'd group horses according to what he thought they were worth, and he had a buy-back guarantee on them. If someone bought a horse from him that didn't work out, that person could bring it back, put it in a designated pen and choose from the next pen up, and give Don the additional money. It was a no-questions-asked policy. If you didn't like the horse, you could trade for another. And if you couldn't find anything you liked, he'd give you all your money back, less maybe $100.

Don really knew how to move horses. There'd be a horse auction somewhere in the Central Valley every single night. He'd send his help (me being one of them) to the various sales with huge truck/trailer rigs, sometimes carrying 20 horses at a time. We'd drop the horses off at designated sales and pick up others. Some days, truckloads of mustangs would drive into his place. Don would never even look at them; he'd just sign the ticket and put them in a pen. His idea was to make at least $10 a horse. Do the math. Running over 10,000 horses per year, that's $100,000 profit and in 1972 that was a lot of money. It still is.

My job was to get horses ready to sell. Do you have any idea how many horses I had to clip, either body clip or clip bridle paths, ears, legs? Hundreds. And, of course, how many of them had behavioral problems around clippers? Hundreds. So I found that either I could clip them, or I had to teach them how to be clipped. I had my work cut out for me.

It was the same thing for horses who didn't want to be caught. I learned every trick in the world about how to catch horses.

Working for Don, I found myself in a situation that forced me to form strategies about lots of different things just to get my job done, and that included hobbling, twitching, blindfolding, etc. In those days, that's what you did. I was there to learn and do a job, and that meant whatever it took.

Don focused on rope horses and was then and probably still is now one of the largest dealers of rope horses in the country. In addition to his sale horses, he'd have around 15 horses in training at any one time. This was my first opportunity to see horses being trained professionally for a particular sport.

Don also had around 1,000 head of roping cattle on his place. He'd supply the cattle for major roping contests, such as the Bob Feist Invitational, the Oakdale 10 Steer and Chowchilla 10 Steer.

He would hold ropings at his place seven days a week in three roping arenas. One of the arenas contained the cattle that were used at one of those big events, so they weren't fresh, but nearly so. Another arena had cattle that were a little more used up, and the third was for practice cattle. After the cattle weren't good for practice, we'd feed them up, then put them across the street at a little arena we used for junior rodeos.

Anything for a Buck

While I worked for Don, he allowed me to hold rodeo schools at his place. I struck a deal with him on the stock that he couldn't sell as saddle horses. In his immense mix of horses, there were plenty of spoiled ones, those that had behavioral problems or were untamed mustangs. All these "back pen" horses were destined for the slaughterhouse. He'd let me buck out all of them that would buck. I'd earn money from guys on high school and college rodeo teams who came to my school to learn to ride bucking horses.

Out of around 100 horses at my school, almost everything would buck once, half would buck twice and from there it dropped really quickly. It was actually difficult to find horses that'd buck more than three times. The ones that could last longer went to rodeo stock contractors. If the animal would buck for the entire season, Don might make an extra $100 profit per horse.

I did the same thing with Don's sour roping cattle. We used them as bucking stock. My rodeo school afforded me a great way to make a little money and to practice myself. I guess you could say that I did anything for a buck.

Buck-Jumping

One interesting thing I learned from my bucking horse endeavors, though, is that most

Pat rodeoed throughout junior college and even ran his own rodeo school, where college kids could practice.

horses really don't want to buck. Knowing this helped me years later in my colt-starting and horse-training businesses. I realized that if I'd let a horse run around long enough, especially with a saddle on, he'd get over bucking rather quickly. That's not 100 percent, of course, but it works most of the time.

In my rodeo career, I'd see horses that'd quit bucking because the riders were too good. Heck, I hardly ever got bucked off. Why would a horse want to keep bucking if it got him nowhere? That's too much like work. Now, if he could get riders off religiously, then that's different. That's why bulls get so good. The percentage of them being ridden for the full eight seconds is low. It turns out to be as much fun for the bulls as it is for the riders.

We've succeeded in breeding the buck out of our modern horses. The only people who've bred the buck back in are bucking-stock breeders, whose business depends on rank horses, and sport-horse people, such as the Dutch and Germans. Horses who want to jump seem to want to buck. To me, there's a correlation between the two. In Australia, they even call it "buck-jumping." Jumping is just bucking over sticks, and bucking is jumping without sticks. Some horses have a lot of jump in them and some don't.

I also learned, contrary to my belief, that mustangs aren't much for bucking either. They usually run as fast as they can and scatter, but rarely ever buck hard, if at all. They might make one jump out of the chutes and then run like crazy.

One of the best bucking horses I ever rode at Don's was a mare who'd been in the dude string for 10 years. When we put a flank strap on her, she came unglued. She bucked high and wild. It all goes to show you that you just never know.

Through my encounters with hundreds of bucking horses, I discovered a common trait: Most horses who like to buck are cinchy or sensitive around the barrel. I have a test that I apply to young horses to find out which ones might buck. I put my arms over their backs and just touch them in the cinch area. The ones that look like Halloween cats are the ones that will buck.

Field Trips Broaden Horizons

In addition to my rodeo activities, I was also active on the junior college livestock judging teams. I got to go on a number of field trips to further my education. On one trip, I remember seeing the famous Three Bars (TB), and on another trip, I saw a fellow named Ron Hawkins (no relation to Johnny Hawkins). He was one of the first people I ever saw use ropes to encourage horses to give to pressure.

Ron was well-known as a starter of Quarter Horse race prospects. I can remember sitting on a fence watching him rope a colt by the hind leg and teach it to yield to pressure. I didn't know it at the time, but it was the type of natural horsemanship technique that Ray Hunt and the Dorrance brothers were doing. I didn't realize until much later that it was that very brand of horsemanship I'd eventually become involved with.

Besides western riding, I was exposed to English riding, as well. Our ag teacher, Tex Longbothum, wanted us kids to see more than just rodeo and roping. It was his goal for us to experience the best of both worlds. I remember a trip to Donna Maddox's stable. Donna and her kids were active in the hunter/jumper scene. We also went to a Gene Lewis clinic. Gene was a noted hunter/jumper trainer, who

many years later would help Olympian David O'Connor with his jumping. Gene showed David how to teach horses to jump on-line first, then under saddle.

Both Donna and Gene were good friends of and big collaborators with Ray Hunt and the Dorrance brothers. All of these people, Ron Hawkins, Donna Maddox and Gene Lewis, whether they knew it or not, were practicing forms of natural horsemanship. I found out years later (at the PRCA Hall of Fame induction ceremony in 2004) that even Johnny Hawkins, my rodeo mentor, studied with Billy Linfoot, who was a great friend of Tom Dorrance. Billy would often tell Johnny about the incredible things Tom Dorrance could do with a horse.

The connections for this emerging horsemanship movement were all there, and, as they say, it's a small world. The epicenter of this matrix was in California between Santa Barbara and Santa Rosa, and between Bakersfield and Red Bluff. I'm just glad I was in the middle of it all, rubbing shoulders with people who were part of it.

Married

I met and later married (in 1980) my first wife, Karen Rivers, during my junior college days. She and I had to decide whether I should finish the last two years of college.

I was doing well rodeoing. For example, I'd won the Folsom Fourth of July Rodeo and earned $1,400, which was a lot of money back in 1972 for eight seconds of work on one weekend. (It'd still be a lot today.)

I decided to invest the money and bought a Limousin steer at the Pleasanton County Fair. I fattened it up to 1,400 pounds, and had it butchered. We sold half to Karen's parents, and I told Karen that "if nothing else, we're going to be able to eat this year." The steaks were huge, and we ate for three years on that darn thing! Typically, meatpackers butcher cattle before their steaks get too big, but I didn't know that at the time.

I'd go to the locker where I had the meat packaged and frozen, bring home two big steaks and try to cook them on a little Hibachi grill in our apartment, along with a package of parmesan noodles. The steaks overran the plate and little, 103-pound Karen would quizzically look at me and say, "I couldn't eat that in a week!"

Itty Bitty Buckles

My first year out of junior college, I won belt buckles at both the prestigious Cal Poly rodeo and the Clements rodeo on the same weekend. During this time, silver prices had really soared. Usually, rodeo belt buckles were good-sized and only about 20 percent of rodeos offered them. But the buckles I won at those two rodeos were itty bitty. I remember sitting in the car looking at those two tiny buckles and saying to myself, "Someday, I'm going to have two little kids who'll like these buckles."

In all, I won about 25 buckles during my rodeo career, many of which I gave away to friends and family, but I kept those two dinky buckles. And sure enough, Karen and I had two children (Marlene and Caton Ryder); they each now have one of the buckles.

Because I won the Cal Poly rodeo, I thought about finishing my last two years of college there, but it was too expensive compared to Fresno State College. Besides, the Cal Poly rodeo team was difficult to get on, whereas the Fresno State team wanted me.

I moved to Fresno and attended college there, majoring in agricultural education. I finally figured out what I wanted to be – a high school ag teacher, so I could have the summers off to rodeo. I was thinking way ahead.

That first year at Fresno our rodeo team beat Cal Poly for the regional finals. Cal Poly had won the region 27 years in a row. I was happy to be a part of that victory.

Assistant Trainer

One of the people I met at Fresno State was Donny Wright, who's a cutting horse trainer today, but at the time he worked in a feed store. He asked me if I wanted a job as an assistant trainer. I said, "I don't know. What's an assistant trainer?"

He told me about a trainer named Chuck Pollard who had a stable east of Clovis.

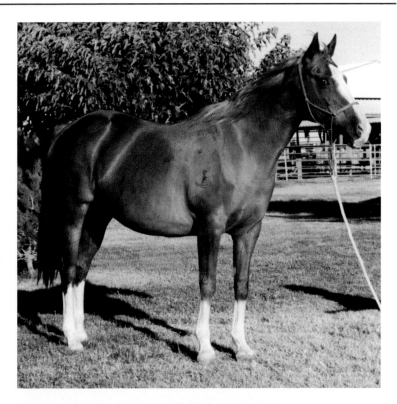

The sorrel Quarter Horse mare Bridget Bar Dough has been in Pat's life in one way or another all of her life. She played a big part in his development as a horseman. She's about 15 years old in this photo, but is over 30 now.

Chuck was looking for an assistant, sort of a colt-starter. I knew that would be right up my alley since I'd started plenty of colts in the past.

I went to Chuck's and did well. It turned out he was a student of Troy Henry's, a horse trainer I'd heard a little about and who later became one of my mentors.

A couple of things I ran into at Chuck's helped influence my eventual career direction. Chuck taught students to ride western pleasure and equitation. So, in my mind, a horse trainer was someone who gave little children equitation lessons. And every Saturday and Sunday you had to take the kids to the show, dress up with a tie and look professional. None of that appealed to me. I decided I just wanted to be a colt-starter.

Running W's

There was an older horse trainer at Chuck's named Ernie, whose last name was Seffell or some such spelling. Ernie was a master of the running W, a restraint device usually used in a cruel way. It's made of a rope with three rings attached. The rope is placed around a horse's stomach. Cuffs with rings are placed on each of the horse's front fetlocks. You take a 30- to 40-foot rope and run it from the first ring on the stomach band down to the first hoof, back to the belly, then on to the ring on the second hoof. With this contraption you could pull a horse's front feet out from underneath him, and he'd fall down.

In the movies, they'd use piano wire instead of rope with the running W's so the audience couldn't see what jerked the horse to the ground. The device was eventually outlawed.

Running W's are something people used on runaway carriage horses. In that situation, you didn't have to pull on the horse's mouth, which could result in no response – instead, you could get the message down to the horse's feet.

Ernie's theory behind the running W was to teach the horse with a verbal cue first before he did anything. The secret was to not pull the rope all at once, but to feather it. With gloves on, Ernie let the rope slide a little bit to give the horse a physical cue. The horse would feel it and stop with one foot in the air.

Ernie was very proficient at this, and together we got a reputation for being able to handle any kind of tough horse. I'd get on the horses in the running W's and Ernie would work the ropes.

I thought I was in heaven because I was around somebody I considered to be really good with horses and in my field of interest to boot. I knew I didn't want to give little kids equitation lessons, and this was fascinating stuff to me.

Thumbs Up

Ernie and I got to be best friends. I remember he once said to me, "Whenever you tie a bowline knot, be careful because you could lose your thumb," as he stuck his thumbless hand in the air. A week later I lost my thumb. Here's how.

I'd purchased a horse for myself at a local auction, but ended up trading him to my Aunt Donna for Bridget Bar Dough, the mare who'd been in my life since her birth. As I mentioned earlier, Freddie Feriera had willed the mare to my aunt when he died. But Bridget proved to be too much horse for my aunt, and the auction horse suited her better. At last, Bridget was finally mine.

One time I took Bridget, my cousins and their friends to a junior rodeo in Springville, California. I unloaded my sensitive mare out of the trailer first and tied her to a fence. As I was tying her, a combination of my flipping the rope and a kid jumping up on the fence scared Bridget. She pulled back. The end of my thumb got caught in the knot and popped off. My thumb bone remained, but all the flesh was gone. I walked over to the ambulance for help and showed my bloody stump to the driver, who promptly fainted. I did get my thumb stitched that day and still have full use of the digit, but it's a tad shorter than the other one.

Once again, the pull-back predicament reared its ugly head for me, but it'd be years before I'd find a solution to that problem.

Injured and in a cast, I was unable to do much work and ended up losing my job at Pollard's.

Entrepreneurial Spirit

I had to start over. What interested me now was having my own operation, where I could board horses, start colts and work with problem horses. I found a piece of property previously owned by Bob Robinson, an ex-rodeo champion who held a rodeo school there at one time. It was on the corner of Cedar and Herndon in Clovis, California. I leased the ranch, 12 acres with a racetrack, some stables, a big rodeo arena with lights and a five-bedroom house.

My objective in renting the place was to make a little money going to school. My entrepreneurial spirit was awakening. I boarded horses, started colts, hauled horses – anything to make a buck. In fact I named my business "Anything for a Buck."

The house was originally a set of military barracks. The owners had purchased the barracks from an abandoned military base, and sided them with aluminum for next to nothing. It actually did look like a house! The whole place was in great disrepair, but I whitewashed the fences and fixed the property up. I decided to call it the Running W Ranch. I thought people would realize I was the one who used to work with Ernie Seffell, and they'd bring me their horses.

I tried to make a go of the Running W Ranch, and even rented my spare bedrooms to college buddies. My home felt like a frat house. Chasing my friends down for their rent money wasn't fun.

One guy could never pay me; he always promised me he would, but never did. At 22 years old, he was an addicted gambler. He had a wife and daughter up in Oakdale and was in school to learn to be a meat inspector. He owed me quite a bit of money and I eventually had to kick him out.

One day a year later, he showed up and proudly exclaimed, "I'm here to pay you."

I said, "Really?"

He said, "Yeah, I got it in the trunk."

I countered, "But I want money."

He shot back, "Well, it's not money, but it's in the trunk." He opened it up and there were 60 pounds of rabbit meat!

Now what was I supposed to do with that? I thought fast on my feet and came up with a workable solution.

I had purchased some panels, and needed them moved to where my stalls were. It would've taken me and another guy 20 hours to take them down, reassemble them and attach them to my stalls. That idea didn't appeal to me, so I figured out a way to get other people to do it for me.

I threw a party for 20 of my closest friends, bought a keg of beer and barbecued the 60 pounds of rabbit that I had marinated for two days. It actually tasted pretty good.

Before dinner, I announced to my party-goers that before they ate they had to march over to the pens, pick them up, turn them around and take them to my barn. The whole thing took about three minutes, and I had my stall runs in place.

After eating the barbecued rabbit, one of my friends asked where I'd gotten all the rabbits. I said, "Oh, I thought I'd told you guys. About a week ago, the Fresno Pest Control guy came by. He gave me a bunch of poison to take care of the jackrabbits out in the race-track's infield. I just picked them up like cabbage the next day."

Pat riding in the Oakdale Rodeo in April 1983, two days before his son Caton was born.

The look on their faces was priceless. My friend was right, he'd paid me in full.

A New Plan

It didn't take me long at the Running W Ranch to quickly realize that managing my own business entailed a big lease to pay, water bill, electric bill, feed bill, shavings bill, someone to clean the stalls and mow the lawns, corrals to buy and build.

And I soon found out that nobody wanted to send me a colt to start either. For two reasons: one, they thought I was just a rodeo cowboy, and all I'd probably do is buck out their horses; and two, there were well-known horse trainers already populating the area – Chuck Pollard, Jimmie Nunes, Les Vogt, Carl Gould, Troy Henry, Bill Wildes, Greg Ward, Leon Harrel. Within a short distance there were a number of good choices to send a colt to.

I needed a new plan.

6 THE KING OF MULES

"I was truly the king of mules because I was riding the queen of mules."

I didn't have many steady clients at this time, but I did have one who was a horse trader and a preacher, which is kind of incongruent, but nonetheless that's what he did. Ray Brown specialized in cheap horses, mules and broncy draft horses. Everything he had was on the snorty side of things and cheap, but he was a wonderful old man, and I really got along well with him.

I made him a deal. If he'd keep two animals in training with me all the time, I'd do it for $125 a month per head. The first animal he brought me was Rosy, a four-year-old wild mule that came off an Indian reservation. The Indians used her for only one thing and that was rodeo. They bucked her out repeatedly, and this mule could buck! Ray paid $300 for her.

I called my good friend Donny Wright and asked him to come over and help me with Rosy.

No Bed of Roses

Ray delivered Rosy in a stock truck and backed it up to my arena, which should've been my first clue. I didn't have a small pen at the time, so the large arena is where we decided to put her.

Rosy had a halter on her with a 20-foot rope hanging from it. Ray said that when they tried to get a halter on her, she kicked like a mule and bit like a crocodile. She wasn't really halter-broke, which was evident from the worn spots on her nose and on the back of her head

where she'd pulled back on the lead rope all the way from Oregon to Fresno.

She'd been in the trailer for two and a half days. When they'd try to feed her, she'd lay her ears back and threaten them. They ended up throwing the feed to her.

Once out of the trailer, Rosy showed her true colors; her self-preservation instincts came through. She came straight for Donny and me; she kicked him and bit me – just flattened us both. When we turned around, she was loose in the big rodeo arena. Brown chuckled the whole time.

Donny and I took turns catching one end of the 20-foot rope. We had to duck and dive so much, it was like being matadors in a bull-fighting arena.

We eventually got Rosy's rope snubbed up around a fence post, and I put a blindfold on the mule as well as four-way hobbles – tricks I'd learned from my Don Gates sale-barn days. It would be a long time before I knew any better.

When we thought we had her completely restrained, I took the blindfold off, and she immediately kicked out. When she did, she jerked her front feet out from under herself. Down she went to her knees. She got back up and kicked again. Again, down to her knees. That was it for her. She'd figured it out.

I left her in the rodeo arena and brought her food and water. As soon as I'd get near her, she'd react like a mad bear. At first, she decided she wouldn't drink from the bucket.

*Thumper,
the super mule,
and Pat competed
against horses at
the Salinas Rodeo
in California.*

However, I was determined she would never drink unless it was from my bucket. I wanted her to depend on me. I felt that was the key to getting through to her, if I had any hope at all of training her. Before long, thirst overcame Rosy, and she started drinking out of my bucket. I could rub her with a stick as she drank, but that was as close as I could get.

"Ca-Chink, Ca-Chink"

When Freddie Feriera died, one of the things I'd inherited from him was a set of Visalia spurs with big rowels. They're still among my prized possessions. They have an "SF" on them and were made in San Francisco, so they're very old, turn-of-the-century spurs.

Every day I'd wear the spurs around the ranch. They made a jingling noise as I walked,

the typical "ca-chink" sound that this type of spur makes.

On the sixth day of her arena captivity, Rosy heard me coming from around the barn – ca-chink, ca-chink, ca-chink – and she bellowed loudly as only mules can do. The look in her eye seemed to say, "I understand now that you're not trying to hurt me."

As she drank the water, I stepped into the arena and petted her all over, including her legs, which still had hobbles on them. I took a leap of faith and took them off, but still left on the halter and lead rope. I then turned away. As I did, she followed me wherever I went, dragging her lead rope. She'd learned to depend on me.

I took off the halter and lead and she still followed me. Even though I'd gotten the right response the wrong way (not the natural way), it was the first time I'd ever had the feeling of pair-bonding or unity with any animal, other than a dog I'd had as a kid.

That was the beginning for us. She fell in love with me and I fell in love with her.

Off to the Races

After that, handling her was easy. She really didn't even buck much when I started riding her. In the next 60 days, she made progress by leaps and bounds. I even felt confident enough that I took her to a mule show in Exeter, California. She won the halter, western pleasure and reining classes and was second in the trail class.

I entered her in the races even though I didn't know if she could run. As we stood on the starting line for the first day's race, we were next to Al Dodds, who was really into racing mules and had three in the race. He was on one, his wife, Donna, was on another and a professional jockey named Celso Camerina was on their third mule.

As soon as the starting gun went off, they were out of there like bullets. I stood, bewildered, with a "huh" look on my face. They'd outdistanced us by five lengths right off the bat. But Rosy and I got in gear, and we actually started gaining on them.

I thought, "This mule can run."

That night I played around with Rosy, teaching her to break fast from a standing start. My cue was to smooch to her and I would start spanking, which meant we were supposed to go somewhere – fast. Soon, all I had to do was smooch.

I was ready for the race the next day. I borrowed an English saddle, so I wouldn't burden Rosy with my heavy western one, and I jacked up the stirrups like a jockey.

The same bunch of mules lined up for the race. Off we went with the starting gun. We broke hard and fast with the rest of them. The next thing I knew, we were a length ahead, then two, then three. I thought I was riding Secretariat. I turned around and saw my competition far behind me. I decided to cruise on in to the finish line.

We came around the last turn and there was a kid sitting on the rail eating popcorn. As I was looking over my right shoulder to see how far back the other mules were, Rosy saw the kid and spooked away from the rail maybe 20 feet. Down I went.

I dislocated my shoulder, twisted my nose a bit and ate a mouth full of dirt. I was okay, although disoriented. Instead of running off with the other mules, Rosy stopped, turned around and came back to me. She started nuzzling me. That was it. I really knew I was in love with her now. I couldn't wait until the next mule show. I got so excited about that mule and our success that I thought I'd found my true calling. I was going to become a mule trainer!

American Mule Association

After the show was over, I found myself talking to several nice mule people, having refreshments and enjoying the camaraderie. There was one man in the crowd who was drunk, and he created quite a fuss about the judging. No one there liked this much and someone said, "If only we had a mule association, we could keep drunk and disorderly people like this from coming to our events." My antenna went up.

As I mentioned earlier, I'd met Al Dodds, who, along with his wife, Donna, had great mules that would win races and reining contests. Still today, to me Al is one of the best mule trainers I've ever seen. He was such a good mule-man. His mules did everything from roping to reining to barrel racing. He took his time with the mules and it showed.

We also met Ray Winters and his wife, Jackie, who had a really nice mule named Molly.

Two months after the show, Ray, Jackie and I sat down to coffee and discussed the idea of starting an organization called the California Performance Mule Association.

I called the secretary of Bishop Mule Days, and got their mailing list of 300 names. We sent each person on the list a letter announcing our new association and how much the dues were going to be.

We selected a handful of well-known people in the mule world – Al Dodds, Johnny Jones, Glen Burns, Bill Shaffer, Leo Porterfield,

Pat and his then-wife Karen competed at American Mule Association shows in the late 1970s. At this one in Oakdale, California, Karen is on Thumper and Pat is on Double Trouble.

Shirley Green and others – and wrote them a separate letter inviting them to a meeting where we'd select a board of directors. The meeting took place at my Running W Ranch.

Out of the blue, a lady named Laverne Ordway showed up and asked to be the association's secretary. I told her, "You got it." Her husband was Ray Ordway, of the famous vaquero family from the Livermore-Brentwood area. He knew Ed Connell very well.

Laverne was passionate about the association. Her and Ray's best friend was Ernie Morris, the artist for Ed Connell's book and one of the most famous vaquero artists of all time.

Twenty people showed up for the inaugural meeting. I told Ray we had an empty bag full of hot air, and we needed to fill it up quickly as we were already receiving membership money from our first letter.

The people who came to the meeting were famous, not only for their mule activities, but also for their other endeavors.

For example, Glen Burns was the Tom Dorrance of packers. He was phenomenal. He packed 300-foot cables for bridges into the backcountry for the government and figured out a way to have the mules carry them so that they wouldn't fall off the switchback mountain trails. He showed me pictures of 30-horse hitches he configured. Glen was instrumental in getting Bishop Mule Days on the map. He was a real go-getter and did a lot of publicity work for the event.

Johnny Jones, also a legendary packer, owned a high-end pack station, sort of the Mercedes-Benz of pack stations, on the south side of Yosemite National Park. Everything he had was top drawer. His clientele included movie stars and even President Ronald Reagan. He was an amazing man – part Indian, part mountain man. He had a reputation for knowing areas of Yosemite's backside that no white man had ever seen. He, too, was influential in the formation of Bishop Mule Days and was one of the event's first judges.

King of Mules

At this formative meeting, someone thought our name was too restrictive and suggested the American Mule Association instead. I became the president and Ray the vice president.

There I was, surrounded by the who's who in the mule business, and they all looked to me for leadership, a 23-year-old kid who was wet behind the ears compared to them. They had faith in me anyway.

Laverne worked for a law firm in Fresno, which enabled us to get our nonprofit status, and Ernie Morris agreed to do the logo as long as he could see a performance mule do a slide stop. He wanted that image for the logo.

Out came Rosy. Ernie watched us perform so he had an idea of what to draw. He wouldn't draw anything that wasn't real. He used the image of me and Rosy as a model for the association's logo.

Basically, Laverne and I babied the new association along. Unfortunately though, shortly after things got rolling, Ray got bucked off a new rope horse, broke his neck and ended up with a halo device on his head for six months. A year or so later they moved to Texas or New Mexico.

But Laverne's and my efforts paid off. Our association went from 300 members the first year (1977) to over 3,000 members in three years.

With the new association and my success with mules, I now decided that this was it. I'd finally found what I wanted to be – the king of mules. I figured that if people saw what I could do with mules, they'd surely send me horses to start.

I'd become passionate about learning how to slide stop, spin, change leads and accomplish other performance maneuvers. I made quite a name for myself in the mule world

and was proud of my achievements. I eventually became the person to beat at Bishop Mule Days.

Bishop Mule Days

Bishop Mule Days began as a packer and outfitter fun get-together, where they'd get on pack mules that'd never been ridden and try to compete in barrel racing and other events. It was hilarious to watch.

But then Johnny Jones and Shirley Green showed up with Rabbit, one of the most famous mules of all time, named in honor of her long ears. Rabbit rode and performed like a horse; she was the mule to beat. At the time, it seemed that everyone who didn't make it with horses got into mules and tried to compete with them. Interest in performance mules was high.

After our success in our first mule show, I felt that Rosy was ready for the big time and could perform with the best of them. I played with her all winter and taught her to spin, change leads and slide to a stop. I couldn't wait until May and Bishop Mule Days.

Rosy didn't let me down. We won the snaffle bit class, which made us the world champions in that event. I was so proud of myself and Rosy. We won a belt buckle, and I just knew I was on my way to fulfilling my dreams.

Well, someone offered Ray $5,000 for his $300 mule, and he certainly couldn't turn that down. But there went my champion partner. Ray gave me about $500 as a commission to ease the blow. He sold Rosy to a little girl, who got along famously with her.

Two years later, Rosy and the little girl showed up at Bishop Mule Days to compete. I hadn't seen Rosy in all that time since she'd moved to southern California.

By this time, my name and fame had spread and I had a half dozen mules to show at Bishop. As I walked down my barn aisle, still wearing my Visalia spurs with their "ca-chink" sound, I heard a "Whoa, Rosy, whoa!"

Here came Rosy, trotting straight for me, the little girl trying to stop her by pulling back on both reins to no avail. Rosy had heard my spurs and came to find me, bellowing in her familiar voice.

I realized right then that mules are just like horses, only more-so. I just wish I knew back then what I know now, with love, language and leadership as my guiding principles.

Thumper, the Wonder Mule

Mules had become a large part of my training business and to capitalize on the performance mule phenomenon, I decided to produce and sell a video of myself and Rosy performing the reining maneuvers I'd learned from reading Ed Connell's book, *Hackamore Reinsman*. This homemade video was my first effort into the realm of film. Karen, who became my videographer for this and many subsequent tapes, stood in the stands after Bishop Mule Days was over one year and taped me and Rosy doing our thing in the arena. (This was some time before Rosy was sold.)

The next year at Bishop, I met Gene Hammerlun, who owned a mule named Thumper. Gene had seen my video and he looked me up at the show. He was entered in the snaffle bit class the next day, and he needed help with Thumper. So I had him ride her around for me to see what his problems were. He was having a hard time getting her to change leads.

I got on her and in short order said to myself, "Whoa, this is one performing mule." She was really something. Extremely handy, she could stick her tail in the ground and cut back the other way. I tried riding her with one rein in the turns, and it really worked on her. Then I picked up both reins, and she ran backward 20 feet in about three seconds. I thought that I'd found a real live wire in her. I asked Gene if I could show her for him, but he wanted to do it himself. Actually, he did a pretty good job. He was way better than the day before.

I made a deal with Gene to train Thumper. I decided I was truly the king of mules because I was now riding the queen of mules.

At this time, I had a lot of mules in training at the Running W Ranch. I'd show up at Bishop with nine or 10 mules and compete all day long. I entered all the classes, from halter and western pleasure to trail, reining, roping and the races.

On Thumper alone I won 50 of the 52 reining or reined cow-horse classes I entered. The two times we lost were my fault; I went off pattern in one and, in the other, I forgot to take off a bosalito under my bridle, which disqualified me. To this day, I still think Thumper is the most amazing animal I've ever ridden and trained. As of the printing of this book, she's just under 40 years old and is living in Gardnerville, Nevada, with owner Gene Hammerlun.

I also rode Double Trouble for Troy Henry and that mule, too, was a snaffle bit world champion. Baby Snooks was another one of my great mules. In all, I think I won in 14 different classes at Bishop Mule Days.

7 AT THE END OF MY ROPE

"I was a typical trainer: I was broke and the horses had all the bucks."

My rodeo activities and training stable provided a decent living for me, but that all stopped when my lease on the Running W Ranch came to an end. The landowners decided to sell the property, and I couldn't gather the money it would take to buy the land. There were 12 acres, and, at the time, it went for $6,000 an acre, much more than I could ever hope to scrape together. The parcel eventually sold to a developer for medical office space.

I had to be out in 60 days before they were going to bulldoze the facilities. I sold every post, board, piece of aluminum, faucet, etc., so that I could pull together some cash. Boy, was my landlord shocked when he drove up and saw just a handful of sticks that used to be a house and a barn. There wasn't much left to bulldoze.

Highs to Lows

Things had certainly changed since my mule days, and I was at a low point in my life. Because I'd lost my lease on the Running W Ranch, I had to move to a place in Clovis called Hixon's Horse World, one of the first indoor arenas in California. But things there didn't work out for long, and I was starving to death. I'd go from seven horses in training to two and then back again. Nothing was steady. I was a typical trainer: I was broke and the horses had all the bucks. And, I was getting hurt. Strangely enough, I got more hurt more often riding saddle horses than I ever did riding rodeo broncs. I found myself looking for another situation.

Clovis Mule Days

I was so despondent about my ailing training career that I actually contemplated getting out of the horse business and doing something else, like being a rep for a western-wear manufacturer. That thought didn't last long.

I then considered doing promotions and marketing rather than horse training. One of my moneymaking schemes was trying to make my fortune with Clovis Mule Days. I founded the event and organized three of them (1976, 1977 and 1978). The first one grossed $26,000 in two days, between ticket sales, entry fees and food. About 5,000 people showed up. It cost me $27,000 to put it on. So I lost $1,000, but I thought that was okay. The event would grow, and I'd build from there.

I lost about $2,000 the second year and $3,000 the next, so I quit. I was $6,000 in the hole. I certainly couldn't afford to play that game anymore. I was trying to do anything I could to stay in the horse business, but nothing was working.

Kung Fu Tony

About this time I met Tony Ernst, who was working for Billy Wildes as an assistant trainer. Billy was a new horse trainer on the scene in the 1970s. He'd been a songwriter and had dated singer Linda Ronstadt, but changed his career to horse training. (He's since returned to the music industry. His last big hit was "One Step Over and Two Steps Back.")

In an entrepreneurial spirit, Pat organized and put on Clovis Mule Days three years in a row. This photo was taken at the 1976 event. In it Glenn Burns, the world's oldest living packer at age 88, is unpacking the world's oldest pack mule. Pat, standing between the horse and mule, oversees the activity. The girl on the horse is Glenn's granddaughter.

Tony walked funny due to an accident he had as a young child growing up in Australia. He was helping his father push their car out of a bog after a monsoon rain, when another car came around the corner and smashed into him, jamming his legs in the bumper. He spent five years in a wheelchair, none of which got him down in the least. A talented musician, he eventually attended a music conservatory, played 14 different instruments and then became a black belt in martial arts.

Tom and Ray Who?

Tony came to the United States and became acquainted with and rode with Tom Dorrance and Ray Hunt, who, at the time, I'd never heard of. He started telling me about these men.

During those years, I didn't know how to properly prepare a colt for riding and was getting a lot of problem horses from around the area. Tony showed me some things he'd learned from Ray and Tom.

59

For example, he showed me how to bend a horse's neck to a stop with one rein and take in a couple of long, deep breaths as I held the horse's head. Soon, any tight, tense horse I found myself sitting on would take a long sigh of relief, as well.

That jogged my memory. I'd seen a guy in Madera, California, doing something like that years before. As it turned out, it had been Ray Hunt. I had attended the last day of one of his clinics and didn't really know who he was. I got there during the last 45 minutes to see Ray have people ride with reins around their horses' necks. Listening to Tony explain what Ray did, I had another one of those "Ah-ha, I remember; I understand" moments.

Focus, My Son

Tony came into my life at a time when I'd reached the end of my rope, professionally. My knowledge of horses was stagnant, my business was declining and my frustration was inclining. I tried everything to make some money; I even leased Hixon's arena to hold dances for the public, but nothing worked. I was seriously thinking about leaving the horse industry.

But along came Tony. What he showed me about horses – the things Tom and Ray were doing – rekindled my interest in learning about horses.

Tony also got me interested in martial arts. He taught me the power of focus and about mental, emotional and physical exercises. He explained that Kung Fu and martial arts are not about beating someone up, but about seeking excellence and how to achieve it in life. Tony encouraged me to stay in the horse-training business, but to do it with excellence.

We would ride horses during the day and practice martial arts at night. Tony had what I called a "kick man." He'd jump up and kick the dummy (for lack of a better word), and as it swung around, there was a part that would hit him in the head if he didn't block it. The whole idea was to kick and block, kick and block.

Tony taught me the basics and the different types and styles of martial arts. Later on, I got

into Bruce Lee's "Jeet Kune Do" style of fighting, which is a compilation of the best things borrowed from many different styles of martial arts. That made sense to me as an approach to horsemanship. Years later when I developed my own natural horsemanship program, I followed the same theory. I took the very best ideas and techniques available in many disciplines and incorporated them into an effective style of horsemanship.

Change in Philosophy

Learning from Tony was the impetus for me to mature philosophically. Martial arts is immersed in philosophy and in the spiritual side of things. Through Tony's guidance, it occurred to me that in training horses, I could cause my ideas to become their ideas through communication and not mechanics.

I think that David Carradine's "Kung Fu" television show was on in those days, and I could relate to it. I saw the parallel: Natural horsemanship is martial arts with horses. The Levels program I created many years later is based on the same system as achieving martial arts belts.

The whole concept was a different track than the one I'd been going down, which was simply breaking and training horses the traditional way. I changed my philosophical stance, and, when I did, that opened the doorway for me to meet Troy Henry.

Tony didn't know Troy Henry, but because he encouraged me to stay in the business long enough, in the next six months I had my fateful meeting with Troy.

Tony went on to work for Bill Freeman, who would one day become a top cutting horse pro and trainer of Smart Little Lena. It was Tony who actually started the legendary cutting horse under saddle.

My world, and how I viewed it, was starting to change. Forces were put into motion that would eventually lead me to my destiny.

People's Perspectives on Pat

Que el Caballo te Acompaque
(May the Horse Be With You)

Normally, horse people are used to looking for and trying to discover new answers to old troubles. The reason for that is clear and easy: We always have problems to solve with our partners, the horses. It is not only a question of bits or technique; it involves vets, feed, arena surfaces, trainers, riding equipment, farriers, schedule of training – thousands of matters

The challenge is to try and find the area to change in order to get better results. But the real area is always the same one, the one that is at the center of our problems: the relationship with our horse.

We, in the dressage world, feel like we are experts in control and in the changing and building up of the movement of our horses. This is especially so in my country where we breed nice Spanish (Andalusian) stallions, full of temperament (spirited), yet easy to ride; but they need some help in the development of the right rhythm and the acceptance of steady bit contact.

In the long process of a stallion's training, we try to explain the challenges we find with answers like "the horse is not strong enough, difficult in his mind, bad in his natural balance, tense, uncoordinated for the flying changes, not easy in piaffe, irregular in passage, etc."

The conversation we always have is about what and how much we can get out of our horses. This is an interesting thing. As soon as someone suggests how to make horses give us more, we just try to ask better or to do less and during a shorter session. But still we keep thinking about asking more in the same way because we don't have another strategy.

Pat Parelli is a real cowboy, no doubt about it. He has the look and the size, well, and also the hat! I really never imagined that behind such a big, strong man I would find so much knowledge about the mental and emotional horse. This man talks about how to get horses to give us everything we want without pushing, by finding a different way. This is the secret to his enormous success.

For him it is all about doing just the opposite, things like don't catch the horse; let the horse catch you. He talks less about controlling the body and more about getting the mind of your horse – try to be its leader and friend and to enjoy all of its offers of generosity and love.

I recommend that everybody involved with horses discover Pat Parelli and his "natural" message. In getting closer to his meaning, we will have more success in our relationship with horses and will contribute to making our horses more friendly and happy.

I will never forget when Pat said to me, "May the horse be with you."

Luis Lucio
Dressage trainer
Spanish Olympic dressage rider

Luis Lucio and Nervi, his new, talented five-year-old Spanish stallion.

Part 2 Overview

SAVVY, THE FOUNDATION

The famous horseman Jimmie Williams had this bumper sticker on his golf cart: "It's what you learn after you know it all that really counts." Nothing could be more true.

I'd like to retool that saying a little and apply it to natural horsemanship: "It's what you experience after you have a foundation based on savvy that really counts."

In my early career I had plenty of experiences without savvy, and wore out many Wranglers,® saddles and horseshoes in the process. But after 20 years of learning and being mentored by some of the finest horsemen of my day, I now notice things and feel things about horses through the eyes of savvy.

With all my mentors' help, I acquired a foundation of savvy, and after that, everything I experienced meant more to me. Then, when I graduated to higher levels of savvy, I found that things were even more meaningful. Horsemanship is an evolving, never-ending, learning experience, and I'm still working at it.

8 MOUSE IN A GRAIN SACK

*"Horses teach humans and
humans teach horses."*

One day in the spring of 1976 while I was watching television, a commercial came on for Continental Western Wear in Hanford, California. It showed a guy riding a horse wide open, then gliding to a long, sliding stop. That got my attention.

I asked a friend who that rider was; turns out it was Troy Henry, one of California's best horsemen. My friend's uncle shod horses for Troy, and arranged for me to meet him.

My Wounded Pride

I was as nervous as a long-tailed cat in a room full of rocking chairs as I got ready to meet Troy. I put on my best shirt and pants, and shined my boots. I arrived on time, knocked on the door, shined my boots again by dusting them off on my pants and adjusted my hat.

When Troy opened the door, I introduced myself. He said, "I know who you are." Well, if

The first real challenge Troy Henry gave to Pat was Salty Doc, a stallion other trainers had given up on. He was considered vicious and not trainable. Pat proved them all wrong.

my head didn't swell and my chest puff up. I figured he'd heard all about my prowess riding bucking horses, training mules and starting colts.

Instead, Troy said, "I heard you couldn't train a field mouse to jump into a grain sack."

I literally had the wind knocked out of me. I almost fell to my knees. I actually thought I'd been impressing everyone in the community with my riding skills.

Before I hit the deck with my wounded pride, he said, "But, I saw you ride that big, yellow horse (Mr. Smith, the famous bucking horse) at a Clovis rodeo last week, and if anybody can ride a horse like that he can probably survive my program."

Troy was the second person who said the words "my program" to me (Johnny Hawkins was the first when I was a young rodeo rider). I remembered how well I'd done following a program before and felt I probably could do it again.

We sat down and talked a long time; it was the beginning of a great friendship.

The Apprentice

About two weeks later, I asked Troy to come to a mule-judging seminar. He did, and it was there that we put together our formal working arrangement. He told me that he thought there was a little more underneath my hood than just a bareback rider, so he'd give me a try.

Troy, who was in his mid-50s at the time, was thinking about his retirement, and he wanted someone who'd trade learning for labor. I was to bring in my training horses, of which I had six or seven, pay him board on them at $225/month and manage the barn help, since I could speak barnyard Spanish. I was to be his second-in-command so he could go on vacations and have time for himself. In turn, he said he'd teach me about horses, riding and the horse business. He said, "I'll help you with clients and to maintain a stable of 10 horses in training, if you do everything I say."

Troy was a fabulous horseman who could think like a horse and feel for a horse, but he was really tough on people. The first thing he insisted on was that I be there at 6:00 in the morning, not five minutes after 6. And I couldn't leave until 6 p.m., every day, with no days off.

At 6:00 p.m., I could go home and eat dinner, but I'd have to return at 8:00 and stay until 11:00. Les Vogt, another trainer who rented stalls from Troy, came at 11 p.m. and stayed until 5:30 a.m. Les was a night owl anyway and trained all night long. That's how Troy's stables operated 24 hours a day, seven days a week.

It worked out that I had 10 horses in training all the time, paid Troy the $225 board and kept the $250 in training fees. I gave Troy the board checks as I got them from the customers. The training fees were separate.

After six months, Troy asked for one check instead of all the separate $225 checks. He was trying to teach me how to become a businessman.

I also got commission checks for horses I sold through Troy. We sold some of the first Quarter Horses to go to Brazil and Hawaii and some of the first to go to Australia and Europe. We shipped them through Bill Verdugo, who operated an export business and later became president of the American Quarter Horse Association. Bill's company was one of the largest animal shippers in the country, mainly of bulls and horses.

Jack of All Trades

Troy had a well-run and multifaceted operation on 10 acres in Clovis, California. On it, he and his wife, Lorraine, built Henry's Stables from a small six-stall barn to a multidimensional stable with over 90 stalls.

When it came to horses, there wasn't much Troy didn't offer. He had a pony ring, rental horses, lesson horses, lease horses, boarded horses, training horses, sale horses, tack store and wagon rides. He had levels of lease and sale horses, depending on their looks, breeding and talent. Some of the more expensive horseflesh went to such famous performance horse trainers as Greg Ward, Les Vogt and Don Murphy.

His tack store had at least 20 saddles at any one time – every kind of saddle and bit imaginable.

The first time Pat competed at the NRCHA Snaffle Bit Futurity was in 1977, in Reno, Nevada. He and his filly had the high mark in the fence work.

Pat and Billy Bar Chex at the 1979 NRCHA Snaffle Bit Futurity.

In the summer he even had a girls' camp near Yosemite National Park.

Troy had around 50 boarded horses and also gave lessons. His student instructors, of which I was one, gave lessons three nights a week to groups of 25, with three groups a night. He had five guys like me working for him all the time. I got in there at the end of this era.

Troy was very miserly with money and managed it well. He was also quite the taskmaster. For example, he insisted his customers clip their horses every two weeks, and if they didn't, he'd have the assistant trainers do it for them and charge them around $15. Also, the horses had to be put on the hot walker three times a week, and if the customers didn't, we would and charge them accordingly.

Customers could be at the stables 25 hours a day and, when they weren't looking, Troy'd find time to put one of their horses on a hot walker or clip one and then charge them for it. He would send a bill at the end of the month with all the extra charges. Usually, the extra charges would equal the board bill.

He had all of everyone wrapped around his little finger. For fun, we had a roast for him and presented him with a prank bill that was several feet long. With his stable logo on top, it read: "Board, so much; lessons, so much; talking back in class, so much; hauling a horse to a horse show, $15; hauling a horse back from the show, $50;" horse stepping on a hose, 50 cents, funny stuff like that.

First Snaffle Bit Futurity

About this time I really got the itch to prove myself in the arena, so I took a horse owned by Freddie Funston to the 1977 National Reined Cow Horse Association Snaffle Bit Futurity in Reno. I told Freddie that I'd ride her for nothing if he'd pay the entry fee. This was the first time I'd ever shown a horse at this caliber of event. Talk about starting at the top. This competition was and still is the premier test of a stock horse. But I wanted to get my feet wet and my name around – that's what all young, aspiring horse trainers want to do.

The mare had the high mark of the first go-round of the fence work, but her stifle locked up and we had to scratch from the competition. Fence work was all she could do, however. If I had to rein her in the futurity's dry work section, I'd still be trying to get her stopped. With fence work, I just "cowboyed up," went out there and did it. The other two parts of the competition – cutting and reining – I really didn't know much about. So, I guess it's just as well I didn't finish the show.

Horses Teach Humans

Troy helped me with my performance dilemma. One of his principles was that horses teach humans and humans teach horses.

He explained to me, "You're trying to teach horses to slide, spin and change leads, but you've never ridden one that did it well. How can you know what you're trying to teach a horse if you don't know what it feels like?"

He put me on good reining and cutting horses, so I could feel what it feels like to be on a high-quality performance horse.

To this point, I'd been trying to teach horses to do things I'd never done before. I made tremendous progress after I felt what I was supposed to be teaching.

Troy had a good system of teaching horses and people to perform. He was a master of horses in the round corral, and in getting them to perform lead changes and sliding stops.

He helped me take Thumper, the mule, from a 10-foot sliding stop to a 30-foot slide. Troy was brilliant at seeing the dynamics of what a rider or a horse was doing. He saw that my stopping dynamics were absolutely backward. He helped me realize that I can't stop something that's in the process of stopping or is already stopped. My typical modus operandi was to gallop, slow down to a canter and then pull back to stop.

Instead, he had me speed up, then drop the reins and say "whoa," not pull back and say "whoa." As I focused on a point in the distance, my horse's body would drop from under me, like a duck gliding to a landing on a lake. That's the visual concept of what he wanted me to do. Thumper was a natural stopper, and once I got the concept, it was easy for me to have her run down to a stop, then drag her butt to a long, sliding stop.

Another good example was Bridget Bar Dough, the talented mare I'd had all those years. She was the first horse I ever cantered backward – nearly on purpose.

The day it happened, I was in the arena riding her. Troy was teaching me how to keep horses in a canter by taking them deep into the corners and letting them turn at the last moment. The barn was in the other direction, and Bridget got antsy about returning to it. When we got to a corner, I held her in it. Her momentum propelled her forward, but the fence stopped her progress.

I'd been on bucking horses that would buck backward. They'd get into a motion where they bucked sideways and then eventually buck backward. Since Bridget couldn't move

any more forward into the corner, she went sideways and then backward. It was an unusual feeling, one few people ever experience, and one I'll never forget.

By the way, Bridget is still alive and well at age 38 (as of 2004). Karen keeps a close eye on her at her ranch in Angels Camp, California. The mare has had a couple of foals – one filly made the non-pro finals of the NRCHA Snaffle Bit Futurity. The other foal was by a Thoroughbred stallion named Knights Honor and ended up becoming horse of the year in fourth-level dressage in California. Her babies were pretty and talented, as was she.

The most important aspect of being his student is that Troy taught me, while he helped me train horses. I realized, very quickly, that his methods provided a good way to train horses and to teach people to teach horses, as well. Troy's philosophy became the basis of my horsemanship program today.

Good, Better, Best: Never Let It Rest

Troy knew five words: Work, work hard and work harder.

I remember one particularly difficult trailer-loading episode. The horse was sweating, and I was sweating. There was dust everywhere. I thought to myself, "Troy is going to be impressed with me. Look how hard I'm working."

Troy was studying the whole thing and said, "You know, son, I've been watching you." I thought to myself, "Oh boy, he's going to compliment me for working so hard." Instead, he said, "If you worked just a little bit harder, I'll bet you could make it even harder for you and the horse."

I said to him, "I'm working as hard as I can," and he said, "Yeah, I know, but you're not working smart, buddy."

That's when my dad's favorite word and his best advice came back to me in spades. There's a "savvy" way to do everything and lots of un-savvy ways of doing things. If you do things the savvy way, it ends up being easier for you and the horse. Everybody has a good feeling at the end of the day. The horse has his dignity. He puts in an effort himself. He knows you did it for him and with him, and then the horse's exuberance starts to come through.

We all know that if a human or an animal feels dignified and is confident about what he's doing, he'll put his energy into doing it – mentally, emotionally and physically. I've seen lots of employees and students, as well as horses and dogs, do things they didn't want to do out of disrespect. They didn't feel dignified and weren't exuberant. They were actually mentally working against the one asking them to do something.

First, Become a Horseman

Troy taught me the difference between a horse trainer and a horseman. He said a horse trainer is a mechanic, and a horseman is half-horse. In his opinion, many of the horse trainers in that day were just mechanics who used gimmicks to train horses.

For instance, if a trainer bit up a horse and tied his head around to teach him to give to rein pressure by trapping him, Troy would consider that trainer to be a mechanic. A horseman would never do that.

Troy told me to quit trying to become a horse trainer and start trying to be a horseman. He pounded that idea into me from day one, and anytime I made a mistake, he'd say, "That's not how a horseman would do it."

He was the first person to build a solid foundation for me. He constantly challenged me in my horsemanship. He'd ask: "Can you lope a circle, not an egg-shaped circle, but a perfectly round one? Can you teach a horse to stop without picking up your reins? Can you get a horse to stand on a trail bridge? Can you get him to take his front feet off the bridge and side-pass with just his hind feet on?" He kept things interesting and challenging for me.

Salty Doc

One of my biggest and most rewarding challenges came in the form of a buckskin Quarter Horse stallion. Troy had a client,

Salty Doc, a grandson of Doc Bar, was five years old when his owner brought him to Troy Henry's for training.

Dick Showalter, who owned Fresnos Salty Doc, a five-year-old son of Docs Dynamo, by Doc Bar.

Salty Doc had been through three trainers who all said he was no good and impossible to train. Troy told Dick to send the outlaw to me, and that I'd get the job done. The first time I cleaned Salty's stall, he bared his teeth at me. He didn't care much for people.

When Salty arrived, I threw a saddle on him and got on. I didn't know enough at the time to prepare a horse with ground work first. I knew he'd been ridden, so I made the assumption that he was well-broke. I stepped on like I knew what I was doing. I rode him around for 15 minutes, then decided to ask him to side-pass. I stuck my spur into his side, which, as I soon found out, was the wrong thing to do. He reached around, bit me on the ankle and held it with a vise-like grip.

I sat there thinking, "Holy smokes. How am I going to get out of this one?" Every time I tried something, he'd clamp down harder. He was mad and had a good hold of me. It seemed like forever, but it probably took me two or three minutes to pet my way out of that deal. Finally, he let go. He definitely let me know who was the boss.

Salty Doc was Pat's partner in numerous bareback and bridleless demonstrations. Pat purchased the horse and kept him until he died.

One day, as Troy watched my progress, or lack of it, with Salty, he came over and said, "You're really trying to master that horse, aren't you?"

I replied that I certainly was. He said, "Well, I can tell you what your problem is."

"What?" I inquired.

"It's in your hands," he explained.

I looked at the calluses in my hands and asked, "Aren't my hands good enough?"

He said, "No. If I were you, I'd take the bridle off and throw it over the fence."

I thought to myself, "Okay, how bad can that be? I'd ridden plenty of bucking horses in the past, so all I had to do was hang on. No problem."

I bent down and took off the bridle, and, before I did, Troy said, "Throw it at least 20 feet away." I did, and what did the horse do? He took off at a full run in a 200- by 300-foot arena, bouncing off the walls, ducking and diving, as I held on for all I was worth. Troy had a real good laugh.

After a while, I got tired and started to relax. We'd been running for a long time. When I did, Troy noticed a change in the horse and said, "Can you feel Salty relaxing?" I could. He said, "Now, look to your right." I

did and the horse went in that direction. Troy had me look left and Salty followed. Troy verbally guided me in a clover-leaf pattern, and Salty began to perform beautifully with me cuing only with my eyes and body position.

Then Troy told me to go to the center and say "whoa." I did and Salty melted to a beautiful stop. It's as if the horse said, "Thank God, you finally said 'whoa.'"

I learned right there that you have to ride a horse as fast as he'll run, and you don't need reins to turn or stop him.

Troy remarked, "Now, put your bridle back on and ride like you don't have reins. Use your reins last. Don't use your reins to turn him, use them if he doesn't turn. Don't use your reins to stop him, use them if he doesn't stop."

This really sank into me. From then on, I used this method with Thumper and all my horses. It became a game I played. I used reins only for reinforcement or refinement.

I later purchased Salty, used him in numerous demonstrations throughout my early career, raised many of his foals and kept him until he died at the age of 16.

Troy was one of the most influential mentors of my life and the first to get me to see things from the horse's point of view. Once I grasped that concept, my whole outlook on horsemanship changed and I never looked back.

Pat showed Salty Doc's three-quarter sister, Dynamay, at the NRCHA Snaffle Bit Futurity.

9 TURNING POINTS

"I knew in my heart that what I really wanted to become was a horseman."

aren and I had been together for eight years and were finally married on a Saturday afternoon in June 1980, and promptly went on a rodeo road trip for our honeymoon the next day. I'd entered a rodeo in Galt, California, near Stockton, and drew a horse named Captain Jack, who'd never been ridden to that time. I won the rodeo on him that day.

We then drove through Yosemite and up to Lake Tahoe, where I entered a few more rodeos. I was late for one of them and remember getting a speeding ticket for going 80 miles an hour. Life for the young Parellis was filled with either rodeo weekends or long days at Henry's Stables.

Thanks to Troy's mentoring, my life had taken one significant turn, and it was about to

Sparky was the next super horse to enter Pat's life after Salty Doc. He's pictured here about 5 years old.

take another. It took me two years to prove to Troy that I was dedicated. He wasn't an easy sell. For one thing, I was still rodeoing. He told me I needed to either dedicate myself to rodeo or to becoming a horseman. Here's how I made up my mind.

Defining Moment

Rodeo had been a key part of my life for many years, and I had experienced a lot of success. But then one day, when I was 26 years old, everything changed, and I never looked at rodeo or anything else the same way again.

At a rodeo in Las Vegas, the stands were packed, and I was the first cowboy out. I drew a National Finals horse that hadn't missed too many meals. He was really fat. I set my rigging on him and called for the gate. It opened, but, instead of bucking, the bronc ran to the other end of the arena as fast as he could. Then, he quickly turned right; my rigging slipped to the left. As I slid off to the left while trying to stay on for the full eight seconds, my right spur got caught on the rigging handle, and the whole rigging turned underneath the horse. As I was dragged around the arena, I couldn't get my hand loose. As soon as I went under his belly, the bronc started to buck!

I tried several times to get free by pulling myself toward the horse. The horse continued around the arena, and my head took a pounding on the fence boards. I had no more strength left to pull myself up, but what I did have was a few moments of serenity as I basically gave up my sense of self-preservation.

The pickup men tried to stop the bronc, but all they managed to do was stomp their horses' feet on my legs. I got kicked, stepped on and thrown into the fence. My chaps and pants were half off me.

After a few minutes, the bronc finally came to a standstill, both of us exhausted. His hind legs were actually standing on my back. He leaned forward and, when he did, somehow the rigging popped out of my hand, but in doing so, it ripped my calluses back almost to the first knuckles. I was finally free at last.

Lying there, I thought I must be dead. There wasn't a sound in the arena. I got up

PHOTO BY FOXIE

Pat riding Too Much Velvet at the Cow Palace in 1980.

and found myself alive, with every eye in the place trained on me, and still everything was deathly quiet. I walked out of my destroyed chaps, pieces falling everywhere. I walked past the chutes. There was complete silence. Once I left the arena, though, the whole place broke out in cheers because they'd just seen someone walking out who shouldn't have lived through the experience.

There was a kid who came along on the trip with me. He tried to pick up all my scattered things, but I didn't really care. I walked to my pickup and started the nine-hour drive back to Fresno. For two hours neither of us said a word. The kid was white and still wide-eyed. I just sat there driving and smiling. Finally, he asked, "Pat, why are you smiling?" I said, "'Cause I'm alive, and I've been trying to figure out how many hours and seconds there are in a year, and I'm going to live every second with excellence until it's over.

"From this moment on," I said, "everything I do I'm going to do with all my heart." I realized then that everything has a purpose.

Surprisingly, I didn't quit rodeoing after that, but was selective about going to only the

At the 1978 NRCHA Snaffle Bit Futurity, Pat dressed up in drag as the Clovis Mule Days Queen to compete on Thumper in the Wild Bunch class.

PHOTO BY SKIPPEN COY

The NRCHA asked Pat to give a demonstration at the 1979 Snaffle Bit Futurity. He did it bridleless on Thumper, the mule.

best rodeos. I knew in my heart, however, that what I really wanted to become was a horseman.

Valuable Lessons

I talked to Troy about my desire and he really started working with me after that – spending time with me in theory sessions, giving me opportunities, putting me on good horses.

The things I'd learned at Troy's were invaluable. I learned what an outstanding facility

was and how important that is. This, of course, jived with my dad's view of class and excellence. His words were coming back home to hit me hard.

Troy had numerous round corrals and five arenas at his place. There was an indoor and outdoor round corral, indoor arena, a 100-foot round corral, good footing, cattle for cutting and roping, broodmares and babies. I was in horse heaven, at a place where I could really, really learn.

And I had a taskmaster to control a guy like me who's apt to be off one place one minute and someplace else the next. With Troy's help, I became really grounded.

For the first time in my life, I had enough money to buy my own house. I could own something instead of rent it. What a great feeling!

I even had my own horse trailer, and I was building my own business. I learned about becoming a horseman and learned about excellence with horses, not only from Troy, but, from time to time, the likes of Buster Welch, Monte Foreman, Bobby Ingersoll, Bobby Knutson and others. I'd love to sit around in the evening, listening to them tell stories and talk "horse." It opened up a whole new world to me.

Wild Bunch

One of the interesting things I did around this time was compete in a demonstration event called The Wild Bunch, at the 1978 National Reined Cow Horse Association Snaffle Bit Futurity in Reno, Nevada. This was a fun class where contestants dressed up as different characters and did wild things. The advertised prize was a million dollars cash.

I entered as the Clovis Mule Days Queen – Pat Parelli in drag. Riding Thumper, the mule, I won the class and actually marked the third-highest score of the entire show, even better than the horses in the futurity and open bridle classes. The crowd went nuts. The Wild Bunch wasn't one of the NRCHA's sanctioned classes, but it was one of the snaffle bit futurity show's favorite spectator classes at the time. When I went to receive my prize, you should've seen the look on my face when what they gave me was a bag of shredded thousand dollar bills from the U.S. Mint – one million dollars' worth. I stayed up nights trying to figure out how to glue those little pieces back together.

I had so much fun I thought about trying the bridle horse class the next year on Thumper. However, the association wrote a rule right after the 1978 show where Thumper stole the spotlight, stating that all the show's entries must be horses. They did ask me to come back the following year, though, and give a demonstration, which Thumper and I did bridleless.

Sparky

About this time, Sparky (registered as King Gray Lynx) came into my life. The gray 1979 gelding was by Docs Tragedy by Docs Lynx and out of a daughter of Royal King. He belonged to one of Troy's students, Tyke (Alice) Carlton, who purchased him as a two-year-old at the 1981 NRCHA Snaffle Bit Futurity Sale from the legendary cutting horse trainer Shorty Freeman, the man who made Doc O'Lena famous.

Troy remarked that he thought the gelding reminded him of me – ambitious and lazy at the same time. When Karen overheard him,

PHOTO BY KAREN PARELLI HAGEN

Sparky as a three-year-old in Troy Henry's yard.

she suggested that we call him "Sparky," my old nickname. Freddie Feriera had given me the moniker years ago because I was always buzzing around the place, running from here to there, charged up like a spark plug.

Troy helped me with Sparky by making sure I kept my fundamentals correct as I trained the young horse. He said that if Sparky had talent, the fancy stuff would shine through. He was absolutely right.

Troy taught me the difference between a true cow horse and a trick horse. To him, a trick horse is an over-trained horse; it moves excessively when the cow moves, like shadow-boxing. A true cow horse moves only to hold the cow; it synchronizes with the cow, no flash and dash and fancy footwork while the cow is standing still.

Troy and cutting horse legend Buster Welch were good friends and both were fundamentalists when it came to working a cow. With Troy's guidance, I made sure Sparky remained a true cow horse.

Pat and Sparky placed high at the Arizona Snaffle Bit Futurity in the early 1980s. Sparky's owner, Tyke Carlton, is standing with them.

I showed Sparky in a lot of snaffle bit futurities and won or placed in almost all of them. He was the kind of horse who mastered all three of the competition classes – herd work (cutting), dry work (reining) and fence work. For example, at the Arizona Futurity in the early 1980s, he marked a 229 in the reining portion and scored equally well in the other two classes.

As time went by, I got more involved in cutting on Sparky. I remember going to the Harris Ranch cutting in 1990; Sparky was probably around 10. I marked a 75 in the open division, riding with chinks and a buckaroo saddle with lariat tied on a mulehide-covered, vaquero-style, saddle horn. I looked a tad different than the rest of the exhibitors in their batwing chaps and flat-seat cutting saddles with tall horns. But then, that was just like me. By this time, I had already started thinking outside the box, thinking of ways to do things differently and hopefully better.

As the years rolled by, Sparky became our family's horse. Tyke traded me Sparky for a good ranch mare; so he came to live with us. After Salty Doc, Sparky was my next super horse, only he had a wider range of talents. Salty was good in roping and reined cow work, but Sparky could do anything. I roped on him, jumped him; you name it, he could do it.

Troy's Legacy

Troy was the first one to teach me the concepts of principles, goals and timelines, and to always put the principles ahead of the goals.

I think that conceptually and philosophically, Troy Henry was a horseman ahead of his time. He was on to natural horsemanship, but he didn't know it. It wasn't a "horsehold" word back then.

About a month before Troy passed away, which I like to now refer to as his graduation to Horseman's Heaven, he said four very important things to me that really changed the course of my career, especially in the show world.

1. Never show your own horse against your customer's.
2. Never show a horse because if you win, they might say it's because of thus and

such. If you lose, they'll say, "See, I told you so." He could see the confusion in my face and said, "I didn't say don't demonstrate."
3. If you became a good teacher, you'll always have a job.
4. Take care of your horsemanship, and it'll take care of you. Those were his parting words to me, and I took them to heart. I quit competing and started demonstrating. I became a teacher, and I started becoming a horseman.

On the day Troy died, I'd shown up for work earlier than usual. Troy and his wife typically got up by 4:30 or 5:00 to eat breakfast and start their day by feeding the horses their grain. That day, however, Lorraine came out of the house alone, and I could tell by the look on her face that something had happened. All she would say is that Troy wouldn't get up.

I said, "What do you mean, he won't get up?"

She motioned to the house. I went into the bedroom and saw that Troy had already passed in his sleep. That was December 1982. Troy died of a cerebral hemorrhage.

The Henrys had known that I had planned to look for a place of my own and were okay with that. My daughter, Marlene, had been born by this time and my son, Caton, was on the way. I was ready to strike out on my own about the time Troy died. After the funeral and things settled down at Troy's, I told Lorraine that I'd stay there at least a year longer to do whatever it took to help her consolidate and liquidate their assets. I promised her that she could depend on me. I felt I owed at least that much to Troy.

I helped sell all the rental and lease horses, tack, rolling stock, everything, so Lorraine had nothing to worry about. She kept the house and property, but the business was disbanded. Before Troy passed, we'd planned to take three horses to the Red Bluff Bull and Gelding Sale. I took them, and they ended up being the first, second and fourth high-selling horses.

I studied and trained with Troy Henry for five years, and the things I learned from him have stayed with me the rest of my life.

After Troy died, one of his friends said to me, "So, I suppose you think you're as good as

Many years after Sparky's snaffle bit debut, he still could hold his own in the arena. At the 1990 Harris Ranch Cutting, Pat and Sparky marked a very respectable 75. Note Pat's stock saddle, rope and chinks. Even then, he rode to a different beat.

Troy was?" I replied as I stuck my thumbs under my suspenders, "Let me tell you something. Anything Troy Henry could do in 10 minutes, I can do in two weeks."

I was proud of that statement because when I first met Troy, it would've taken me two years to get anything done. Thinking I could accomplish it in two weeks meant I was on my way.

People's Perspectives on Pat

Quite a Feat for a Mule

I first saw and heard about Pat in the late 1960s and '70s when he was riding broncs in rodeos. Later in the '70s, I met him while showing at some of the major reined cow horse events.

I remember at the 1978 NRCHA World Championship Snaffle Bit Futurity, Pat showed a mule in the Wild Bunch class and won first place. This was quite a feat for a mule because he was competing against some very good horses.

Pat and I have remained very good friends, and I always enjoy sitting in on his clinics. They're very good for people, helping them to understand horses and have more fun with their horses.

Bobby Ingersoll
Three-time winner and reserve, NRCHA World Championship Snaffle Bit Futurity
Only NRCHA Triple Crown winner (won snaffle bit, hackamore and bridle divisions in same year, 1975.)
NRCHA Hall of Fame
Trainer, 22 AQHA Champions

PHOTO BY JOHN BRASSEAUX

10 THE EIGHT PRINCIPLES

"Horsemanship can be obtained naturally through communication, understanding and psychology versus mechanics, fear and intimidation."

I put on my first seminar in Hollywood, California, for R. M. Bradley, a veterinarian and American Mule Association board member. He always kept about six horses or mules in training with me and was fascinated by the things I did with them, so he asked me to put on a seminar for his clients. I didn't even know what a seminar was, but said I'd try it.

I needed help in putting together something like this, and fortunately ran into a longtime friend of mine from high school and junior college, Mike Adian, D.V.M., who said he'd help me with the seminar. His idea was to invite some of his friends so I could practice my presentation on them.

Rehearsal Dinner

The only way we persuaded Mike's buddies to come to the rehearsal seminar was to bribe them with a sparerib dinner, which I

Pat put placards on the round corral walls to make it easy for spectators to see and remember the Eight Principles.

The Eight Principles and other tidbits of wisdom were visual aids for Pat's early presentations.

cooked. About 12 people showed up, and I stumbled and stammered for two hours in my "seminar," talking in circles, not knowing at all how to get my points across.

We audio taped it and later Mike made me listen to myself. It was painful.

But Mike came up with a good plan to help smooth out my delivery. He took notes, and every time I said something conceptual or important, he wrote it on a three-by-five card, and threw it on the floor. By the time we were done, there were cards scattered everywhere. We went through them and grouped the ideas into similar categories. We might find four that seemed to be talking about the same thing, another three that focused on something else and maybe six on yet another topic.

Eight Principles

We came up with the Eight Principles, guiding concepts I still use today. I made placards and wrote a principle on each one.

1. Horse-Man-Ship is natural.
2. Don't make assumptions.
3. Communication is two or more individuals sharing and understanding an idea.
4. Horses and humans have mutual responsibilities.
5. The attitude of justice is effective.
6. Body language is the universal language.
7. Horses teach humans and humans teach horses.
8. Principles, purpose and time are the tools of teaching.

Salty Doc was Pat's demonstration horse for his early seminars.

The day of the seminar rolled around, and I was ready. My thoughts were in order. I tacked up the Eight Principles around the round corral for all to see. It made quite a visual presentation.

My opening line, which I practiced for two weeks prior to the seminar so I wouldn't forget it, was "Horsemanship can be obtained naturally through communication, understanding and psychology versus mechanics, fear and intimidation." (This same sentence is still the heart of my horsemanship program today.)

Once I said that, I was over my nervousness and began with the first principle.

"Horse-Man-Ship is natural," I started out. "Notice the order of the words. 'Horse' is first, out of respect for the animal. 'Man' means

human, and 'Ship' is a vessel with which we travel." And so on went my talk.

I used the Eight Principles tacked up on the walls to guide my audience around the seminar. They were the heart of my talk and demonstration. For example, when I came to the principle that "responsibilities are mutual," I sent the horse I had with me around the round corral, and told the crowd that the horse's job was to not change gaits or directions and to watch where he's going. My job was to stand out of his way.

I used Salty Doc to demonstrate and then played with a couple of the spectators' horses to make my Principle points.

In giving this seminar I realized how deep my interest in horsemanship was and that I had many things to say. All I needed was a structure, and the Eight Principles provided me with just that.

Dr. Bradley told 30 of his friends and customers to pay $50 apiece to attend that seminar. I made $1,500 that day, and all I did was share my passion for horses. That really left an impression on me.

I got a good feeling during the seminar. I loved it, the audience loved it and the horses loved it. "This is it!" I said to myself. "I've found my calling."

It's in the Toes

My efforts at producing a videotape of this seminar were fairly comical. It was about this time that I began to realize how important it was to capture things on video, and so we made attempts to video most everything I did.

For this venture, I borrowed my father-in-law's huge video camera that used three-quarter-inch black-and-white film. It also had a live microphone on the end of it. As I walked around and demonstrated on a horse, the live mike recorded my words and any surrounding noise with them. Unfortunately, it was Saturday, and one of the neighbors living

next to where I was giving the seminar was mowing his lawn. I didn't realize it until much later when we viewed the tape, but all we heard on the tape was the sound of a screeching lawnmower!

Following that, a company by the name of Video Velocity approached me and produced some videos of me. They put together one video that was a collage of things I did in my demonstrations. At one big cutting in California, they used this collage video as entertainment during the cattle changes. There would be 20-minute breaks between go-rounds, as the cattle were being settled. A large screen was set up to show the videos to the audience, while they waited for the competition to resume.

I just so happened to be sitting in the grandstand when they showed the video of me performing sliding stops, spins and lots of other fancy maneuvers, all without a bridle!

The two ladies sitting in front of me didn't know I was behind them. One lady turned to the other and said: "That's nothing; he's using his toes." That cracked me up. I thought to myself, "Let's see you get a horse to do that with just your toes, lady."

People's Perspectives on Pat

Help the Person Help the Horse

My association with Pat Parelli started in the early 1980s. Pat had a lot of ability and a lot going for him before he ever met me.

His keen interest in the horse kept him searching for ways to communicate his knowledge to help the person help the horse.

Ray Hunt
Horsemanship clinician

PHOTO BY ROBERT DAWSON

Ray Hunt has dedicated his life to helping the horse.

11 THE KIDS

"Love, Language and Leadership give you tightness of bond and lightness of response with people as well as with horses."

During my tenure with Troy Henry, Karen and I were able to purchase our first home in the suburbs about a mile from Troy's stable. I felt my career was secure and our life was stable. Our thoughts ran to starting our family.

Home Birth

We had decided to have our children born at home and had a husband-and-wife doctor and midwife team come out to assist us. Both experiences were fabulous.

PHOTO BY KAREN PARELLI HAGEN

Marlene fell in love with Sherlock, the diminutive horse.

A proud papa with his pretty little girl.

Marlene was born June 9, 1981. Her right foot turned in, like a clubfoot. After months of going to the doctors, the foot wasn't getting any better. They decided she needed a cast on it, but before we did that, we took her to a naturopath. He suggested putting two left-foot shoes on her, which we did and that quickly straightened out the foot. When you're the parent of a child born with any imperfection, somehow you just feel guilty.

Never Make a Cowboy Dad Mad

My training business was in full swing, and I was on the road a lot, but I always wanted my family with me. In her first three months of life, Marlene must have traveled 6,000 miles going to rodeos, cuttings and mule shows.

Marlene was a very athletic little girl, even as a baby. She used to balance herself standing on the edge of her highchair. Later, she was active in gymnastics.

Raised around horses, Marlene was good with them, but was somewhat timid and didn't like to go fast. She preferred to play with horses on the ground.

She had a little pony named Ladybug. One summer I took the family to Silver Lake, California, up in the Sierra mountains, for a trail ride. After we'd ridden awhile, I persuaded Marlene to let me take the lead rope off Ladybug so she could ride by herself.

We hadn't gone more than a half-hour when some kids on motorbikes roared by and

Caton had a passion for riding early on. He's shown here, at about 7 years old, riding Thumper with nothing but a Carrot Stick at a clinic in Likely, California.

purposely scared the horses. The pony was terrified and ran off with my little daughter, who was about six at the time. The pony didn't go far, but the whole incident traumatized Marlene.

We got Ladybug back under control, and Marlene was unhurt. I heard the bikes revving in the distance and took off after them on my horse. I was so mad. I saw the boys in a field, yakking with one another.

I took down my rope and ran straight for them. They didn't see me coming until it was too late. As one tried to get his bike started, I roped him, dallied around my horn and jerked him off his bike backward. I dragged him 50 feet or more, then stopped and cussed him for a while. He was one scared-to-death 12-year-old when I got through with him.

Pat and Marlene having fun on Marlene's pony at a mountain horsemanship camp.

It turned out his parents owned the resort where we parked our trailer. By the time we made it back to our rig, his parents were waiting for us, more than a little peeved. In their explanation, the kids had left out the reason why a big, bad cowboy had roped them. I set everyone straight pretty quickly.

A Real Miniature Horse

Someone sent me a cutting horse prospect, a son of Dry Doc, to start. Cutting horses can be small, but this one was exceptionally tiny. I had to put a pony saddle on him; a normal-sized saddle literally went over his tail. Because of his diminutive size, the owner gave me the horse. We called him Sherlock.

Marlene fell in love with Sherlock. One time she and her friends went to a barrel race for fun. Marlene and Sherlock won second by trotting the cloverleaf pattern. They were efficient and stayed close to the barrels.

The other competitors were angry about someone beating them at a trot. They thought the timer must be off. They made Marlene go again. She bettered her first time, so that ended the squabble. She proved that slow and right beats fast and wrong.

At a clinic in Red Lodge, Montana, Marlene coaxed Sherlock across an irrigation ditch. Marlene is about 10 or 11 years old.

Grown and Beautiful

Years later, Marlene worked for a pack outfit and even drove a team of horses in the winter to feed livestock. The pack station was at the same resort where we'd gone trail riding when she was a little girl. She ran into the owner's boy who had scared her so badly on her pony, and they became friends.

Marlene was a cute little girl who grew up to become a beautiful young woman with model-like features. My biggest fear was that some jerk would sweep her off her feet because she was so gorgeous. Luckily, that didn't happen. She picked a nice young man, Angelo Delanini, and the two were married at Lake Tahoe in the summer of 2002.

At the wedding, a young man came up to me and said, "Sir, you probably don't remember me but one time I was riding my motorbike in the mountains, minding my own business and you roped me off it."

I said, "Yeah, I remember you, but that's not how I remember it." We had a good laugh.

Marlene likes horses, but they're not her passion as they are for my son, Caton.

Wise Horseman

Caton Ryder was born April 10, 1983, two years after Marlene. He's named after Cato, the philosopher, and Ryder is an old English word for horseman, so his name means "wise horseman."

The delivery was difficult for Karen, and Caton had what is called "extreme molding" of his head. Many newborns have elongated heads that mold later into a more normal shape, so we didn't think anything about it. Caton's head stayed abnormally long, however, and he was a very quiet baby.

Also, his eyes were crossed and kept getting worse. The pediatrician we were using didn't say a thing about his condition, only that we should have Caton checked out by an eye doctor. Our boy was three months old by that time.

Pat and Linda celebrate Marlene's marriage to Angelo Delanini at Lake Tahoe, 2002.

Sparky helped Caton develop his riding skills.

Even as a little boy, Caton went everywhere with Pat.

Well, the eye doctor knew immediately that something was wrong and that Caton had more serious problems than strabismus (crossed eyes). He called Oakland Children's Hospital and told them we were coming. We didn't have any money; I'm not even sure we had insurance.

We drove to the hospital and by the time we arrived, Caton had gone into a coma. His whole body was contracting. I couldn't pry open his little curled-up hands. Karen and I both had that sick-to-your-stomach feeling parents get when their child hurts and they can't do anything about it.

We found out that he had hydrocephalus or water on the brain. One of the ducts going into the brain was closed and the spinal fluid couldn't circulate normally. It could come in, but was blocked going out, hence his head was large. His skull had been increasing by a centimeter a day.

The doctors put a shunt in his skull, and said if he did live, he'd probably never walk or talk; he might be nothing more than a vegetable. I remember thinking to myself that I would not let that be the case. The shunt worked its magic and relieved the pressure in Caton's head. By the next morning he was a different baby, still affected, but at least he was alive.

We stayed with him for about a month at the hospital and during that time, he got increasingly better. His eyes were completely crossed, however, and he had to have surgery later to straighten them.

As Caton got older, normal gross motor skills were really a challenge for him. He was behind other children his age in walking and talking. He was a big baby with a big head, which made him clumsy; his limbs just didn't work properly for him.

As a youngster, Caton grew so quickly his shunt would break and he'd land back in a coma again, as he did when he was three years old.

The Littlest Buckaroo

Despite his physical challenges, Caton was a happy little boy. He always had a smile on his face and he loved to ride. My good horse, Sparky, eventually became his horse.

One of my most indelible memories of Caton riding Sparky was at a cattle roundup on the French Ranch, near Hollister, California. Caton was only about six or seven years old at the time. So he'd stay put, I seat-belted him onto the little buckaroo saddle I'd purchased for him.

Caton really got into the swing of things, playing the part of the littlest "buckaroo," slapping his chaps and shouting "He-yah, he-yah!" like he had seen cowboys do to get cattle to move.

There were about 30 calves on top of a knoll, bawling for their mothers. Before I could stop him, Caton left the main herd, loped up the hill, rode around the back of the calves and started chousing them to move down the hill. I could hear him shouting the

PHOTO BY KAREN PARELLI HAGEN

Caton rode Sparky in a lot of Pat's demonstrations and horse courses. This one took place on the Clements ranch.

Caton rode Scamp in the 1999 4th of July parade in Pagosa Springs. He was part of the bridleless mounted unit made up of Parelli students.

words to a famous western tune, "Get along, little doggies, it's your misfortune and none of my own."

Later on that day, we got into some really rough country, so I put a lead rope on Sparky. We saw that the ranch manager, Ira Reed, was having some trouble herding two bulls, so we dropped off a steep ridge at the lope to help him. Caton was behind me, hollering "Daaaaaad, Daaaaad, Daaaaad." I didn't look back until we caught up with Ira. When I turned to look, all I could see was Caton's head. He'd come out of the saddle and was hanging on Sparky's side, with the seatbelt straps under his arms. As I look back on it now, I should've listened to his call. Caton's always been such a tough little kid, and I was so proud of him for "cowboying up" that day.

Caton rode Sparky for years during all my road trips across the country. Caton's always been a part of my demonstrations and clinics, and the old gray horse took real good care of him. Today, Sparky is retired and living with

Bridget Bar Dough at Karen's California ranch.

As Caton grew older, he continued to catch up physically, and he always was mentally fast. When he was 12, he had a stroke, which was unrelated to his hydrocephalus condition, but it compounded his coordination problems. He lost all function on the right side of his body. Through therapy and a lot of horseback riding, today he has about 85 percent mobility on that side and is improving all the time.

High School Grad

We decided to home-school both our children and it worked out very well for all of us, plus it gave us the freedom to travel and develop our business. Marlene went all the way through high school that way, but Caton had other ideas.

Caton attended public high school because he wanted to be socially active. He's a very personable kid, likes to be around people and just wanted to be like every other teenage kid.

PHOTO BY COCO

Father and son on father on son. Pat and Caton make a good team at tours and demonstrations. Caton (left) is riding Pat's stallion Liberty Major, who sired Aspen, the horse Pat is on.

At a school of about 600 to 700 students, everyone knew everyone else, and Caton was a well-known figure.

At his high school graduation, all of our family was on hand to watch him walk down the aisle and accept his diploma. The most touching thing happened: When Caton stood up to get his diploma, all of the students cheered for him. Every time I think about it, it brings a tear to my eye.

When I was young, school kids would make fun of someone like Caton, but that wasn't the case for him. Everyone loved him.

Levels Graduate

Caton, my wise horseman, graduated our program in Level 2 and, so far, the liberty and freestyle portions of Level 3. With him, I've always made sure I followed Principle 7 –"Humans teach horses and horses teach humans" – and I always put him on the best horses I could – Sparky, Scamp, Liberty Major, Aspen.

Caton lived with his mom until he was 18, but he now lives with me full-time. He rides with me every day, sometimes spending six hours a day in the saddle. He has a driver's permit and he drives everything on the ranch, including his dad crazy.

If you ever get a chance to meet him, you'll find out he's quite versed on the subjects of horses, trucks and football.

Caton's Gift

Caton travels with us everywhere and is as much a part of our team as anyone. He is a huge part of the inspiration we try to offer at our seminars and demonstrations. It's a challenge for him to get on a horse barcback, but he gets it done in front of 3,000 people.

Caton's goal is to preserve the foundation Quarter Horse though a selective breeding program and to have his own yearling division that sells pre-saddle trained two-year-old horses. His business card reads: "Your source for the world's smartest yearlings."

PHOTO BY COCO

Caton and his horse Aspen. Caton's plan is to selectively breed foundation Quarter Horses and to develop a yearling program.

I actually think that Caton is a gift from God to me. Sometimes, as a parent, you blame yourself. I've gotten over that and cherish the strong father-son relationship we both have.

Caton has also given me a gift. He's taught me how to break things down in small steps, how to be 10,000 times more patient and to recognize the little steps of progress that people make.

People love horses; it's their passion, but it's not necessarily their talent. So, for them, I've got to break things down into manageable steps they can follow. Caton taught me how to do that, and that I must do that.

I use Love, Language and Leadership in equal doses with Caton. I have to be firm with him; I have to be focused and have a plan. Love, Language and Leadership give you tightness of bond and lightness of response with people as well as with horses. My friends tell me that I've done my best work with Caton.

People's Perspectives on Pat

Studied with the Best

I once told Pat that he was a genius, a term I don't use lightly. He said, "I don't know about that." I think in his heart, he'd like to believe that he is. Who wouldn't? In any case, I still think he is.

I've know Pat for a lot of years. He's a man of enormous charm and charisma. He has a great sense of humor, a quick wit, intelligence and enough "savvy" to have found the most perfect woman in the world for him and to somehow get her to marry him. No mean feat!

I've been a dedicated horseman all my life. I've shown jumpers, played serious polo for 20 years, shown cutting horses, and am an active team roper. I've studied with some of the best people in the world.

In the summer of 2004, my wife, Susannah, a dressage trainer, and I spent about 10 days at Pat and Linda's spectacular place in Pagosa Springs, Colorado. I think I learned more in those 10 days than I have in 60 years of pursuing a perfection one can never achieve.

That said, I believe the thing I admire most about Pat is what he has accomplished in the raising of his wonderful son, Caton. Pat should write a book about that. I'd sure like to read it, and recommend it to every parent on the planet.

I treasure my friendship with the Parelli family.

Alex Cord
Actor, 25 feature films, 300 television shows,
Three television series, including "Airwolf."
Novelist, Sandsong and A Feather in the Rain
Founding Member, Chukkers for Charity
Celebrity Polo
Chairman, Ahead With
Horses Therapeutic
riding program

PHOTO COURTESTY OF ALEX CORD

Alex Cord has been an avid horseman all his life.

12 HAVE HELP, WILL TRAVEL

"I found the solution to my problems by thinking outside the box."

With my business starting to grow, I went hunting for my own place. I found the perfect property in Clements, California, which I purchased from Dick Randall with help for the down payment from Karen's father and my dad. The ranch included 65 acres, a modular home, an eight-stall Elkins barn and a Butler building. Previous to Randall, it'd been owned by roping champion Leo Camarillo and well-known rodeo-announcer Bob Tallman, who had a rope-horse training business and rope-manufacturing factory on the place.

It was an expensive piece of property for me at the time, around $300,000 with $3,000 in monthly mortgage payments. But everything was set for my operation. I had clients and was ready to roll.

PHOTO BY KAREN PARELLI HAGEN

The Clements ranch was the site for numerous clinics, demonstrations, colt-startings and several Natural Horsemen's Rendevous.

End of a New Beginning

The day after we went into escrow, our son, Caton, who was three-months old, went into a coma. (See Chapter 11 titled "The Kids".) During the month or so we tended to Caton, I lost all but two of the dozen clients I had. They'd all promised to move to Clements with me from Troy's, and I depended on that income to get me through the first winter. Unfortunately, the little bit of down time I had dealing with Caton's condition gave them the impetus to go other ways.

I started hustling and got a few things going, but then the $3,000-a-month mortgage payment came due. Also, I had to buy hay, and then the rains came and I had no indoor arena. It seemed to be the rainiest season ever. The whole thing was like a nightmare. I was really destitute, and thought I was going to lose the place.

I found myself looking for help in lots of different places and one was in listening to motivational tapes. One in particular I remember was called "The Psychology of Winning" by Dr. Denis E. Waitley, a well-known motivational speaker. These tapes addressed the 10 qualities of winners, and how true leaders always continue to grow and improve. I'd go to bed at night listening to tapes that were based on subliminal learning (the ability of the mind to take in and process information while unconscious, as in sleeping).

The tapes did what they were designed to do; they motivated and inspired me. They gave me the way out of my dilemma. I found the solution to my problems by thinking outside the box. I woke up in the middle of the night, and I knew the answer. Instead of trying to make my money right there on the ranch, I decided to take my message to wherever it was needed.

With Help from Dr. Miller

I called Dr. Robert M. Miller (noted veterinarian and speaker/lecturer from Thousand Oaks, California) the next morning with the idea that came to me in the middle of the night. I wanted to do workshops to help people with their typical horse problems, such as trailer-loading, clipping, catching, pulling back, jigging and other behavioral issues – whatever.

I first met Dr. Miller at the 1981 Bishop Mule Days when I did a bridleless demonstration on Thumper. Dr. Miller was there to do a story on the event for *Western Horseman* magazine, and he saw my performance.

At Bishop, I sat down with Dr. Miller at his camp area, and we talked philosophically for what seemed like hours. We found ourselves on the same wavelength. He got so excited he decided to do an article on me as well, and, on top of that, he put a mule in training with me. His article, titled "A New Look at Old Methods," was basically on my Eight Principles seminar, and it proved very popular with the *Western Horseman* readers, something I'll touch on in a later chapter.

$100 an Hour!

When I called Dr. Miller with my idea, he said it was a good one, but I'd have to charge what he told me to charge. I was thinking at the time that it should be about $20 an hour, but I braced myself for the possibility that he might suggest $10. Instead, he told me I had

PHOTO BY KAREN PARELLI HAGEN

Dr. Miller (middle) has been Pat's treasured mentor and true friend for over 20 years. Dr. Miller's wife Debby is to the left.

From left, Ronnie Willis, Ray Hunt and Pat. Pat started hosting Ray Hunt clinics in the spring of 1984.

If I had to do it again, though, I'd call it "Have Savvy, Will Travel." I got the idea from my dad's favorite television show when I was a kid, "Have Gun, Will Travel."

Even my pickup had my clinic name on it. The pickup had an insert in the bed that formed a one-horse trailer of sorts. I'd have my horse jump up into it and away we'd go.

Then, I bought a three-horse, gooseneck horse trailer from Charmac. With horses in tow, Karen, the kids and I lived in the gooseneck part for six years as we traveled the clinic circuit. I still have that trailer today, just for a keepsake. It's a wonderful reminder of my early days on the road.

Ray Hunt Horsemanship Clinics

My clinic business expanded, and soon I was asked to give demonstrations at various equine events on the West Coast. At the 1983 California Livestock Symposium in Fresno, I gave a bridleless demonstration on Thumper, the mule. The symposium attracted around 5,000 spectators.

Ray Hunt was the headliner at the symposium and gave a colt-starting demonstration. To this day, I still think that's the best demonstration I've ever seen him do. The late Tom Dorrance agreed with me on this matter.

I'd never personally met Ray before then, but I was well-acquainted with his reputation and methods by this time.

After my demo, I was hungry so I stood in line at the café. In front of me were Tom, Ray, their wives and Ronnie Willis. I asked Ray if he'd be interested in doing a clinic at my Clements ranch. He said, "Talk to my wife."

In the spring of 1984, I started holding Ray Hunt horsemanship and colt-starting clinics at my place. (I put them on until 1990, at which time my own business really took all my available time.) Before putting on my first one, though, I remember being concerned about it coming off perfectly. I wanted to make sure I crossed all my "t's" and dotted all my "i's."

Ronnie Willis, who had ridden with Ray and knew him well, had moved from Montana to central California because he'd come down

to charge $100 an hour and have a three-hour minimum with a money-back guarantee.

I thought he'd lost his mind. No one would pay me $100 an hour! But I trusted Dr. Miller and took his advice. He said he'd help me with the first couple of clients, and the rest would be up to me.

I went to his facility, called the Conejo Valley Veterinary Clinic, and put on a couple of days' worth of clinics, working through various typical problems – trailer loading, clipping, hard-to-catch, pulling back, rearing, hoof handling; you name it, I tackled it. After that, Dr. Miller would send me to various clients' homes to help solve problems right on the premises. The whole thing caught on fire, and I did at least three and sometimes four three-hour sessions a day.

I offered clinic participants a deal wherein if someone brought five people, I'd do the clinic for $75/hour instead of the $100/hour; and if they brought 10 people, I'd do it for $50/hour. I knew the clinic-goers would be potential clients, so I gave volume discounts.

The concept of the weekend clinic was born. It was an instant hit, and the next thing I knew I had people following me around, lining up and signing up for more. A big head of steam kept building, and within a few months I was a hit up and down the California coast. I was able to branch out of state, as well, with clinics in Arizona and Colorado.

I called the clinics "Have Help, Will Travel."

with diabetes and couldn't live in a remote part of the country anymore. He needed more accessible medical attention. He trained horses on a Clements ranch, owned by a man named Rink Babka, who was a gold medalist in discus throwing or shot-putting, I can't remember which one.

Since Ronnie was now my new neighbor, I sought his advice about the Hunt clinic. He said not to worry, that if I got people there it would all happen naturally. But he advised me, "If I were you, I'd pay attention to the way Ray teaches big groups of people."

Getting people to come was no problem. Ray was so popular, he'd easily attract 400 people at a time, and I found my pasture turning into a huge parking lot.

Ray was in his heyday at this point and had been doing clinics for years, but I was just starting with my Have Help, Will Travel clinics, figuring out a system that worked well for me. Therefore, I made it a point to watch the way Ray taught people in groups, as Ronnie suggested. I'd wondered how to teach 20 to 30 people at one time. Ray was very good at group orchestration and psychology. I immediately started emulating that in my clinics.

Here Today, Gone Tomorrow

Ronnie and I became friends, and either I'd go to his place, or he'd come to mine. During our visits, he'd graciously explain to me what Hunt and Dorrance meant with their theories and methods. I'd heard what they said, but didn't fully understand what they meant. Ronnie really did a great job of mentoring me, and we spent hours and hours, talking philosophically and conceptually.

Philosophically, I'd already made the move toward communication, understanding and psychology, but I had a lot to learn. I mean, I had a lot to learn. I'd been working on basic riding skills and was always very good at them, but I was still conceptualizing the natural horsemanship methods.

One day, Ronnie asked me why I didn't give my own colt-starting clinics. I explained that I didn't think I was all that qualified, and Ray

PHOTO BY KAREN PARELLI HAGEN

Sparky helped Pat in many colt-starting clinics. This one was at the Clements ranch, about 1984.

Hunt was a guy who really knew what he was doing in that area.

We talked and talked about it, and I finally agreed that if he'd help me, I'd do one. So we did; we had 16 colts to start at my ranch. We worked very well together, and when the clinic was over he said to me, "From now on neither one of us will ever have to put our heads below our butts again."

In my mind, we were going to be like Ray and Tom, doing colt-starting clinics all over the country. Surprisingly, that was the last time I saw Ronnie Willis for 14 years, because the day after our clinic he apparently had a diabetic episode. He went into the hospital and almost lost his life. No one told me. He and his wife moved, and they got out of horses entirely. I lost track of him and didn't have any idea where he was. It wasn't until years later that I'd run into him again.

Trailer-loading Unlocks Secrets

On my own, I started doing colt-starting clinics from Saturday to Wednesday with a horsemanship class in the afternoon, like Ray did. It was a really good formula, and I got tons of experience.

I also made trailer-loading part of my clinics, and my goal was to trailer load every horse. I had between 12 and 20 colts per week

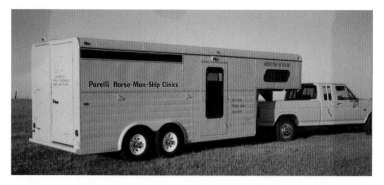

The first Parelli touring rig in 1984 took Pat and his family all over the West for their first horsemanship clinics.

to start and an average of 30 people in the horsemanship classes. Therefore, I trailer-loaded somewhere between 20 and 50 horses every week.

Along the way, I learned I had to empower people to do things. It occurred to me that you dis-empower people by doing it for them. So, I found ways to coach people to trailer-load horses themselves.

I tried to see how clever I could get with trailer-loading and made a sport out of it. Then, I made a sport out of me trying to get people to do it, without me even touching the horse.

This gave me lots of practice with different types and breeds of horses and, over time, in different parts of the country and even different countries.

Over the years, I discovered that every place has its own variety of people and horses. I found disparate "normalities" wherever I went. Whatever is normal in the north might not be normal in the south. Whatever is normal in the United States isn't normal in Europe. I started seeing the similarities and dissimilarities, all of which has really given me enormous scope and depth in the world of horses.

I realized that Troy Henry was right when he told me that if I could learn to trailer-load horses naturally, it would unlock all the secrets to horsemanship. Troy explained that horses throw every objection possible, every move, every evasion they have when they refuse to load in a trailer. He said that everything I'd ever need to learn about horses would be embodied in the psychology that's needed to trailer-load horses. I'd understand the dynamics of movement, of following a feel and following a suggestion. He was certainly right about all that. No matter what I wanted to learn – spins or sliding stops, back up, side-pass, piaffe, passage – it was all in teaching horses to trailer load as your partner. Through the trailer-loading process, I realized the principle of the horse having self-carriage, the principle of lightness and the principles of dignity and exuberance the horse must have in order to excel. I learned all these principles through trailer-loading literally thousands of horses over the years.

The Foundation Station

Besides my clinics and demonstrations, I developed another part of my business called the Foundation Station. After the rainy fall and winter of 1983-84, I went to all the local horse trainers within 20 miles, of which there were at least 30, of every type and discipline, from cutting and reining horses to Thoroughbreds and Arabians. I proposed a unique deal to the trainers: I'd start all their young horses and never promote myself to their clients. They'd basically outsource the first-ride process to me, and I'd return the horses to them, broke and ready for more advanced training. Horse trainers are always afraid of other horse trainers stealing their clients, so my premise intrigued many trainers, who didn't really want to bother with foundation training anyway. Like most high-level performance trainers, they wanted to con-

In the mid-1980s, Pat gave clinics at mountain horsemanship camps, owned by Doc Grishaw (middle). Still today, every chance Pat gets, he'll strum his guitar, which he often does around a campfire while his students sing their favorite tunes.

PHOTO COURTESY OF KAREN PARELLI HAGEN

People's Perspectives on Pat

A Century from Now

My wife, Deborah, and I were at Bishop Mule Days in Bishop, California, 25 years ago when I saw a young fellow starting a colt. I watched him for about a half hour, and then went to our camper and asked my wife to come watch. I said, "I don't know who this young man is, but I've never seen such natural talent with a horse. If this guy sticks with it, I predict he'll be one of the best horsemen in the world by the time he's 40."

We watched until he was done and then I introduced myself. I asked him if he'd like to do an article for *Western Horseman* magazine with me. It ended up a three-part series titled, "A New Look at Old Methods," and it was one of the things that helped launch his clinic career. Some years later he thanked me for it. I said, "You're welcome, Pat, but I didn't do it for you." He looked at me, puzzled.

"I did it for the horses."

He understood.

I've attended many of Pat's clinics over the years and witnessed amazing things. Pat is a genius with horses. The hallmarks of genius are brilliance, creativity and eccentricity. That's Pat!

Often imitated and criticized for his showmanship and entrepreneurial skills, Pat never stops learning. He has a passion for horsemanship, a compulsion to share his knowledge and the vitality to inspire students. He has tremendously influenced some of our top clinicians. He's had many mentors and learned from them all, but he's also come up with his own original and ingenious concepts.

Pat, along with his contemporaries, has changed horsemanship forever. They've advanced civilization and given mankind a lesson in relationships.

I predict Pat Parelli's name will be known a century from now.

Robert M. Miller, D.V.M.
Internationally renowned speaker, equine behaviorist, consultant and author of Imprint Training of the Newborn Foal *and the newly released* The Revolution in Horsemanship.

Dr. Robert Miller and his wife, Debby.

centrate on the fancy stuff.

Very quickly I had more demand than I had the capacity to fulfill. I couldn't ride all the colts myself, so I started working in conjunction with Lee Rosser of the Mammoth Lakes Pack Station. He needed good help in the back country in the summer and early fall, and I needed colt-starters from late fall to spring. This liaison arrangement worked out well for both of us. I had at least five guys working for me at any one time, which allowed me to take care of business at home, yet still go on the road when I needed.

1984 Olympics

Interesting invitations started coming my way as my reputation and business grew. In 1984, the Olympic Committee asked Dr. Miller and me to go to the Olympics in Los Angeles. We were dubbed as the official equine behaviorists of the 1984 Olympics. In that capacity, we walked through the barns, making observations, answering people's

Pat drove all night to get to his clinic in a little mountain town in southern California. Here he's catching up on his sleep; his brand new Gary McClintock Wade-tree saddle made its debut on this trip.

questions and helping where we could.

One thing that struck me as odd was watching some of the riders mount their Olympic-caliber horses with the help of two people, one on each side, holding the horse's bridle, and a third person hoisting them into the saddle. It really shocked me to see that at this level of competition.

One lady came up to us and asked why we thought her horse wouldn't go forward anymore. I asked her how often her horse got out of the arena and onto the trail. She remarked indignantly, "My word, he isn't a cowpony! He's a dressage horse."

I said to myself, "I get it. We're on two different planets here." Obviously, I couldn't offer her any help – none that she'd accept anyway.

Most sad, however, were the atrocities Dr. Miller and I witnessed as we sat near the warm-up arena – things like grooms wiping blood off horses' sides from abusive spurring before they went into the arena. Not all of them, of course, but the number was still appalling and not what we expected at such an event.

I also remember doing a trailer-loading while I was there. I wondered, "How could anyone think about going to the Olympics if they can't even get their horse in the trailer!"

Chinks in the Dressage Arena

The dressage portion of the Olympics took place at the Santa Anita Racetrack. I believe the grandstands held 86,000 people. In between the dressage tests, there'd be intermission, and I was part of the entertainment. For four days, I performed a bridleless dressage and reining demonstration on a mule named Sissy, one of the best mules I've had the good fortune in my life to ride. We performed half-passes, flying lead changes, canter pirouettes, sliding stops and the like. I was dressed up in my cowboy attire – hat, boots, chinks and all. What a sight I must have made to the flat-saddle crowd.

There were a lot of foreigners at the event, as you might expect. I'll never forget some Japanese spectators coming up to me after the

Pat made trailer-loading a part of every clinic and demonstration. Troy Henry once told Pat that learning to trailer-load horses successfully would reveal the secrets to most horsemanship challenges because horses pull every trick they've got to avoid loading.

demo, speaking rapidly in their native tongue, cameras clicking away. All I could make out was the word "mule." They were obviously fascinated by this cowboy and his mule.

E-Myth Lessons

Things were really starting to pop for me. I'd hung in there and finally could make the payments on my ranch.

In my first year I grossed $300,000, but it cost me $325,000 to run the place. I felt like I was back in Clovis Mule Days, taking two steps forward and three steps back.

I was traveling all over the place, mainly in California and Arizona, and busier than a one-legged man in a butt-kicking contest. But as business grew, so did expenses.

I didn't know how to run a business, and I finally realized that. Running that type of operation is more difficult than simply balancing your checkbook.

My mom suggested I enroll in Michael Gerber's business development course. He'd written a book titled *E-Myth* and another called *E-Myth Revisited*. The books' premise is about the entrepreneurial myth in which people believe that if they're good at something, they can make a business out of it. I found out that this is true; it's absolutely a myth.

I took the course at Michael Gerber's headquarters in the East Bay Area – an 80-mile drive one way, a couple of times a week, but it was well worth the effort. It was the first thing that made a difference in my business life. I realized that growing a business is like growing a child or starting a colt. When you start, you've got to have the end in mind. Like a human or a horse, a business goes through infancy, adolescence, maturity and a decline. If you don't know how to reinvent your business, it'll die.

It takes four things to be successful in any business. You must first be competent in what you're doing. Then, you must have people skills, marketing savvy and business expertise to pull it all together.

I had competency and good people skills, but I didn't understand about marketing at all. I thought it was simply advertising. I learned that marketing is everything. It's how you build a brand. It's the perception people have of what your business is all about.

What Michael Gerber brought into my life was the marketing and the business skills. I learned to present myself and my program to people effectively. Then, once I made the money, I had to learn to keep it, how to capitalize at the right time and for how long – that sort of business expertise.

The above four things are crucial to any business, whether it's plumbing, building houses, selling cars, being a doctor or a horse trainer.

I also found my Eight Principles of horsemanship important in developing my business. For example, I learned that you must put principles in front of goals. If the goal is achieved without principles, the business has no integrity and won't last. Also, you've got to allow the time it takes so it takes less time. In other words, do whatever it takes to do it right the first time, so you won't have to do it over again and again.

My Eight Principles have taught me to be a good teacher and a good businessman. I built my business team on the same concept I approach horsemanship – love, language and leadership, in that order and in equal doses. This results in tightness of bond and lightness of response. In other words, horses and people become willing partners when given love and respect, communicated with openly and freely, and offered positive leadership.

Over the years, Pat polished his presentation skills and fine-tuned his weekend clinic format. He became a hot property all over the West. Conquering the rest of the country and the world would be next.

13 WHEN YOUR HORSE BECOMES YOUR PARTNER

*"If there was ever a time when
a horse could leave, it was then."*

PHOTO BY COCO

Scamp was the first horse Pat was able to take all the way through natural horsemanship.

In the early 1980s, Scamp, my second super horse, came into my life and forever enriched it.

A friend of mine trained most of Dick Gilbert's horses for cutting competition. I went to his barn to meet with Dick to see if I could contract with him to start his horses, not to train them for cutting, but to start them under saddle.

Dick sold insurance and later on we did quite a bit of business together. He became my insurance agent, and I became his colt-starter.

Dick owned a stallion named Roan Star Bar, a son of Nu Bar who'd placed third at the National Cutting Horse Association Futurity. He was quite a horse.

Like Riding a Border Collie

One day Dick showed me his horses, including a little red roan filly, six months old and just weaned. Registered as Roan N Royal, she was square on every corner and had muscles on top of muscles. When I first set eyes on her, I recognized she had something special about her.

I'd moved up to Clements by this time and 18 months later Dick sent me the roan filly for starting, along with a couple of other colts. I fell in love with that roan filly. I had to have her. I asked Dick if she was for sale, and she was, for $5,000. My heart sank because that was all the money in the world to me, way more than I could scare up. But by hook and by crook, and riding a few more horses, we arranged the sale and I bought her. I named her Scamp; what else could I name a horse that moved so quickly?

She was very sensitive around her mouth and didn't much care for the snaffle bit. She also bucked quite a bit when I first saddled her.

I'll never forget the third or fourth ride I had on her. I had some cattle in a pen next to where I was riding her. One of them sauntered into the adjacent round corral, so I took the opportunity to see if the filly would look at a cow.

Oh my! Have you ever watched a Border Collie when it sees a cow or a sheep for the first time and realizes that it's a stock dog? Well, that's what happened to Scamp. She took one look at the cow and wanted to pounce like a cat on a mouse.

Of course, I had very little control of her at the time. She didn't know what she was going to do with the cow, but she was going to do something. I stayed out of her way and encouraged her. When the heifer trotted off, Scamp took after it, put her nose on its tail and for the next 20 minutes, I felt like I was riding a Border Collie. Wherever the cow went, Scamp went. I couldn't pull her off the cow.

While she was locked onto the cow, I tried for a little lateral flexion. I bent her head around to the right and her hind end disengaged. She flowed right around and landed on the cow again. I did the same thing to the left with the same pretty movement. No matter how I directed her, she'd land right back on the cow. She was a natural cow horse.

I knew that the filly had more cow in her than any other horse I'd ridden in my life.

It was love at first ride for Pat. He just had to have Scamp.

Pick a Cow, Any Cow

My neighbor behind me had 300 acres and I had about 120. He made a deal with me that if I'd let his cattle eat my grass, he'd let me work my horses on his cattle. This was a good arrangement for both of us. I'd work Scamp out in the open, in the various pastures and she learned to hold cattle anywhere. Her confidence escalated.

I entered the talented filly in the 1986 Pacific Coast Cutting Horse Futurity. The event was held at the Los Angeles Equestrian Center, which I think is 150 feet across. That's really large by cutting pen standards because the bigger the pen, the harder it is for the horse to hold cattle.

I was no cutting-horse showman, for sure, but I was really confident of the foundation I'd put on Scamp and that she could hold a cow, anytime, anywhere. In practice, I'd seen

97

PHOTO BY COCO

Riding Scamp was like riding a Border Collie, Pat says.

her put her head down close to the ground and paw with one front hoof, daring a cow to move. She reminded me of a bull, pawing the dirt before he charged.

Besides our regular workouts, I used her at brandings where we had to separate mother cows from their calves. I'd probably done a lot more with her outside on cattle than most of the other cutters with their three-year-olds.

I was as green as grass at showing a cutting horse, and it cost us. When I went to cut my cattle, two popped out. I chose the black one and Scamp picked the white one. Unfortunately, I'd already indicated which cow I wanted, so in the first 12 seconds of my cutting debut, I'd incurred a five-point penalty by switching cows.

I knew I didn't have a snowball's chance in Hades to win anything, so I got over my nerves real quick. I took Scamp off the white cow she was on and put her on the black one. It was as if she said, "Okay, pick a cow, any cow." She really went to work. She got down on the cow, and we let it all hang out. The place went nuts. The people in the stands knew they'd seen a great horse. She marked a 72 and with the five-point penalty that

would've been a score of 77, enough to win most any cutting anywhere, including that one. But with me being a novice showman, it was like saddling Seattle Slew with a fat jockey. If Scamp had had the benefit of a better jockey, she could've won the futurity.

People followed us out to the parking lot. One man even offered me $40,000 for her. That was a lot of money to a guy like me, but I've never, ever regretted not taking it.

Out of Retirement

Scamp turned into a terrific family horse. We've ridden her in the mountains, and she's taken really good care of my son, Caton. Her main job, though, was to be my demonstration horse. I hauled her a million miles, literally, going to clinics and seminars across the country.

One day I went to the pasture and noticed Scamp wouldn't put any pressure on her hind leg. Somehow, she'd managed to shatter it. Our vet X-rayed it and found 27 small fractures. I took her to the University of California vet clinic at Davis, where they said she could never be ridden, but she'd be serviceably sound for breeding.

If it had to do with a cow, Scamp could do it. Note that in this photo and the one below Pat is riding bareback and bridleless.

I retired her to pasture for about three years. One day, however, when Linda and I went to check on her and all the mares and foals, she came galloping and bucking down the hill ahead of the rest of the herd. She was completely sound. She'd amazingly healed herself with just time. I thought to myself, "I think that mare could go back on the road again."

Mustangs at the NFR

With Scamp back in commission, I took her out on the road again.

At the National Finals Rodeo, 1992, I did a demonstration to raise money for the Special Olympics. About 3,000 people showed up in the Thomas & Mack Arena in Las Vegas,

Scamp had been one of Pat's best demonstration horses. Here she shows how cutting is done naturally.

PHOTO BY COCO

Scamp has had several foals for Pat, including this one, Aspen, by Liberty Major. Aspen is now Caton's horse.

Nevada. The demo was free, but I asked everyone to put $10 in the hat if after the performance they liked what they had seen.

The Bureau of Land Management was celebrating its 100th anniversary and brought in a bunch of range mustangs for us to start. The owner of the *Nevada Sun* bought one of the mustangs. Despite her skepticism, she donated the horse to my horse-taming demonstration.

Three mustangs were brought into the arena, one being the newspaper owner's buckskin. I had only an hour and 45 minutes to accomplish my task because the arena had to be readied for the NFR competition that night.

On Scamp I cut the buckskin out of herd, and BLM staff members held the other two. Scamp had done so many colt-startings over the years, she could almost do it blindfolded. When the buckskin looked at her with both eyes, she'd back up. She knew to back off and release the pressure. We played approach-and-

retreat and pressure-and-release games with the mustang, which he understood completely.

What made my demo even more interesting was that I did it bridleless. I used my flag and a rope to direct the mustang's attention on us, and pretty quickly the horse started following us around the arena.

As we walked, I swung my rope in a reverse arc, something called a "houlihan." When I released the rope, it fell around the buckskin's neck. He didn't even know he'd been roped.

The rope had a breakaway honda on it and just to show people that it took only two or three pounds of pressure to release it, I gave it a pull and released the horse.

Unity

As we played with the mustang, Scamp was focused on what we were doing. I really felt true unity with her at that moment. Scamp

PHOTO BY KAREN PARELLI HAGEN

In the early 1980s, Pat (left) was invited to give a demonstration at the Reno Rodeo. For fun, Pat loaded Sparky into one of the bucking chutes and burst out like a contestant, but instead rode around the arena bridleless. Announcer Bob Tallman (right) was in on the charade.

PHOTO BY KAREN PARELLI HAGEN

Pat gave demonstrations during the early 1990s at the National Finals Rodeo. Here, he's on Benny Binion's stagecoach, seated next to PRCA world champion saddle bronc rider and Hall of Fame member Clint Johnson and his son. Pat's son Caton is up front with the driver.

knew what I was thinking and what I was feeling. When we got next to the buckskin, I rubbed him all over with my Carrot Stick and then with my hands.

I stood up in the saddle, as Scamp stood motionless. I put my foot on the buckskin's back, then put it back on the saddle, then back on the mustang again. Finally, I put both my feet on the wild horse's back.

If there was ever a time when a horse could cheat ya' and leave, it was then. I would have been hanging there with nothing but the famous words to Hank Williams' song, "Your cheatin' horse will tell on you," ringing in my ears.

I stepped back and forth between Scamp and the mustang, then quietly slid down on the mustang's back. I asked Scamp to move and off we went.

That all happened in one hour and 44 minutes. I made the deadline, slid off the mustang, tipped my cowboy hat and said "Please, everyone, put $10 in the hat."

We raised about $30,000 for the Special Olympics that day, but what I got out of it was a memory of Scamp I will never, ever forget. Thanks, Scamp.

The mare is 23 years old now and has raised seven foals for me, probably the best of

PHOTO BY KAREN PARELLI HAGEN

Pat used Sparky during a mustang demonstration in front of the Thomas & Mack Arena in Las Vegas during the National Finals Rodeo, about 1990.

which so far is Aspen, the horse Caton rides.

In 2004, Scamp foaled a sorrel colt by Sailing Smart, a champion reining stallion campaigned by top reiner Craig Johnson. That same summer I became partners with Craig on the son of Smart Chic Olena. I have high hopes for Smart Seven and intend to chronicle his life on film as it unfolds.

101

14 OPEN DOORS

"After 20 years, I'd become an overnight success."

Doors started opening and opportunities started coming my way in the mid- to late 1980s, putting me more in the public's eye. Finally, I'd become somebody who people would want to take a clinic from or send a horse to train.

I realized that after 20 years, I'd become an overnight success. My mother once said that to me jokingly, but it's true. I'd paid my dues over the years, made some good and bad choices, learned from all of them, and found myself growing in the right direction and developing in a movement that would take the country and the world by storm.

Breakthrough in *Western Horseman*

Dr. Miller's three-part series titled "A New Look at Old Methods" in *Western Horseman* (November 1983 through January 1984) was a

Dr. Miller (left) and Pat collaborated on numerous seminars and demonstrations, including tours to Australia and a presentation before the American Association of Equine Practitioners. This photo was taken at Colloque, held at the Cadre Noir, Saumur, France. It was a scientific meeting on the etiology of horses.

At the prestigious, invitation-only Rancheros Visitadores ride, Pat gave horsemanship demonstrations and started wild horses.

huge breakthrough for me; it made a significant impact on my career as a clinician. (This was the series of articles Dr. Miller conceived after our meeting during Bishop Mule Days.) In that series we talked about the Eight Principles and much of what my first seminar for Dr. Bradley's clients in Hollywood was based on. We covered natural horsemanship techniques and how they integrated with modern concepts of behavioral science.

It was interesting that we got a lot of response from that article because it didn't have a lot of how-to training information in it. What it did have, however, was a lot of why-to information – philosophy and concepts. People were very receptive to a humane line of thinking as it pertains to handling horses. It was an idea whose time had come – again. I still have people tell me that that's one of the best series of articles they've ever read.

I had other subsequent articles in *Western Horseman* and made the cover of *EQUUS* magazine in February, 1989. That article, too, dealt with my Eight Principles.

One-Shot Wonder

Selling your own videos became the thing to do in the '80s, and I started producing my first educational videos in June 1985. We called them Home-Spun videos. They had very short lifespans because the master tape was capable of duplicating only a few hundred copies.

I found out that trying to produce a video was easier said than done. Because editing is so expensive and time-consuming, I used (and still do today) what I call the "one-shot-wonder"

At the Rancheros Visitadores ride, Pat met many celebrities and influential people, one being the great rodeo rider Casey Tibbs (middle). World Champion bull rider Gary Leffew is on the right.

103

technique, meaning that whatever topic I'm expounding upon I tape all at once, which eliminates a lot of editing. If something happens during the taping, such as an airplane flying overhead ruining the soundtrack, instead of editing it in the studio, I just do it all over again from the beginning. I've been within two minutes of completing a 45-minute video when something silly would happen, and I'd have to start all over again.

The good thing about the Home-Spun videos and being a one-shot wonder is that it forced me to learn to prepare what I was going to do and say. It made me very efficient in my speech and aware of what it takes to be on camera. This, in turn, made me more confident in front of any audience. My presentation skills were growing by leaps and bounds.

Today, my video business has grown into a private multimedia company. We have our own production division, with television- and movie-quality cameras, editing equipment and the professional personnel capable of running it all. One couple on the production team, Michael and Diane Killen, have won Emmys for their documentary work. We video almost everything I do to chronicle events and archive them for our media library.

Special Invitations

I'd become a hot property in the horse world by the mid-1980s and started getting some very interesting invitations to speak and demonstrate at high-profile events.

For example, my friend Dr. Burt Johnson invited me to the famous and exclusive Rancheros Visitadores ride that takes place annually in Santa Ynez, California. Open only to members and invited guests, the weeklong ride generally has approximately 600 riders show up for one big party. Some of the people on *Fortune* 500's list of richest Americans were there. I met Ronald Reagan, Gene Autry, Doak Walker, Casey Tibbs and other famous people.

Typically, ride management brings in entertainers such as George Strait, Red Steagall and others. What I did was horsemanship seminars and demonstrations, usually on a wild horse that hadn't been touched – my specialty.

Another special invitation came through Dr.

Miller. For years he'd been trying to get the topic of equine behavior on the agenda at the American Association of Equine Practitioners Conference, an annual meeting that brings together around 2,500 veterinarians from all over the world. The AAEP board didn't want to include a non-medical topic at the conference, but finally agreed to Dr. Miller's proposal. With his help, I was invited to speak at the 1986 convention, a venue that offers major presentations, and dozens of minor seminars and demonstrations. To give a major talk, most speakers have doctorates in their chosen fields. I was probably one of the first, if not the first, person to give such a presentation without a doctorate.

My speech, which attracted around 2,000 veterinarians in the main auditorium, was about the etiology of equine behavior, how and why horses do what they do. I used video footage to help illustrate my points.

This presentation led to others, for many years running. Dr. Douglas, president of the California Veterinary Medical Association, had me give a talk to his group; I also did one at Purdue University and other colleges and universities with equine programs.

These two experiences opened doors for me for many years to come, from the top down versus from the bottom up (this is meant just as a figure of speech). My appearance in magazine articles made me well-known to a vast audience of horse owners, but by going to such affairs as the AAEP Conference and the Rancheros Visitadores ride, I became acquainted with people of position and influence, who, in turn, paved the way for other exciting opportunities over the years.

European Tours

I experienced popularity on foreign shores, as well.

One day, back when I was still working at Troy Henry's, a European girl named Sylvia Furrer asked if I would give her lessons. I promptly said, "No" because I'd already gotten a reputation around town for giving somewhat avant-garde lessons. The few people I'd given lessons to were disappointed because they weren't what they expected, which was the typical equitation lesson. That was definitely not my style.

Sylvia asked if she could watch me in the round corral, and I said she could. She came around for the next several days in a row. I noted her tenacity and finally agreed to give her a lesson. I charged $25, or some such amount, which was about all the money she had. She was on her way back to Europe and didn't have much money, so I told her we'd work something out. I had her do things like clean stalls in lieu of payment.

She returned to America the next couple of years and continued to take lessons from me. We struck up a good friendship. When she asked me to consider coming to Europe, I was quite eager to do so.

Sylvia had quite the eclectic background. She lived in Switzerland, spoke five languages and worked at a guest ranch. The ranch had a therapy program in which they used horses to help clients in a variety of ways. They'd bring in high-powered executives who needed to chill out from their stressful jobs, or they needed some humble pie because their heads had grown too big for their hats.

At the guest ranch, Sylvia used the horsemanship techniques I'd taught her in the round corral and at liberty to teach horses to respond in natural ways. Europeans were intrigued by this approach.

Our clinics that first year went over very well, and we promptly got invited back. From Switzerland, we expanded our reach to Germany and other European countries.

You Are the First

On our second trip, Sylvia had invited Fredie Knie, the most famous circus trainer in Europe, to watch my demonstration. After it was over, he asked to meet with me the next day.

European riding halls and stables are quite different than in the States. Most have indoor arenas, and you have to schedule time as you'd do at an American racquetball court. If you don't show up at your appointed time, you have to pay anyway. Also, the stables all have restaurants and Fredie and I met at one

of them.

Fredie's English wasn't great, but I did understand him. The first thing he did was put his hand on mine, look me straight in the eye and say, "You are the very first." Curious, I asked, "First what?" He said, "The first American not full of B.S. What my great-grandfather taught me you were able to tell the people." (The Knie Circus is a fifth-generation circus.)

From that point on, we had a great relationship. Every year after that I'd have the chance to go to his circus training ground in Switzerland, where he'd share things with me, especially how he played with horses at liberty. Fredie taught more than horses, however. His brother and partner in the circus would handle the predatory animals (lions, tigers, bears) and Fredie dealt with the prey animals (giraffes, camels, zebras, etc.).

Having been raised to think that a circus is not far from a carnival in terms of credibility, I didn't think much at first about a circus in Europe. But on that continent, being a circus master is a highly regarded profession, and from Fredie I learned incredible things about horses at liberty.

A typical circus ring is two feet high and only 40 feet across. That's pretty small, but despite the size, Fredie would have horses do amazing things, such as lead changes every stride.

Fredie Knie (here in a 40-foot pen) inspired Pat to learn more about what can be done with horses at liberty.

The late Fredie Knie, the famous Swiss circus master, could do amazing things with horses. Watching him, Pat realized how much of a willing partner a horse could really become.

Phenomenal Feats

One truly remarkable feat I witnessed: Fredie brought in eight white stallions and turned them loose. They'd squeal and fight with each other until he walked in and asked for their attention. He'd have them all trot in one direction around the ring's perimeter;

Pat and Colonel de la Porte du Theil, who succeeded Colonel Carde as the ecuyer nen chef (head riding master) of the Cadre Noir, Saumur, France.

then he brought in eight black stallions and had them trot in the opposite direction, weaving in between the white ones. Then he brought in four zebras and had them circle in the middle. Lastly, in came two miniature horses, a white one and a black one, who performed figure-eights between Fredie's legs.

Another astounding feat: Fredie trotted four Friesian stallions on the circle, stopped them on cue, asked for a synchronized pirouette, had them resume trotting, stopped them again, backed them around the ring and had them lie down in unison. With one quiet cue, he'd have them sit up and with another barely audible cue, he laid them down again. He'd clap his hands loudly and they'd all jump up, run around, bucking and kicking and playing. Then he'd ask them to join him in the middle. What a sight! The coordination and respect that man commanded of his horses boggled my mind.

Most of Fredie's horses were once problem horses. The circus would come to town and people would tell Fredie about their troubled steeds. If Fredie could use the horse in his acts, he'd purchase it, rehabilitate it and make it part of his act. Many of his horses were in their 20s and early 30s still loving what they did.

Watching Fredie expanded my world as to what horses can do. It sank into me that if you create an environment that's provocative and fun enough for horses, they'd do anything willingly and forever. They loved performing for Fredie. This made a big impression on me and, consequently, I've added this dimension to my horsemanship program.

One time, when I was in Europe, Fredie invited my students and me to bring our horses to his training grounds. As we entered the arena, he opened his arms and said, "Welcome Circus Parelli." That was a high compliment because he'd never allowed anyone else to use his facility.

VIP Treatment

Once it became known that Fredie put his stamp of approval on Pat Parelli, doors immediately opened for me then and in the years to come. I've been invited to visit the Spanish Riding School in Vienna, where I was

Thin yachting braid was the right dimension for the effective rope halter Pat created.

treated like a VIP. I got to watch the 6 a.m. practice and sat in the royal box down on the main floor. Most people never get to see the Lippizans schooled, and must sit in the upper levels of the school's riding hall to watch a performance.

I got a similar reception at the French Riding School in Saumur, but, unlike Vienna, the French wanted me to give them a demonstration. Colonel Carde, the school's head rider, had me meet with the officers, who were in full military dress.

The school had a four-year-old Selle Français (breed of French horse) they couldn't get a saddle on or ride. Of course, they tried to do it "in the box" or stall, as is their custom. I wasn't prepared for a demonstration. I had no halters, lead ropes or equipment with me, but I gave it a go anyway.

They brought out the horse, which appeared to be introverted and goosey – the kind that would do nothing, then explode, then do nothing and explode again. I played with him on the ground, used my "drunk"

cowboy routine on him, where I walk around as if I were in a drunken stupor, tripping in a haphazard fashion. He finally tolerated my uncoordinated movements and grew roots where he stood. I crawled up on him and stood on his back, all of which took 20 minutes. Of course, the officers thought I was nuts at first, but when I could sit on the horse and back him up with just a savvy string around his neck, they were all eyes.

Colonel Carde was just blown away. He took me to lunch and asked a million questions, and, of course, invited me back. I've been back several times, including the time I participated in a debate with French behavioral scientists on equine etiology. Dr. Miller went with me, and we both had to listen to the eight-hour-long debate in French. This was another collaboration with one of my best and dearest friends, Dr. Bob Miller.

Cottage Industry

My clinics fostered other businesses for me, as well. In May 1986, at one of my Have Help, Will Travel clinics in Yucca Valley, outside of Palm Springs, California, I helped a lady who had a horse with a trailer-loading problem. I asked her where her halter and lead rope were and she showed them to me. The lead rope was the strangest I'd ever handled.

"My husband works for the Edison Company and they pull cable with this rope,"

The 12-foot lead line with brass hardware was another innovation of Pat's.

107

PHOTO BY KAREN PARELLI HAGEN

On their first Australian tour, Pat (left) and Dr. Miller (right) visited Morris Wright's station (ranch). Wright (middle) was a follower of Kell B. Jeffrey, one of the first Australian horse-whisperers.

she explained. "They use it once and then throw it away. It's really strong stuff." And, of course, it's the type of rope boat owners use on the docks to secure their boats, called yachting braid.

At this time I was making my own rope halters, the kind I'd learned to make in FFA. I used them on my own horses and found them to be much more effective than the typical store-bought rope halter or the flat nylon ones with cheap, breakable hardware. The problem was that the rope I was using at the time was stiff and thick.

I really liked the feel of the yacht braid. The lady gave me 300 feet of it. I experimented with the rope, making a bunch of reins and leads out of it.

I later found the company and purchased the thinner version to make my halters.

Every time I'd trailer-load a problem horse, I'd put on my unique halter and lead rope. Soon, people asked where I got the rope, and I told them about the guy in Yucca Valley. Poor guy probably got 100 phone calls.

Finally, it dawned on me that I ought to manufacture them myself. Bingo! The birth of my own cottage industry. I found myself in the tack business. On the way to my clinics, I'd tie halters and lead ropes if I was the passenger, and, if I drove, my assistant would tie them. We'd figure out how many we'd need between clinics and tied like little elves until we had enough to sell.

From that humble beginning, I've grown my business to include an entire line of first-rate horse-handling equipment, including halters, lead ropes, saddles and bridles, as well as clothing. It's a complete collection of all the things that I use.

The Land Down Under

In 1986, Dr. Miller and I were in Colorado Springs, Colorado, for the North American Trail Ride Conference year-end awards. Dr. Miller gave a presentation, and I worked with a couple of problem horses.

Bob Berg, whom I hadn't seen in 10 years, was in the area to buy some Watusi cattle. He wanted to export them to Australia to start a roping-cattle business. (Watusi grow their horns quickly.)

Bob stopped by the convention to see what I was doing. He was very impressed by what he saw and came up with the idea of taking it on tour in Australia. Bob suggested that we (he, Dr. Miller and me) become partners and split the proceeds in thirds.

We took both of our families to Australia in 1987 and stayed there 30 days, traveling about 2,000 miles doing demonstrations, seminars and videotape presentations. The whole tour was very successful, and I've been going to Australia twice a year ever since.

Bob did a really great job of promoting the tour. Australia is the size of the United States, but has only 17 million people, as compared to 265 million in the States, and most are concentrated along the southeastern coastline. There were about four horse magazines and only two television stations, so if you get on TV there, most everyone sees you. Bob was able to get us coverage in the newspapers, magazines and on the Australian television equivalent to "Good Morning, America." We became well-known, almost celebrities, in no time.

On the first tour, the truth is that most people came to see Dr. Miler; they'd never heard of me. Dr. Miller would present his ideas first with the aid of videotapes. I would usually do a talk and a trailer-loading or riding demonstration afterward. The funny part was we grossed $30,000 and our expenses were $29,900. We split $100 three ways. Big business!

Dr. Miller chose not to come on the second tour. In order to get people to come to see me, we offered a $500 reward to anyone who'd bring a horse I couldn't handle. The upside of this whole thing was that we got all sorts of interesting horses and lots of people came to watch, so our audiences were huge. The downside is that some of the horses were really rank; many were on their way to the killers. Some of the clinic attendees thought they could kill the "Yank" and make a little money on the side.

One of the horses they brought was from the country's biggest and best rodeo, called Mt. Isa. The custom at this rodeo was to offer $1,000 to the station (ranch) that could bring the best buck-jump horse (their term for bucking horses) to the rodeo.

One big palomino had won the honor a couple of times, so someone got the bright idea to bring it to my clinic the day after the rodeo and challenge me for the $500.

A big crowd gathered for what they thought would be my demise. I told the person who brought the horse, "You'd better not want this horse to buck anymore."

The palomino had what's known as an "abo strap" on him – much like a dog collar with a strap hanging down. It got its name from Aborigines who'd crawl on the ground near a horse, grab the strap and capture the horse.

I played approach-and-retreat games with the horse, but when I got too close to him, he struck and took off two buttons from my shirt. I mean this horse was tough. He was about 10 years old and knew how to handle humans.

We went round and round; I played with him and within an hour I was standing on the horse's back. Another hour later I rode him around the arena. The next day I did a lead-change demonstration on him, riding him with two Carrot Sticks and no bridle in the same arena where he'd won the $1,000 two days before for being the best station buck-jumping horse.

At another one of our Aussie clinics, an attendee brought a horse that could really buck. I saddled him in a little cattle pen, which had a six-foot-high rail. All the spectators were perched on the fence, and, when the horse bucked, his saddle hit the bottom of their feet. That's how hard and high he bucked! Some people were even knocked off the fence. There were people scattered everywhere.

I did get him ridden that day and managed not to lose my $500. Furthermore, I ended up buying the horse for $200, which was the going killer-price. I kept him for years, but changed his name to "Rub." Reason: He was the kind of horse who taught you never to lean over and pat him while riding. This horse could buck high, wide and lonesome.

On his second Aussie tour, Pat offered $500 to anyone who could bring him a horse he couldn't ride. "Rub," the horse that could buck high, wide and lonesome, was one of them. Pat liked him so much, he bought him.

109

When Tom Selleck needed help preparing for his movie, "Quigley, Down Under," Pat was called upon to help him with lessons and general horse-handling skills.

"Quigley Down Under"

A couple who worked for actor Tom Selleck got wind of my clinic business and contacted me about helping him with his horsemanship. He was preparing for the movie, "Quigley Down Under." Although he'd been a Marlboro Man and ridden on the television series, "The Sacketts," he wanted to improve his horsemanship skills.

I spent four days with Tom, and was totally impressed with him as a person. He's the same person we all saw on screen in the "Magnum, PI" television series. That's him. What you see is what you get.

We'd start lessons at 9:30 or 10:00 in the morning and go till 11:00 at night. These were not just the usual riding lessons. He learned to polish his all-around horsemanship skills, such as trailer-loading a horse, picking up the feet, saddling, bridling, the works. He also wanted to learn how to crack a whip and swing a rope.

Tom had heard that Australian ringers (cowboys) could be tough. He wanted to go over there with enough savvy to keep himself out of trouble. I gave him a series of tests he could do to determine if a horse was legitimately a good one or worthless.

Sure enough, in Australia Tom was brought some tough horses. They couldn't pass the tests, so he refused all the junk they sent him. He could tell they just wanted to see the star get bucked off. He told them he'd shut the whole project down unless they got him a horse that could pass the Parelli tests. He gave them a couple of days to find a suitable mount.

The show was being filmed in western Australia, not exactly close to the country's civilized eastern seaboard. But it just so happened that a few months earlier I'd given a clinic to some movie stunt riders there. One of them had a good horse that he loaned Tom. Tom liked the horse so much that, after the movie was filmed, he bought him and brought him back to the States. The last time I talked to Tom, he still had him.

Off-Site Office

Even though I was fairly well-known in Australia and Europe, my American clinics, for the most part, were West Coast affairs. One clinic grew out of another in a networking fashion. All that began to change in the late 1980s.

At a clinic I gave in Colorado Springs, Colorado, around 1987, one of the students, Marty Marten, had a horse with a trailer-loading problem. I helped him with it, and he was so excited about what he'd learned he wanted to become a dedicated student, and asked how he could do it. He ended up becoming my marketing manager, and we situated our company's marketing department with Marty in Lafayette, Colorado.

This was my first foray into having an office off-site. It was really interesting to have someone promoting me deeper into the country. This was my first giant step into moving my business from the mom-and-pop variety to a more full-blown business with employees.

Marty worked for us for several years, and did a wonderful job booking clinics in lots of states east of the Rockies – Missouri, Ohio, South Carolina. My clinics were taking on a very national and international scope, and my name was becoming even more recognizable and respected.

People's Perspectives on Pat

Clever Cowboy

I've been involved with horses for the past 55 years. I've ridden for pleasure, worked cattle, played polo and competed in rodeos, hunter-jumper shows and in steeplechases on an amateur basis. I began my equine veterinary practice in 1966 working on Thoroughbreds all along the East Coast and in Kentucky. I entered the Thoroughbred racing business in 1967, and have purchased, bred and campaigned numerous successful horses, including the 1977 Triple Crown Champion Seattle Slew and many of his offspring. I've experienced every facet of the horse world. It's been my life.

At the 1986 American Association of Equine Practitioners convention, I was introduced to Pat Parelli by his longtime friend, the famous Dr. Robert Miller. Pat was a young cowboy with a great smile. Dr. Miller informed me that the horse world would soon hear from this cowboy.

Later that day, Pat spoke to the assembled equine practitioners and then presented a trailer-loading demonstration on film. I remember the horse was a particularly obstinate fellow that definitely wanted no part of the trailer. In a surprisingly short time, Pat had the horse calmly walking into the trailer and backing out at his slightest suggestion. Pat had used none of the techniques that we normal horsemen were familiar with. The horse was transformed from a wild, scared beast to a relaxed, confident animal that trusted the situation and followed Pat's direction. I thought to myself, "What a clever fellow this Parelli cowboy is." We were all impressed. But the fact of the matter is I missed the point, and I believe that most of my normal horseman/veterinarian colleagues missed the point, as well. What Pat was attempting to convey to us was that to be good with horses, you must learn to think like a horse!

In January 1998, I had the good fortune of having dinner with Pat and Linda. By that time, Pat was becoming more well-known in the horse world, and I looked forward to renewing my acquaintance with this clever cowboy. The dinner was a delightful experience. Linda was bright, beautiful and charming. Pat was a natural-born entertainer, who led the conversation into diverse subjects, mostly fun but some serious. Always, the conversation drifted back to his passion to share his knowledge of natural horsemanship. That dinner was a turning point in my life.

In the spring, I traveled to the Parelli Center in Pagosa Springs, Colorado, where I took my first steps on the exciting journey that is transforming me from a lifelong normal horseman to an accomplished natural horseman.

Over the years, my journey and learning experience have continued. I appreciate Pat and Linda's friendship and generosity. I admire Pat's devotion to his family, especially the attention and affection he gives to his son, Caton, who has overcome tremendous challenges. I marvel at the progress of the Parelli Natural Horsemanship program; its impact on the horse world is nothing short of phenomenal.

Dr. Miller was right many years ago. The world is hearing from Pat Parelli, the clever cowboy.

Dr. Jim Hill
Equine Veterinarian
Thoroughbred owner/breeder
Owner/operator J.B. Hill Boot Company

Dr. Jim Hill with Seattle Slew

15 MEDIA MOGUL

"The hardest thing I had to learn was to be efficient with my words, not just prolific."

On stage, in print or on television, my education as a teacher, presenter and speaker was ongoing. In the 1990s I really gained experience as an in-demand personality. Through public appearances, on the screen and in print, I learned to deliver my message to the world in an effective, informative and fun manner.

On Top, Down Under

In 1993, Rob Woodard, an event/expo/trade-show promoter in Australia, came up with the idea for an Australian Horsemanship Congress, a traveling seminar all about horses. He invited Captain Mark Phillips (United States Equestrian Team chef

Filming for "Burke's Backyard" in Australia helped hone Pat's speaking skills in front of a camera.

d'équipe, three-day eventing coach and British Olympic gold medalist), Andrew Hoy (Australian Olympic gold medalist), Dr. Hilary Clayton (well-known Canadian veterinarian and locomotion and fitness expert), Dr. Chris Pollitt (world-renowned veterinarian and hoof specialist) and me to go on a tour of the country's five major cities – Melbourne, Adelaide, Perth, Brisbane and Sydney. Each stop attracted audiences that numbered in the thousands.

We all met in Melbourne first. I've never kept up with celebrities or royalties. I have a terrible time remembering movie stars' names, unless I've actually met the people and get to know them personally.

All of us got invited to an organizational dinner at an incredibly fancy place in Melbourne. Everyone dressed up in a suit and tie or dress. Linda dressed for the occasion, too.

Me, I always dress the same. I had on a western shirt, blue jeans and cowboy hat.

When I walked into the place, Capt. Mark's eyes popped open at the sight of this cowboy with the handlebar mustache. Mark seemed quite stuffy at first, being a former member of Britain's royal family and all. He was once married to Princess Anne, quite a horsewoman in her own right.

I thought to myself, "Oh, oh, I'm going to blow this party wide open." I didn't mean to stick out like a sore thumb, but I did.

I introduced myself with a big handshake and an even bigger smile. At the dinner table, I pulled out my savvy string and showed off a few of my rope tricks.

I did a trick with a wine bottle and had Mark hold the bottle. He got the biggest kick out of it, so I showed him more tricks. A few drinks later, we were best of buddies and had a blast.

The next day, Rob held a rehearsal for all of us to practice. Everyone decided I would be first presenter to kick off the whole seminar with something dynamic. I had wonderful footage of Thumper, Salty and Sparky to put up on the three giant screens behind our podium. My scenes with Sparky showed us bareback and bridleless jumping out in a field and changing leads. The music Linda had selected for our presentation was from the

Don Burke (left) with Pat before filming a segment for Don's popular television show, "Burke's Backyard."

buffalo-chase scene in "Dances With Wolves." It was breathtaking, if I say so myself. Every time I hear that music, it brings back memories of the Congress tour.

Rob wanted us to practice exactly what we were going to do. I was first and as I was announced along with my credentials, the music started and the video played, I came on stage, faked a fall and slid across the stage on my belly.

Rob yelled, "Stop, stop, stop!" And he made me do the whole thing over again – the introduction, the song, the video, the works.

Mark and Andrew were in the stands organizing their speeches for their turns, but at the same time cackling at my Laurel and Hardy antics. Linda was right behind them operating

PHOTO BY KAREN PARELLI HAGEN

Larry Mahan (left) hosted "Horseworld" on television for many years. In one segment, he featured Pat and Salty Doc.

the video projector. The two Olympic gold medalists were attentively watching my bridleless jumping on the huge screens. Linda noticed Mark nudge Andrew with his elbow, as if to say, "Geez, look at that."

When it came Andrew's turn, he was visibly nervous over what he was going to say. Linda and I offered to coach him on giving a speech. We told him that the first thing he needed was an opening line.

He came up with one that was really catchy about how Australians won 13 gold medals in Barcelona by sitting down and going backward. He was referring to the fact that the medals were obtained in riding, rowing and

other sports that involved a seated position. We became very good friends after that. Once he got past his opening statement, he relaxed and was actually quite good.

A Lot of Levity

In my presentation, I brought a little bit of levity to the seminar, as I usually do in my talks. I got people laughing and loosened up, sort of like the opening-act comic.

I told a funny story comparing riding a horse to riding a walrus, and that a person probably wouldn't care how scared their horse became if he didn't have legs. Could you

Pat poses with the publicity horse in front of the World Congress Centre, Melbourne, for the 1993 Australian Horsemanship Congress.

imagine riding a walrus on the beach? Mark just lost it and laughed his head off at that story at each stop.

Mark turned out to be quite the clown himself. On our flights to the other cities, Mark flew first class and we were in business class. During the flight, a bread roll would come hurtling from first class to our compartment. Mark instigated a food fight on the plane somewhere in the middle of the Australian skies!

After the first night of our tour, I told Linda that before the tour was over, I'd get Capt. Mark Phillips to do a handstand while wearing his suit.

She said, "What? How?"

I said, "Leave it up to me."

Sure enough in Sydney, Mark and I got to talking about exercises horsemen could do to improve things, such as balance, and I mentioned doing a handstand. I showed him how and helped him do one himself with his legs propped up against a wall. So, Capt. Mark Phillips wasn't so stuffy, after all.

On all the tour stops, Mark liked to use my Carrot Stick as a pointer during his talks. I was to leave it in a certain place at each seminar so Mark could locate it easily when it came his turn to present. He was always last on the agenda. I was on at 9:00 in the morning and he was up at 3:30 in the afternoon.

The very last stop was in Brisbane. Andrew and I decided to play a practical joke on Mark. I told him the Carrot Stick would be right in front of him on the stage but near the edge. All he had to do was lean down and pick it up.

Andrew and I rigged up a fishing line to the Carrot Stick. I sat way in the back of the theater with the fishing pole.

Mark stood up to give his speech and reached for the Carrot Stick. When he did, I reeled it in a little at a time, and he couldn't make out what was happening to the stick. His eyes were blinded by the bright stage lights to begin with and here the stick kept moving farther and farther away.

Mark quickly thought on his feet and shook his finger at the naughty Carrot Stick for moving away from him. The whole place just cracked up.

We all became really good friends and to this day, we see each other a couple of times a year.

PNH - the Book

Western Horseman approached me in 1991 to write a book about my horsemanship methods. Then-editor Pat Close was familiar with my techniques, remembered the impact my previous articles had on the readership and proposed the project.

115

From left: Pat, Australian Olympic Gold Medalist Andrew Hoy and Captain Mark Phillips at the 1993 Australian Horsemanship Congress.

It was a significant opportunity for me to write *Natural Horse-Man-Ship*. I probably never would've done it if the magazine hadn't promoted the idea. I've never written down anything. I probably haven't sent three letters in my life. I probably still have an English teacher in high school waiting for one of my reports.

The only way I was able to accomplish the book was working with the magazine's associate editor, Kathy Kadash (now Swan, also the writer for this book), who'd been to some of my clinics and believed strongly in my methods. She came to my Clements ranch, tape-recorded my conversation and got my words down on paper for me.

The book's content and structure were all important to me. I wanted to present my *Natural Horse-Man-Ship* concepts in a way people could grasp them easily. That's where the Six Keys came in. We shaped the book to follow the keys, which are things I'd learned were necessary to being successful at anything in life. They are attitude, knowledge, tools,

techniques, time and imagination. Just like the combination to a lock, I could prove to you that if you got all six of them lined up in a row, you could open up any success story you wanted. If it didn't work or the door didn't open, I could show you which one of those six keys wasn't used: Maybe you don't have enough knowledge, maybe your attitude isn't good enough, maybe you're using the wrong tool, maybe your technique isn't right or your timing is off. The book offered *Natural Horse-Man-Ship* within the framework of those Six Keys, with sections on the ground and in the saddle.

The book was published late in 1993 and still sells well today. It's *Western Horseman's* all-time best-seller.

Lights, Camera, Action

In Australia from September 1993 to February 1994 I got a chance to work with Don Burke on his television program called "Burke's Backyard." It'd been that country's highest rated show for 15 years. It's basically a gardening show, and about people's back yards, which often contain animals. Sometimes those animals are horses. Australia has a strong horse culture. You can pick up almost any newspaper and read news about horses in it, so having equestrian talent in the news is fairly common "down under."

How I came to be on "Burke's Backyard" is a rather interesting story. I'd been on the morning television shows in Australia – "Good Morning, Australia" and the "Today" show several times. Linda and I had even gotten some notoriety by being in *Who*, the Aussie version of a supermarket tabloid. Our faces were fairly familiar to most Australians.

We were invited to be on the "Wide World of Sports" television show that's broadcast in Australia. On it, I was asked to tame an untouched horse, my usual demonstration act. The guy who produced the show was adamant that he'd pick out the horse to prevent any smoke-and-mirror tricks on my part. He located a seven-year-old wild mare and, in 45 minutes, I was able to stand on her back. I proved I was no charlatan and did the broadcast in one take, with no need to go back and do it again. I got it right the first time.

Don, who's a bit of a Geraldo Rivera, (sometimes controversial American newscaster), didn't know this when he saw this show and thought it was a hoax. He decided to expose me on his show.

He called my office in Australia and asked if I'd be available to be in a segment on "Burke's Backyard." He had some horses lined up that he knew were tough. One that showed up was the property of a manic mother-and-daughter team. The horse was totally neurotic, a space cadet, but mostly due to his owners. I was in his stall trying to get a halter on the horse when the mother reached over to grab the halter's nosepiece to help me. However, in doing so, she spooked the horse badly. He ran over the top of me and through the stall door to freedom. Within seconds, the mother had a syringe in her hand; she was going to sedate him if she caught him. I finally got control of the horse and the demo again. I put the horse in a round corral and within minutes I had him responding to me.

Kathy (Kadash) Swan co-wrote both Natural Horse-Man-Ship *and* Raise Your Hand if You Love Horses *with Pat for* Western Horseman *magazine. A longtime fan and friend, she's shown here on her horse Nick at the 2002 Horseman's Experience Course at the Parelli Center in Pagosa Springs, Colorado.*

Don confessed to me later that it took him only five minutes to see a change in the horses. By the time he'd finished filming me with two horses, he knew I was the genuine thing.

We worked together and put out short, three-minute segments, about eight times a year. Topics included the usual – catching, bridling, saddling, picking up feet, etc. Soon,

117

At Equitana, Germany, Pat presented before standing-room-only crowds.

Venues such as Equitana and horse expos helped Pat to spread his message worldwide. This photo is of the PNH booth at one of the Equitana events.

I'd become a household name in Australia. I'd walk down the street, and people recognized me. They'd stop me and want to talk about seeing me on television.

One of the most important things Don did was teach me how to talk in front of a television camera. Since I'd done videos in the past, I thought this would be easy. No problem. Oh, did I get a lesson.

The hardest thing I had to learn was to be efficient with my words, not just prolific. Don's a master at it. He can say more in one minute than any person I've ever met.

It's taken me years to get really comfortable in front of a camera, but I finally feel I can look at one and start speaking and make my point without being wordy. Don gave me tips and coached me through the TV episodes. It was one of the best things I'd learned in my continuing education as a teacher and clinician.

Equitana Experience

Parelli Natural Horse-Man-Ship became a big name in Australia and Europe long before it was a big hit in the United States. Maybe it's because those two continents constitute a much smaller horsemanship pond than the large ocean of America, but nevertheless, I earned my stripes abroad before I did in the U.S.

In Europe, my biggest impact came from my performances at Equitana, the every-other-year equine extravaganza in Germany. There, I performed in front of standing-room-only crowds of over 6,000.

My success at Equitana Europe opened up doors to appear at Equitana USA, which debuted in Louisville, Kentucky, in 1994. Fortunately, all of my peers were there at the same time. Spectators could compare and contrast the messages and styles of several popular clinicians. My goal was to dominate the show.

I hit my stride at the horse expos, including Equitana, Equine Affair and the various state horse fairs, and they really put me on the map in the United States. It didn't take long to go from last billing the first year to top billing the following years.

16 TIME WITH TOM

"Never, ever knock the curiosity out of a colt."

Tom Dorrance was one of the most interesting and enigmatic people I've ever met. He was beyond genius, but that doesn't mean complicated. He took everything to its simplest level, yet he was esoteric. He could explain something in simple terms and you'd think you understood him, but

On his "visits," Tom Dorrance (standing) would show up at Pat's colt-starting clinics at the Clements ranch during the mid-1980's.

PHOTO BY KAREN PARELLI HAGEN

after you thought about it more, you might think, "I heard what he said, but what did he really mean?"

As I mentioned in a previous chapter, I met Tom, Ray Hunt and Ronnie Willis in the concession line at the California Livestock Symposium in 1983. The three of them had spent a lot of time together over the years in Montana, and Ronnie was basically one of Tom's and Ray's students.

Ronnie had moved to the Clements area about the same time I did. Tom would make the rounds for one of his "little visits," as he'd call them, to see Ronnie and me. When I started my Foundation Station colt-starting business, he'd come through once a month or so and stay for a couple of hours and sometimes he'd stay all day. At other times, I and some of my students would drive down to Merced, where he lived, and he'd conduct a little workshop or "get-together." His wife, Margaret, called them "Pony Parties."

So between Tom visiting Clements, me visiting Merced and seeing him at every Ray Hunt clinic I'd go to or put on, I spent some quality time with Tom.

The Importance of "Feel"

Tom was an enigma to a lot of people, especially in the way he looked at horses and horsemanship. I had a young man working for me by the name of Jim. At the NRCHA World Championship Snaffle Bit Futurity Show one year, he said he'd like to meet Tom Dorrance, so we walked over a couple of alleys and there was Tom. I introduced Jim, and then Jim proceeded to ask Tom a long-winded question about what he'd do if he had a horse that did this and did that. Tom looked at him with a blank look on his face. Finally, when Jim got done asking his lengthy question, Tom took his two hands and shoved a deck of cards at him. He said, "Pick a card, any card."

Jim looked at him as if to say, "What does this have to do with anything?"

Jim picked a card. Tom put the deck down and asked Jim for his card, face down, of course. Tom felt the card, trying to "read" the card with his fingers. He spent about a minute and said, "King of spades." He flipped the card over and, sure enough, it was the king of spades.

Jim exclaimed in complete surprise, "How'd you do that?"

Tom looked at him, said "Feel," turned and walked away.

Exasperated, Jim called after him, "But what about my question?"

Jim failed to understand that "feel" was the answer. That was my first real glimpse into how Tom thought.

Chicken Wire

Another example of Tom's terseness displayed itself in Jamestown, California, when Ronnie, Tom and I sat on top of a hill, looking down at Ray doing a colt-starting clinic.

I gazed over to my right and there was a brand new round corral. It was about six feet high and had plywood sides with a few pipe rails on top. I had designed one similar to it years ago with Freddie Funston. I wondered what Tom thought would make a good design for a round corral. I figured he might say, "Oh, there's a good one over there." I was just sure I knew the answer.

I said, "Excuse me, Tom. If you were to design a round corral, how would you do it?"

He looked at me without blinking an eye, without a half-second going by, without raising his voice or changing his inflection whatsoever,

Tom Dorrance's wife Margaret said, "There will never be another Tom."

and so quickly it was as if he'd been waiting for years for me to ask that very question. He said, "One made out of chicken wire."

I was floored and almost fell over. I said, "Chicken wire? Why would you make one out of chicken wire?"

He said, "For cowboys like you who are too strong in the arms and not strong enough in the head. With chicken wire, you won't put too much pressure on the horse."

That hit me like a ton of bricks, and I pondered it a long time.

Near-Death Experience

Years later I got a call from Oscar and Judy Thompson, who worked for me during my Foundation Station days. They lived in San Juan Bautista, not far from where Tom was living. They told me he was in the hospital. A

Tom Dorrance (standing at left) at one of Pat's horse courses, held at the ranch in Clements, California.

month earlier he'd had a five-way heart bypass; and because he didn't take his medicine properly, he ended up with a blockage and a stroke. He lost his eyesight and couldn't hear well either. They said he probably had only hours to live.

I was out of state at the time, but I hopped on a plane, got in a car and drove to Carmel to the hospital. When I got there, he wasn't in his room. The nurses said he'd been moved to a hospice, a place where patients are cared for until they die.

In his hospice room were Margaret, his nephew Steve Dorrance and a couple of other people. Tom was just skin and bone. I doubt he weighed more than 65 or 70 pounds. He went in and out of consciousness. He didn't know I was coming; so he really didn't know when I entered the room.

When he regained consciousness, Margaret motioned me to go over to him. He couldn't hear or see me because of his condition, so I reached over and felt for his hand. He felt mine, explored it like he was reading Braille, and in a short time said, "Pat Parelli? I was hoping you'd come."

I was blown away and mumbled something. Then the nurse came in to take his blood pressure. She couldn't get enough for a reading, he was so frail.

Throughout our acquaintance, Tom had always given me riddles or jokes, fun stories with secondary meanings. So, I thought it was my turn to try.

I said, "So, Tom, what's your next project going to be?" Tom always referred to the things he did as his "projects."

He said, "What?"

I repeated my question.

He said, "My next project is I'm going to die, and it's going to be today. I'm tired. I hurt and I want to see my brothers."

The whole room full of people broke down crying, throwing daggers at me with their eyes, as if to ask, "Why would you ever ask that question?"

I felt awful. I tried to keep my wits about me and countered with, "No, I've got some wild horses I need help with. Don't you want to start some more horses?"

He came back, "Naw, I'm going to die," and went unconscious again.

Curiosity and the Colt

A little time went by before he woke up.

I leaned over to him and asked, "Do you have anything to tell Pat Parelli before you go?"

Without hesitating, without any inflection or changes in his voice, as if he'd waited for years for me to ask, he said, "Never, ever knock the curiosity out of a colt."

That stopped me cold, but I said goodbye, told him I loved him and how much he meant to me.

I walked outside his room; the others followed and I talked to Margaret. She thanked me for coming, and I apologized for the inadvertent question. She just brushed it off.

She said, "I want you to know something. Tom's always had a special interest in you. There will never be another Tom. There will never be another Ray, and there will never be another Pat."

I got in my car and drove to Sacramento to the Western States Horse Expo, where I was giving a presentation. I pondered Tom's last words to me, and what he meant eventually dawned on me. He'd seen me "knock the curiosity out of a colt" before! I thought back to the times he might have seen me do something like that and remembered when I'd flipped a foal on the nose for wanting to nibble on me. Tom always had a way of deflecting things like that. He didn't punish a horse for transgressing; he just made it so it was hard for him. Tom would get the colt's feet busy so he didn't have time to do such things. If a foal moves his feet, it's hard for him to move his mouth at the same time.

This concept is important because it takes confidence to have curiosity, and we want horses to be confident around us. Confidence and curiosity are powerful things to be instilled in a horse, not driven out. It took some thought, but I finally understood what Tom meant.

"It's Your Fault"

That day I'd given Margaret and the other members of Tom's family my cell phone number so they could call me about Tom. I never got a phone call, not the next day, nor

Pat (right) shakes Ray Hunt's hand at the Tom Dorrance Benefit in Fort Worth, Texas, 2001.

the next. Finally, two weeks went by and I couldn't stand it any longer. I called Oscar and asked, "What about Tom?"

He said, "Oh, he lived. He's back home."

Months later I got a message that Ray had called. I phoned him and he explained about the benefit he was putting on for Tom, as he and Margaret didn't have any insurance and their bills were high. He wanted to know if I'd participate and I said, "Absolutely. No matter what I've got going, it's cancelled." And I did just that.

This was February 2001. The benefit was held at the Will Rogers Complex in Fort Worth, Texas.

Tom couldn't be there, of course, but dozens of clinicians put up their $1,000 to participate in a colt-starting demonstration for the public. Spectators paid to get in, as well,

Pat in the colt-starting portion of the Tom Dorrance Benefit. That's clinician and friend Dennis Reis in the background.

the day you were going to die, and I believed you. So, what happened?"

He answered me without changing the inflection in his voice, as though he'd been waiting a year for me to ask the question, "It's your fault."

I was taken aback and asked, "How could it be my fault?"

He replied, "You asked me that question (about his next project) and after you left, I thought about it. What else could I do? And I realized that I was 90 years old and trying to act as though I were 45. I decided that it was okay to be 90, and I got curious about what it would be like to be 91. As soon as I told myself it was all right to be 90, I decided to get better."

Like This, Pat

I was having trouble with my stallion Casper (see Chapter 19, "Something for My Soul"), and I had brought along a video tape to show Tom. In it, the horse was going around in a large, 180-foot round corral. He'd be with me and follow me (hooked on), but all of a sudden he'd just take off and leave me.

As Tom watched the tape, he'd take his hands and move them in an up-and-down motion. His voice wasn't good and he whispered, "Like this, Pat, touch him like this." He was pointing to the jugular groove on the horse's throat. He claimed that touching him like that would make all the difference to that horse. It was an intimate thing and Casper would really like it.

After I left Tom's, I went to the Western States Horse Expo in Sacramento, where Casper was. I played with him in a pen, and the horse ran off just like he did before. When he returned to me, I stroked him three times as Tom suggested, and the horse never left me again.

That was the last time I personally saw Tom. By the next year, he was declining rapidly, and Ray had just been to see him. I asked Ray how he was doing and he said, "Not well. I wish he'd turn loose because he's really suffering."

I called Margaret and asked her if she'd like for me to come. She said, "You two had such a

and there was a dinner and auction. The whole affair garnered a couple hundred thousand dollars for the Dorrances.

The following June, I visited Tom at his late brother Bill's ranch in Hollister, California. He and Margaret had moved there after the hospice stay.

By this time, some of Tom's vision had returned and he could see me. His hearing still wasn't good, but he could make out enough of what anyone said.

I said, "Tom, you've never lied to me. But exactly a year ago, you told me that that was

People's Perspectives on Pat

With Class and Style

On February 25, 2001, at the Will Rogers Memorial Complex in Fort Worth, Texas, an event called "Friends of Tom Dorrance Benefit and Colt-Starting" took place.

Western hats from all over the United States and Canada rode into "Cowtown." There were skeptics and believers; there were the egos and the ego-less.

I was one of the many who paid to participate in both the colt-starting and the horsemanship sections. I drew a nice colt who gave me an opportunity to watch some of the action in the other two round pens.

For the horsemanship part, I brought Matlock, an eight-year-old gelding I'd raised and had only 50 or so rides on, back when he was four. After starting him, I turned him out. Like a lot of young kids who have a chance to run loose without constant supervision, he got on drugs – locoweed, and was a mess for years. He didn't know any better. In rehab over the years, he improved but hadn't been to town. Well, now it was time to go to town. I took him to the benefit. Every time a horse in the arena would come up behind or near him, he'd scatter and away we'd go.

Matlock and I were reprimanded and sent to the middle of the arena. It felt as if we were in the penalty box. We had become a no-no. Matlock would walk in small circles, ahead a few steps, then back, while I observed all of the other riders. I found myself focusing on a man, who many years before, pulled into Burbank, California, to be on "Horseworld," a monthly television show I hosted that highlighted the horse industry. He was driving a funky old motor home pulling an old, four-horse, bumper-pull trailer.

Inside the trailer was Salty Doc, his buckskin stallion. The horse was obviously a partner in helping this young man to develop his tremendous skills in equine communication.

Fast forward about 10 years. The day of the benefit that man rode a gorgeous black stallion named Casper in the horsemanship portion. He rose above the egos and rode with class and style.

The event ended and on my way to my old trailer, the U.S.S. Mahan, I stopped by that young man's now-fancy, beautiful motor home, stuck my head in the door and said, "Pat Parelli, you are as good as you think you are."

Larry Mahan
PRCA six-time All Around Champion
1965 & 1967 PRCA World Champion Bull Rider
PRCA Hall of Fame
Saddlesoar.com

great visit last year, why don't we just leave it at that."

The next day Tom graduated to Horseman's Heaven.

I feel privileged to have spent time with Tom and honored for his help with me and my horses. Like Margaret said, "There'll never be another Tom."

DREAM BIG ENOUGH

After 20 years of "savvying savvy," I now feel confident to share what I've learned with others. It's my turn to contribute as my mentors have contributed their time and knowledge to me.

As I look back over the first part of my life, I realize that all I was doing was getting ready. I'm proud to say that many people have said I'm one of the most confident people they know. Being confident is knowing that you're prepared.

The TSTL formula – Talent, Skills, Try and Luck – comes into play in any successful venture. I discovered my talents and worked hard to perfect my skills through the years. The two things that have propelled me to the success I've achieved are Try, which is my dedication to my passion, and Luck, which is spelled "w-o-r-k," also defined as when preparation meets opportunity. All I've really ever been is prepared for opportunities.

The opportunities that have presented themselves to me and I've capitalized on are phenomenal. Those opportunities have allowed me to enjoy awesome experiences and good fortune. I now realize that by putting one foot in front of the other, I followed the opportunities in an absolutely logical and natural sequence that allowed my dreams to come true.

The one thing I've learned, though, is that as big as my dreams or my visions are, I might be pleased at the time, but I'm still not satisfied. Every single time I think I've achieved something significant, I sit back and ponder, "I just climbed the Matterhorn and that ain't nothing compared to Mt. Everest." I wonder, are my dreams big enough?

17 WE GAVE IT A NAME

"Every other word that comes out of your mouth is 'natural.'"

PHOTO BY COCO

Pat and Linda Parelli have coined the term "natural horsemanship."

Probably the most important turning point in my life came in September 1989, when I met Linda. It was during one of my clinic tours in Australia, which I thought might be the last because the organizer, Bob Berg, had other business obligations. His silversmith company had taken on a life of its own, and he had his hands full. He said he wouldn't be able to host any more clinics because they involved too much time and work.

That's Trouble, Boys

This last tour Bob organized included Dennis Reis, Wayne Banney, Oscar Thompson and myself. We drove a Hi Ace van, the Aussie equivalent of a minivan, to the tour stops. The vehicle needed a ring job or something because it spewed a lot of black smoke everywhere. We called it "Puff, the magic wagon." Merrily, our little troupe puffed our way through Australia.

In that country many people transport their horses in cattle trucks, instead of horse trailers. At this particular tour stop there were a few cattle trucks around the place and people were milling about, waiting for the clinic to begin.

Then my eye caught sight of a brand new Range Rover, with a nice horse trailer attached and a well-groomed horse tied to it. Standing next to the fancy horse was a pretty blond gal tending to the immaculately turned out

In front of the mare and foal bronze statue in Scone, Australia, from left, friend, Oscar Thompson, Dennis Reis, Pat and Phil Rodey. Bob Berg is standing behind Pat with his arm on the bronze.

Thoroughbred. She, too, was all spiffed up, with white jodhpurs on.

I took one look and said, "See that, boys? That's trouble."

To my way of thinking, someone who had that fancy of a rig, that fancy of a horse and was all dressed up in fancy white riding pants would probably never get along with my clinic program, which entailed getting dirty from time to time.

I asked the clinic participants to lead their horses into the arena. The girl (Linda) was one of the last ones in. Her horse led her and was getting higher by the minute. A lot of Thoroughbreds that come off the track lead their humans around. She held on tightly to the chestnut that was now leaping on the end of his lead line. All the other clinic horses were walking quietly, like seasoned cow ponies.

Linda had found out about my clinic at a local tack shop. She saw a video of me riding Salty bridleless, performing sliding stops, spins, lead changes, etc. She asked the tack-

store sales person who I was and did I have any books for sale. They said, "No," but that I was giving a clinic down the road.

Curious about a cowboy who can get horses to do things without a bridle, and desperate for some help with her flighty and dangerous Thoroughbred, Linda signed up for the clinic. All the traditional methods of training had failed her with this horse, so she looked for other answers to her problems.

As I usually do, I asked the participants to stand in a horseshoe shape around me, so I could talk to them easily. I asked Linda to stand over to one side because her horse was making circles around her, and it was the only safe place for her to be.

I went around the horseshoe and asked each participant to explain who they were, and what problems they were having with their horses, so I would know how to help them.

The lady standing next to Linda said that her horse was perfect, but that she was having trouble catching it in a pasture. To answer her

129

Bob Berg (left) and Pat are shown here by the Hi Ace van in Tamworth, during Pat's Australian tour in 1989, the year Pat met Linda.

question, I talked about a horse's right and left brain, how a horse thinks, how to look at things through the horse's eyes, etc.

Evidently, Linda had come to the clinic prepared with two written pages of complaints about her horse: "My horse has this problem...; My horse has that problem...; My horse won't...; My horse can't... and so on." But after listening to me answer the lady next to her, she quickly tucked her two pages in her pocket. It dawned on her that the problem was not with her horse, but with her!

When it came Linda's turn, she said, "Hi, I'm Linda. This is Regalo, and I'm the one with the problem, not him."

As the clinic continued, all my helpers (Bob, Dennis, Wayne and Oscar) surrounded Linda to help her. Not only was her horse the most troubled, but Linda was the prettiest participant. Naturally, the guys swarmed around her like bees to honey.

I had the class play the Seven Games with their horses. All got along well, with the exception of Linda, who still had problems with the first game, the Friendly Game. She had trouble throwing the rope over her horse's back. I told her she must accomplish that task before going any further. Her skittish Thoroughbred would have none of it, and Linda got fairly frustrated. Things weren't working, and the horse was getting worse, jumping around, almost out of control.

In my typical witty fashion, I said to her, "You're doing fine. I've never seen this take longer than two days."

Eventually, the horse got to where he could tolerate it, but by this time, the rest of the class was way ahead of Linda. They'd been through the Seven Games three or four times by now.

In due course, Linda was able to throw the lead rope over her horse's back and withers while she was standing on the ground, but what she failed to do was throw the rope over the horse's head. After lunch, all the horses were saddled and ready to ride, including Linda's.

The Runaway and the Bronc

I said to the class, "Is there anyone who's not comfortable riding their horse with just one rein?" looking more at Linda than anyone else. No one said anything, including Linda. As the class went along, I wondered if she didn't hear me, didn't understand me or if things were okay with her.

I had the class bend their horses with one rein, right and left, while mounted. To do so, they had to throw their lead ropes over their horses' heads, something they'd all (except Linda) done successfully on the ground.

When it came time for Linda to pitch her rope over Regalo's head, she tried to sneak it past him, and the rope's end slapped him on the side of the head. He snorted to let her know what he thought of that. She tried again, but this time she threw it too strongly and it caught on her stirrup. Regalo took off with Linda, galloping around the arena at 90 miles an hour.

I hollered, "Bend him, bend him," but she couldn't.

I was sitting on the problem horse that had been brought in for me to fix. He wasn't

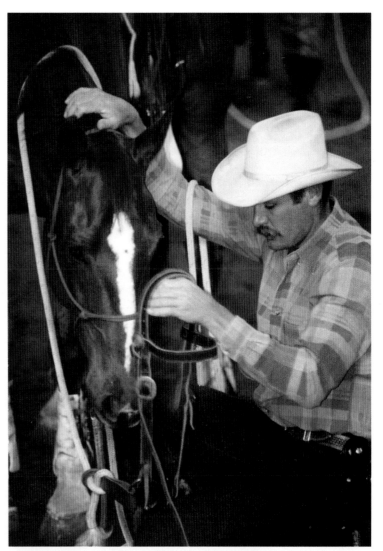

Pat bridles Regalo, Linda's high-strung Thoroughbred, at an Aussie clinic in 1991.

exactly the best prospect to work another horse from. I tried to head Linda off, and my horse started bucking. So, there we were – Linda on a runaway and me on a bronc.

Regalo headed for the gate, and I thought for sure he'd try to clear it. Instead, Linda finally got him to bend and they came to a screeching halt. She immediately got off and went out the gate.

I told Wayne to see if she was alright and to give her her money back. I felt she'd probably had enough.

When Wayne asked if she was okay, Linda said, "Yes, but can you get me my 'crash cap'?"

When she came walking back through the gate with her riding helmet on, I thought to myself, "This girl's got guts."

She wanted another go of it, so I helped her with getting the lead rope over Regalo's head.

By that afternoon, she rode her horse with only one rein at a walk, trot and lope all over the arena. Linda made big advancements in one day.

That night I did a trailer-loading demonstration at the same place. They gave me Snowball, a 26-year-old dude-string horse whose trick was to turn around and return to the stable. They'd curbed that vice with a standing martingale, which he evaded by backing all the way home.

Snowball had more tricks than a magician. He got loose from me three or four times during the demonstration. I rarely had horses get away from me once or twice, but never three times. He even pulled me off my feet and dragged me on my belly. By the end of the night, though, we saw eye-to-eye.

The next day I gave a clinic at the showgrounds in downtown Sydney. Linda came to that and brought her horse.

I did another demo that night for "Good Morning, Australia," and she came to that as well. She'd spent two full days in clinics and watched two demos in the evenings.

From Cosmetics to Cowboys

At the time, Linda worked for a company called Ella Baché, a French cosmetic corporation that has an innovative line of skin-care products. Linda worked her way from secretary to executive in the 12 years she was there and helped grow the Australian distributorship to a multimillion-dollar business.

Part of Linda's job entailed her giving seminars around Australasia to beauticians who use the products. In Australia, a beautician is someone who helps clients with skin care regimens, does facials, etc., not someone who cuts and styles hair, as we call them in the United States.

In her seminars, Linda demonstrated how to use Ella Baché products, why they work and how to prescribe them. One thing she always stressed to beauticians was to wait for their customers' permission before telling them what to do.

By the same token, what Linda heard me say in my clinics was, "Ask permission of your

Linda and Regalo, the challenging ex-racehorse that brought her to Pat.

horse to put the halter on. Ask permission to put the bridle on. Ask permission to get on, etc."

Linda told me later that the parallels in our presentations were unbelievable. She, too, did short segments on "Good Morning, Sydney," only hers were on skin care.

She asked me if I knew who Tony Robbins, Robert Kiyosaki and Stephanie Burns were and I said, "No." I later learned about these motivational and inspirational writers and speakers. She'd been studying these people, their philosophies and approaches to business and life, and she felt mine were similar as they related to horses and horsemanship.

Between the first clinic with me and the evening seminar with Snowball, I went over to visit with Linda at her trailer. I told her I couldn't help notice that she was paying attention in a different kind of way. It seemed as though she were studying the way I was teaching or something.

She said, "I was. I was very intrigued, not just with your message, but how you delivered it."

Instantly, we connected on the parallels in our philosophies and our way of thinking. We had similar teaching styles and were involved in comparable instructional programs – hers with cosmetics, mine with horses.

Just before I left Australia, I told Linda that this might be my last time, as Bob Berg no longer had time to be my promoter. Linda asked for a chance to handle the Aussie clinic business Bob was giving up. From scratch, she organized my whole company in that country. She literally breathed life into it. One of the first things she did was put out a newsletter to keep clinic-goers in touch with me and my horsemanship program. She networked, let people know when I was coming to Australia and secured hosts for my clinic tours. Linda did a fabulous job of getting the word out. She ran the Aussie tour business for three years before she came to the United States.

"Natural"

As I gave my seminars and demonstrations, I began to realize that people didn't really like following some person's methods. I called my

clinics Pat Parelli's Horsemanship Clinics in those days. It seemed that if my methods and techniques didn't work out for people, they'd get upset with Pat Parelli.

So, in talking to Linda one day as we were driving down the road heading toward Melbourne, I remarked I needed a name for what I was doing.

She said, "Pat, every other word that comes out of your mouth is 'natural.'" And, that was true. Even the cover of *EQUUS* magazine referred to my natural methods.

"You should call it 'Natural Horsemanship,'" she exclaimed.

And we did. I hyphenated the word "horsemanship" and added Parelli in front of it for Parelli Natural Horse-Man-Ship or PNH. It wasn't long before the rest of the horse world adopted the term as the name for this brand of horsemanship.

The name even reached the ears of the Dorrance brothers, Tom and Bill, the senior statesmen for this movement. I was at Bill's house about nine years before he died. I think he was 86 at the time.

He said, "You did it."

I said, "I did what?"

He said, "You gave it a name, this horsemanship thing. For 50 years, my brothers and I have been calling this 'it.' It's now got a name. It's natural horsemanship."

I'll never forget how excited he was about "it" having a name.

I think it's done a lot of people a lot of good to identify with something – to be able to say that "natural horsemanship is what we're doing. We're doing things naturally for the horse."

That made me feel good back then, and it still does today. And I've been pleased to say that my program is Pat Parelli's version of natural horsemanship.

Change the World

Because of Linda's efforts on my behalf in her country, I went to Australia twice a year for clinic tours. Linda was still working her full-time job, but would take time off to go to the seminars she organized. All the while she promoted natural horsemanship, she lived it as well.

Linda made great progress with both her horses, Regalo and Siren, another Thoroughbred. She was an extremely dedicated student. If I told her to ride bareback an hour a week, she rode 10 hours. She put her heart and soul into it, and got fantastic results. When she hit the dirt trying to do what I asked, she dusted herself right off and climbed back on.

Linda was criticized and ridiculed by her dressage friends for doing something silly and different and western, as they thought "it" was, but none of that dissuaded her. Her dedication to natural horsemanship was real. She saw how her horses benefited, and that's all it took for her to press on and excel in something she believed in.

I could tell that between the two of us, we had the chemistry it took to really change the world with horses. As our relationship matured, we often talked about just that – changing the world.

My clinic schedule in Australia, Europe and the United States was in full swing by the early 1990s, and I found myself traveling more and more, often taking Karen and the kids with me on the road. More and more, Karen wanted to stay home and raise our children. We got to a place where either I had to change and stay at home, or she had to change and travel more. Our visions were different, and there came a point in time when it was best to call it quits. It was one of the most difficult decisions of my life. But as I look back now, I think it was one of the best decisions for all of us. Karen, who lives on a ranch in Angels Camp, California, has found her soul-mate in her husband, Jim Hagen, and I've found mine in Linda.

PHOTO BY COCO

Linda and her Dutch Warmblood, Remmer, are familiar figures on the seminar tours.

People's Perspectives on Pat

$5,000 Bet and a Testament

Pat invited me to join him on Bob Berg's 1989 promotional tour in Australia. Two things really stand out in my mind about that trip.

One is that Bob arranged a wild horse demo each night of our monthlong tour. He offered $500 to anyone who brought a horse that Pat couldn't ride.

I had a lot of faith in Pat's abilities and encouraged Bob and Pat to make the bet $5,000. Bob agreed and upped the ante to really get people to bring out their worst horses.

On our last night, a gal brought in her rank two-year-old stud colt. About 500 people were watching and "Good Morning, Australia" was there to film the "horse psychologist," as Pat was called, tame the horse for the $5,000 bet.

I'd never seen Pat tired or unable to handle any horse. He was very fit and always in control. But he was in a huge arena, not a small round pen. Two hours into the program, Pat seemed "aired out" and almost on the ropes with that young horse. I thought, "Oh my God, it's not going to work. My hero is failing on national television!" Then Pat did something I'd never seen him do. He put his Progress String (now called Savvy String) above one of the colt's hocks. The colt sat down, and then Pat caused him to lie down. Pat rubbed and petted the animal. You could've heard a pin drop.

Pat took the halter and lead rope off the colt's head and the string off the hind leg. Then he got on. I knew he was a good bareback rider, but there was absolutely nothing on that colt to hold on to.

The colt got up, froze for a second, looked at Pat on his back, then moved out at a trot. Before long, Pat had him cantering in circles and changing leads.

That's what Pat Parelli stands for. He always does the extraordinary.

The other notable thing on that tour was the clinic in which Pat met Linda. She had a high-powered, out-of-control Thoroughbred. Sincerely, it was the worst horse in the class, with absolutely no respect and no ground manners. But Linda had one thing going for her and that was she rode well enough not to fall off.

Ten years later I saw her at a demonstration, and by that time she and Pat were married. She did things that impressed me beyond belief, things that I couldn't do with horses. It showed me just how well Pat's techniques work. That inspired me to learn more and become a better student.

I'm one of Pat's biggest admirers. He truly deserves whatever accolades he gets. I don't think anyone has done more for natural horsemanship than he has. He's made it mainstream and attainable for the back-yard horse lover. Through Pat's methods, people can have safe, productive, happy relationships with their horses, and that's a testament to how much Pat has changed the horse world.

Dennis Reis
Universal Horsemanship®

PHOTO COURTESY OF DENNIS REIS

Pat and Dennis Reis (right) in North Dakota in 1988. Both are sitting on two troubled horses that they ended up riding bridleless.

18 HORSEMAN'S HEAVEN ON EARTH

"The conference allows people to make a migration, sort of a pilgrimage to Mecca, to return to the source, so to speak."

The December 1996 issue of *Western Horseman* magazine ran an article titled "Horseman's Heaven on Earth." Writer Kathy (Kadash) Swan described her experience taking a course at the newly opened Parelli Center in Pagosa Springs, Colorado. Evidently she saw our vision in the making just by what she titled her story. The dream Linda and I had for years finally had come true, but we had a few nightmares along the way.

Meetings, Marriage and the Morning After

We'd moved our corporate headquarters from Clements, California, to Delta, Utah, temporarily. Frankly, we were experiencing serious financial difficulty at the time.

I proposed marriage to Linda and thankfully she accepted, but then we had to figure out a good time to propose to get married, considering

Pat and Linda opened their center in Pagosa Springs in the summer of 1996.

our hectic schedules. Secretly, I devised a scheme. Linda and I had gone to Delta to do some instructor and staff development. Our next clinic was to be in southern Oregon, and I knew that one of the best routes to get there would be through Reno, Nevada, so I concocted a plan to have our wedding there.

After our time with the staff, we all went to a honky-tonk, where the staff had a cake delivered to celebrate the upcoming wedding. Since the staff development had taken more time than we had predicted, Linda said to me, "Let's get married another time, when we have more time." Little did she know that I had already set up plans for the wedding. I just smiled and agreed with her.

Long before this, I had called Linda's sister, Vivienne, and asked her to come to the United States for the wedding, as a surprise for Linda. Her husband, Barry Black, was already in the States to collaborate with us on our Australian business. Barry and Viv ran Parelli Australia for us.

After the staff session, Linda arrived at the honky-tonk later than I did, and, when she walked in, she saw me dancing with a beautiful blond lady. I kept the gal's back to Linda for a bit, then twirled her around and Linda saw that it was Viv. She couldn't believe her eyes. Linda burst into tears – not only over Viv being there, but also in now knowing the wedding was on.

The next morning we left Delta and drove across Nevada to get to Reno. When we arrived, I said, "Why get married in Reno, when we could get married at Lake Tahoe. It's just one hour's drive over the mountain and one hundred times more beautiful."

We made the decision to do it, but we had to decide what to do with our entourage, which consisted of a motor home pulling a horse trailer with three horses and four dogs in it. We found a place that had been abandoned, put up some electric fence to contain the horses and staked the dogs out.

I made a phone call to one of those chapels that marry people conveniently and in a hurry. They asked me if we wanted to get married in the chapel, on the mountain or by the lake. I chose the lakeside because I'd been to Lake Tahoe before and knew how beautiful it was.

Pat and Linda were married in July 1995 at Lake Tahoe, Nevada.

We met with the marriage coordinators to sign the papers and make all the arrangements. The officiating couple was a little different. The man was a tiny guy with no hair anywhere — a bald head, no eyebrows, no eyelashes even. All we could see were eyes and ears. His wife, on the other hand, was a big-boned woman, who had big hair, big earrings and shoulder pads, and looked a little bit like Elvira, the television hostess for scary movies. The first thing they did was show me a picture of Tom Selleck, who'd gotten married with them. Of course, I told them the story of me helping Tom with "Quigley Down Under."

We all went down to the lake, where they held the weddings and had a beautiful ceremony. Linda wore an elegant, yet simple dress and cowboy boots, and I was in my standard attire – jeans, cowboy hat and boots.

On our trek to the wedding spot, we were giggling about the bizarre situation. But as soon as the officiating couple turned on the music in their boom-box, both Linda and I started bawling like babies. Barry was video-taping and Viv and Kaye Thomas were watching. Kaye was one of our Australian employees who later became a Parelli instructor. Pretty soon all the girls were crying. With everyone weeping, it looked like more of a funeral than a wedding!

"Run down" doesn't begin to describe the conditions of the Pagosa Springs ranch when Pat and Linda purchased it in 1995.

Following the ceremony, we ate a late dinner, after which Linda and I went to a honeymoon suite we'd rented for the night, and Viv, Barry and Kaye stayed in the motor home. We had to leave the next day at 6:00 a.m. if we had any hope of making our clinic in southern Oregon.

The next morning Linda and I arrived at the motor home; I started the engine and we all took off. About 10 minutes later, Viv joined us in the front of the cab, had some coffee and then Linda said, "Where's Barry?"

It turned out Barry had gone for an early-morning run by the lake, and we'd left without him! We'd driven about 30 miles before we realized it. We all had a big laugh, turned around and found him sitting in the parking lot with a knowing look on his face. With him safely loaded in the motor home, we drove all day and just barely got to the evening demonstration in time.

Homeward Bound

For two years, Linda and I traveled around in that motor home, giving clinics and spreading the PNH word, 367 days of the year. Somehow we always managed to stick a few more days in the year than there actually were.

We searched for a long time, looking for an appropriate place to situate a school for our students. It'd been our dream to have dedicated students come to a center to study horsemanship under our watchful eyes.

We had looked in British Columbia, Washington, Oregon, northern California, Montana and Wyoming. We finally found just what we were looking for in Pagosa Springs, Colorado. The property was a run-down old ranch, but it was situated on 130 beautiful acres, bordered on three sides by the San Juan National Forest and framed by an incredible view of the San Juan Mountains. When Linda and I first saw the place, we both started humming the familiar song from the television Western series "Bonanza." The atmosphere looked and felt like the home of the Cartwright family. Ben and his boys could've come bursting out of the ponderosa pines at any

PHOTO BY COCO

Karen Scholl was the first president of Pat's company. She did a tremendous amount of work to get it up and running and paved the way for a lot of PNH's early success.

The old red barn was a landmark until it was torn down.

moment. It was truly the perfect spot for our dream to come true.

We had just enough money for half of the down payment and arranged to pay the rest in yearly payments for three years. I told Linda that if we didn't get enough people to come the first year, then we could consider the $100,000 a lease payment and walk away.

We named it the PNH International Study Center and immediately made plans to develop the business and infrastructure, but we needed help. One night, as Linda and I were sitting in the ranch house, I thought out loud and I said, "Mark and Karen Scholl. Let's call them." Linda asked why, and I said that's who I thought should help us run our office and build our business. She agreed. I phoned the Scholls and left them a message; they lived outside Phoenix at the time. I told them to call me any time of the day or night and sure enough, they returned our call at 11:00 p.m. that night. We explained what we had in mind, and they agreed to get on a plane the next day to fly to Pagosa Springs.

Both Karen and Mark had been good students. I just had a feeling that they'd be right for the job. Their business backgrounds at Intel in Scottsdale, Arizona, dovetailed nicely into what we needed to help us develop our center. Karen became president of our corporation, and Mark was responsible for the operations and finance end of things.

We already had three other employees, and,

with the Scholls, we now had five people working for us. We were good to go.

We rented a mechanics garage in Pagosa Springs as office space and installed two computers. The first snow melt flooded the shop. It was cold and the roof leaked – an inauspicious beginning to our burgeoning international business.

What a Dump

We'd arrived on the ranch in October 1995, and spent the winter tearing it down and cleaning it up. The ranch needed a lot of work; I mean a lot of work. Within the first week, we had six semi-loads of junk cars and old tractor parts hauled out of there.

Within the next six months we hauled 36 semi-loads of garbage from out of the ground – batteries, refrigerators, barbed wire, bones, all sorts of trash. The place had been used as a public dump. My first clue should've been the fact that the fellow who sold us the place wouldn't sign the piece of paper stating that the ranch had never been used as a dump site. It didn't bother me at the time because it never dawned on me that that's what it was. I figured all old ranches had a dumping grounds

One of the covered arenas next to the old red barn before it was razed to the ground. The pond in the foreground is in front of Pat and Linda's home.

139

somewhere. But we found them every 25 feet!

After making the down payment, we didn't have enough money left to buy a car, but there was an old Scout on the ranch that the previous owner let us keep for six months. There was also an old tractor that didn't have any brakes. On all the hills the place had, we had to use the bucket and the backhoe as brakes! The machine ran away with us a couple of times. We were lucky we didn't kill ourselves.

Barter Could Be Smarter

We had 15 months to make the first annual payment, but only 10 months until the students would arrive for our first course the following July. We had to erect a facility in that short amount of time – cabins, arenas, round corrals, horse pens, tack rooms, you name it, we had to have it all to conduct our courses.

I wrote and called everyone I knew who I thought could help us. I explained what we needed and that, in lieu of money, "barter could be smarter." Naturally, that worked for me, as money was tight.

Like magic, things appeared. For example, we got a 10,000-gallon water tank from Arizona, and the cabins came in kits from Canada. Our working students helped put them together.

Our original idea for the ranch was to have a place we could come home to for three months during the heat of the year. We'd hold various weeklong courses throughout the summer for a handful of students, say 12 to 15 per week, with a couple of very serious students staying the 12-week period. To our surprise, we had 27 people sign up for the entire summer and only two or three people enroll in the weeklong courses – just the reverse of what we thought.

This meant that every week we had to do what we said we were going to do for each course for just two or three new people. But we made it work.

Opening Day Nightmare

We opened on July 1, 1996. We'd had a very dry spring that year and the ranch was a dustbowl. It hadn't spit one drop of rain in months. We had no gravel on the roads, and the arenas and round corrals were like concrete.

But the day people arrived for the first course, the skies opened up, and we had six inches of much-needed rain. However, the place turned into a quagmire. Trucks and trailers were jackknifed everywhere in the mud. People couldn't even walk up to their cabins because of all the slippery slop they had to plow through.

An aerial view of the International Study Center during its first years of operation.

Live-in courses have been popular at the center from the start.

The lodge, where we planned to feed everyone, wasn't finished. We had volunteers for a 12-day work party, after which we were going to offer them a three-day riding clinic. We'd all put in 15 days and it still wasn't completed. Jill Matthews, one of our employees, saved the day by bringing in hot soup to feed the troops.

Yet another disaster: We'd stored our supplies, foodstuffs, toilet paper, etc., in the basement of one of the old ranch houses. It flooded, ruining about $3,000 to $4,000 worth of goods we needed for the courses.

At 11:00 that night, Linda and I finally fell into bed. We just hugged each other and cried. We felt our dream and investment had just gone down the drain. That was our first day.

Fortunately, despite the opening-day nightmare, we made it through our first season, paid our mortgage and have continued to hold our summer courses ever since. While the center was a success, it still ran in the red for five years. We made more money out on the road than at the center. Nonetheless, we kept investing in our dream until we had it right.

The Lodge and dining hall is the main gathering place for students.

The top of the Lodge hall with the cabins in the background.

141

Pat (left) works with one of the students over the challenge course.

Today, we have the facility and the faculty of a world-class educational institution. We hold a variety of courses and programs to fit anyone's schedule: weekend, weeklong, two weeks, 10 weeks, one-year, two-year and four-year. The center is accredited as a university in the State of Colorado, and is the only accredited natural horsemanship university in the world.

Building an Industry

Long before this dream came true, however, I'd had another dream, in which the center would one day play an important part.

When I first realized how important natural horsemanship was as an industry, I wanted to do some things that would be industry-builders. The reason: I'd seen the NRCHA almost deplete itself from 300 to 400 entries at its futurity to between 30 and 70. What happened in my estimation was the dog-eat-dog syndrome. People started caring about themselves more than they cared about the industry. You've got to be able to do both for an industry to survive. If you're a reined cow horse trainer, a cutting horse trainer or a polo horse trainer and your industry goes out of business, you're out of business.

Natural Horsemen's Rendezvous

My idea was to do something that would create unity among the natural horsemanship followers. I decided to hold a Natural Horsemen's Rendezvous and invited all the natural horsemanship clinicians I knew to my ranch in Clements. Those who came included Bill and Tom Dorrance, Dennis Reis, Richard Winters, Alfonso Aguilar and others. I held three of these rendezvous in the early 1990s, but they never really came together in the way I'd hoped. I gave up the idea for lack of solidarity among the group. My hopes that everyone would join together really didn't pan out.

The closest thing I've seen to unity among natural horsemanship professionals was the Tom Dorrance Benefit that Ray Hunt put on to help pay for Tom's medical bills. (See Chapter 16, "Time With Tom.") That event gave the public a chance to see who's who in this new zoo, and, just as important, for everyone in the zoo to see each other. It was very interesting for all the clinicians to see what their compatriots were about. Most clinicians are so busy they rarely get a chance to take in another clinician's clinic.

Students enjoying a ride on a beautiful fall day in Pagosa Springs.

Framed by the San Juan National Forest in the background and affording an incredible view of the San Juan Mountains out the front, the Big Top, a Cover-All building, went up in 2002. It provides ample, lighted space for courses and events and holds over 2,000 people in bleachers.

People's Perspectives on Pat

Love, Language and Leadership

Some people learn how to compete before they learn how to ride, and they learn how to ride before they develop a language with the horse. Pat Parelli has developed a program where all horse people, no matter what skill level, can easily learn how to create a language with their horses.

Karen and I had been looking for a way to demonstrate our teaching philosophy, and we found an allegiance with Pat and Linda Parelli. At our presentation at the 2002 Rolex in Kentucky with Pat and Linda, when I took the bridle off Giltedge, it was an amazing feeling from the crowd's reaction. I had taken away the one method we humans think controls the horse. Giltedge, who has been to the Olympics, World Championships and Pan Am Games, allowed that communication to become visible for the audience. That, in turn, permitted them to see that the message of natural horsemanship is to redefine communication with horses. Fear and intimidation are short-term paths; they're unfair to the horse, and they don't work. Giltedge brought the crowd to its feet as he sailed over the jumps, bridleless.

By developing a language and therefore confidence in the horse, we allow the horse to begin to solve puzzles by himself, which makes our jobs easier. If we teach communication and language on the ground, by the time we hop on, most of our job is done. Pat's program is a great tool for that foundation.

We have taken horses out of their natural social environments, and we have become their social environment, the leader of their herd. What Pat has developed is a way to learn how to create a fun language for everything we do with horses. Pat's program shows how to develop a language before you do anything else — jump, cut a cow, trail ride, run barrels. Horses and riders understand one another through love, language, leadership, trust, respect and lightness — all the things Pat teaches.

PHOTO BY COCO

Olympian David O'Connor has represented the United States in numerous international-caliber competitions. Here he's shown co-instructing a three-day eventing course at the Parelli Center in Pagosa Springs.

Pat's a remarkable teacher, entertainer, motivator and horseman. Even after all my years in three-day eventing, Pat got me excited about cutting cows and learning slide stops!

David O'Connor
Three-day eventing rider
USA Olympic gold, silver and bronze medalist,
Pan Am Games, silver medalist

PHOTO BY COCO

At the 2002 Savvy Conference, Caton plays with Pat's stallion Casper while a proud father looks on.

Savvy Conference

When Linda and I moved to Pagosa Springs, we revisited the idea of developing a horsemen's get-together and came up with the Savvy Conference concept. The thought was to give people the opportunity to have an intellectual experience, versus a hands-on or seat-in-the-saddle experience.

When we go on the road, we show people Levels 1, 2 and 3, which is the hub or foundation of our horsemanship program. The objective of the Savvy Conference is to demonstrate what people can do with it. The agenda includes a variety of activities: foal and yearling handling; colt starting; demonstrations of people who've taken liberty or freestyle to new heights; high-performance riding, such as reining, jumping, dressage, cutting and more.

Also, in our travels, Linda and I see a world full of new programs, products and people. When we find those that are congruent with what we're doing, we offer them to the public at this venue. We've brought in Dr. Miller, David O'Connor, Craig Johnson, various health-care professionals, manufacturers of innovative products, etc. The event turns into a mini horse fair for natural horsemanship devotees.

The conference allows people to make a migration, sort of a pilgrimage to Mecca, to return to the source, so to speak. They can immerse themselves in natural horsemanship and natural horsekeeping for three days. Annually, it's become the best and biggest thing we do.

19 SOMETHING FOR MY SOUL

"Casper is the most challenging horse I've tried to make a lifetime partner with."

Linda and I put on a clinic in a little Canadian town called Olds, just west of Calgary, in the summer of 1995. We had about 30 participants and about 300 spectators. During lunch break in our motor home the first day of the clinic, we both turned to each other and said, "Did you see that black stallion?"

The Black Stallion

I usually don't allow stallions in my clinics, but somehow this one's owner signed up through the host or something and slipped through. However, we had no problems as the Quarter Horse stallion behaved himself. (He's not known to be a noisy stud horse, but he's not shy either.)

We watched him throughout the day and evening; our curiosities were piqued. When it came time to ride in the clinic, the black stallion's owner, Hazel Street, asked if she could simply sit on her horse bareback. I said she could, but asked her why. She explained that when anyone put a saddle on him, he'd really buck. He'd gone through six trainers, and no one had been able to get a second ride on him.

I said, "Ah, really, well then, why don't you sit out the session, and afterward I'll saddle him and see how it goes." To myself I said, "I really want to get a feel of this horse."

Linda and I had just completed a weeklong wilderness course, which we put on in Banff for some friends of ours who owned a pack-outfit concession in that area. My slicker was still attached to the back of my saddle, and on the right side I had my rope and a Sierra cup (small, brass water cup). The latter was hooked to the saddle, and it made a tinkling noise whenever a horse moved.

I played with the handsome, race-bred stallion on the ground for a while. He was familiar with the Seven Games because he'd been through the course all day. When I put the saddle on him, I noticed that he got a little tight. I didn't think much of it until I started to cinch him, at which time his eyes bulged out of their sockets. He started to look like a Halloween cat – his back up, eyes wide open and a scared expression on his face.

I realized I'd better "let some air out," as they say. I had a rope halter and a 22-foot rope on him. I figured that with the rope I'd be able to double the stallion back when he bucked. No problem. I'd done it hundreds of times before with other green or difficult horses.

Tinkle, Tinkle

When the black stallion saw my lariat out of his right eye, he moved away from it, and, as he did, the brass cup made a little "tinkle-tinkle" noise. When it did, the horse lost it and launched himself into the air. As he did, I was prepared, or so I thought. I set back and held

PHOTO BY COCO

"There's a special thing between us," says Pat.

onto the rope. Rope halters are usually effective in this kind of situation because they're thin. When a horse feels the pressure, he normally bends around to give to it. But the black stallion wasn't a typical case. The halter pressure didn't even faze the airborne horse. He hit the rope with so much force that he pulled me off my feet. I flew 10 feet before I landed on my belly. This horse had launched me in the air, and I'm a fairly big man. I can usually stop most anything!

He bucked for at least a minute and a half – now, that's a long time. Most rodeo horses have flank straps on them to encourage them to buck for eight seconds, but by the seventh second, they often start to slow down, stop bucking hard and run instead.

Finally, after what seemed like an eternity, the black stallion stopped and took a deep breath. Then he moved again and, when he did, he heard the tinkle, tinkle. Oh boy, did the bucking ever commence. This went on for an hour! He'd stop, catch his breath, hear the tinkle and explode again, and every time he

PHOTO BY LINDA PARELLI

According to Pat, Casper can buck higher, harder and longer than any other horse he's ever seen.

which in him is very strong.

After a while, I was confident enough to get on him. And, as I'd expected, he felt like a wonderful horse to ride.

Casper, the Friendly Ghost

At the clinic the next day, I asked Hazel if she'd consider selling the five-year-old stallion to me. She said, "Well..." and hemmed and hawed around. It turned out her husband, Brian, specializes in breeding and selling horses, and they'd purchased the horse to breed black and white Paint Horses. The stallion is a true blue-black color, not a fade-to-brown type of black.

Linda and I thought that his name was a play on words. Casper, the ghost, is white, and this horse was anything but white. So, I asked Hazel why they called him "Casper." She remarked that he was a spook, but a friendly spook. It's almost like he's two horses, she explained. He can be one way one minute and something totally different the next. There was no in-between. She's absolutely right. He's juxtaposed in every aspect.

But, in my estimation, he was (and still is) one of the most magnificent-looking horses I've ever seen. He's one of those "can't-take-your-eyes-off-him" kind of horses. We came to an agreement with the Streets to buy him. And, at the time, he was one of the most expensive horses I'd ever bought. I didn't get him cheap. I really wanted him.

We had a Canadian veterinarian perform a pre-purchase exam on him. On the X-rays, the vet found some changes in one of his front feet, so he didn't declare him 100 percent sound. I didn't care, though, and bought him anyway. The horse has never taken a lame step. He's solid-footed.

I bought Casper at the same time we were in the process of buying the Pagosa Springs ranch. The place was literally falling down around us. Barbed-wire fences lay on the ground everywhere. Every gate had baling wire holding it together. Some were just baling-wire gates! We put the horses where we could, in the run-down, old red barn or in cor-

put his heart into it. There was no bottom to this horse. I thought to myself, "Oh my God, this is incredible."

I already had a sore foot that day. I don't remember how it happened, a sprained ankle or something. I was sore that morning, but by this time, I was hobbling around.

We were in an indoor, rodeo-size arena, and I had a crowd of 300 watching this whole procedure. Sore as I was, I played the Catching Game with the scared and distrusting stallion. Finally, he composed himself enough to canter around, turn and face me. I played with him until he got left-brained. (The left side of the brain relates to calmness and thinking. The right side is emotional and reactionary.) He'd been working out of the right side of his brain,

PHOTO BY LINDA PARELLI

Pat and Casper ride through the snowy fields the first winter in Pagosa Springs.

rals, held together with aspen logs attached to posts with, what else, baling wire. The whole place was just in shambles.

We'd been there about a week when we had to fly off to give a clinic. Jim Smith, who owns Boot Hill Saddlery in town, had become our friend early on and said he'd come out to feed the horses for us.

When we returned home, we found that somehow the horses had gotten loose during the night. Casper had arrived from Canada by that time, and apparently he and Scamp had had a romantic interlude. The following summer she foaled a filly we called Touche because she had a beautiful "tush."

My Biggest Challenge

The first time I saddled Casper after he'd arrived in Colorado was in back of the old red barn, which had a makeshift round corral attached to it. Linda had a camera on hand, ready for the explosion we both expected would come. After I cinched the saddle, Casper bucked hard enough to jerk the lead rope from my hand again, as he'd done in Canada. He jumped so high you could see the top of the barn door under his belly! Linda has the pictures to prove it. He eventually came back to earth. I still say he's the bucking-est horse I've ever seen.

Casper is very popular with the crowds at my seminars and demonstrations. He now has a Breyer model horse created in his likeness. Everyone always asks about the brand on his hip, which consists of a rafter, an anchor and a 4. The rafter stands for the Street family's household, there are four of them and they're anchored together. I like that concept and wish I'd come up with it.

Casper was raised in northern Canada. He has a scar on his left hind leg; it's not bad,

149

If Pat doesn't play with Casper a couple of times a week, he's got his hands full.

more of a thickening than anything else. The story goes that when Casper was a yearling, he and another horse were trapped in a corral by a grizzly bear. Casper jumped a five-foot fence rail to save himself. He's a very intelligent horse; he figures things out. But at the same time, if he goes a week without being ridden, he'll buck. He's bucked with me several times in the past and three times hard enough to get me off. In my life, he's the only horse that's bucked me off three times. Even throughout my 14-year rodeo career, I've never had any horse buck me off twice.

Fortunately, Casper usually doesn't buck with me on him anymore. The last time he did I was in a round corral at a colt-starting clinic. I'd roped a colt that moved around us, and,

when he did, the rope caught under Casper's tail. Oh boy, did Casper jettison me into the air. I can remember coming down, grabbing a corral panel and landing with my feet and hands on the panel. I never hit the ground! But there was Casper, jumping straight up and down in one spot. He's an unbelievably athletic horse, who's been a real provocative challenge for me, not just to get along with him, but to get him to perform. He hates to go backward and sideways, so maneuvers such as lead changes and the piaffe are exceptionally problematical for him. My saying has always been, the worse your horse goes backward and sideways, the worse he does everything else.

I've played with difficult horses for a day or two, but Casper is the most challenging horse

Pat and Casper enjoying a lope across the Colorado pastures.

I've tried to make a lifetime partner with. It's not because he bucks, is spirited or sensitive. Partly, it's because he's aloof. He's not gregarious. Even when he's with the mares, he'll stand at the other end of the pasture. They can leave, and he often doesn't care. That makes it hard because pair-bonding isn't important to him. Still in all, there's a special thing between us. He comes to me when he sees me in the pasture. He does something for my soul.

Casper has wowed the crowds countless times over the years.

151

20 LEARNING CURVES

"I realized that what I did in Natural Horse-Man-Ship was follow an invisible ladder."

As I developed my version of natural horsemanship, I found myself heading down a road of frustration. It became apparent in my clinics that half the participants had been to previous clinics and heard about natural horsemanship and half hadn't. I had to repeat the same information and stories for the benefit of those who hadn't heard it, but that left the initiated bored. However, if I advanced the lessons for the people who could keep up, then I left the uninitiated in the dust.

PHOTO BY COCO

Pat instructing a course at the center in Pagosa Springs.

Pat's classes can be a little unorthodox, but always a lot of fun. This was taken at the center in Pagosa Springs.

Levels 1, 2 and 3 packages and specialized tools are all part of the Pat Parelli program.

Belts and Levels

I desperately needed to find ways to group people according to their needs and skills. That's how I came up with the Levels program. I went back to my martial arts training as a model. I realized how simply brilliant the martial arts discipline is by making people progress belt by belt and attaching colors to each step, so everyone knows where they stand.

I decided to put students together in learning groups. It didn't matter what age people were or how much experience they had; if they had certain fundamentals, then it was easy to address them as a group and teach them the next set of fundamentals.

In an effort to put all this together, the concept of the Levels program in Parelli Natural Horse-Man-Ship was born. What I did was go back in time and trace my own steps. I tried to recall what I'd learned, what kind of skills and knowledge I had and at what stages.

I organized the basic skills into segments and, in doing so, developed the first three Levels in the horsemanship program. In my clinics, I concentrated on those Levels first to be able to get people really up to speed and

build a good foundation. The program gives people a skill set to learn and achievable goals to strive for.

I realized that through the Levels program I was doing for people what Troy Henry had done for me. He'd given me a philosophy, important horsemanship concepts, theory and enough skills that I could be considered a horseman. He'd often ask me, "Son, what do you want to become?" I'd say, "I want to become a better horseman." He'd say in return, "Then, you've got to become a horseman first before you can become a better one." That's what the first three Levels in our program are all about – becoming a horseman.

Invisible Ladder

After doing thousands of clinics and demonstrations, and generating hundreds of articles, I realized that what I did in natural horsemanship was follow an invisible ladder. And all my dedicated students who'd been successful found this invisible ladder, as well, and were able to climb it.

The problem with an invisible ladder, though, is that it's hard to follow. And people

PHOTO BY COCO

Pat developed the Seven Games based on what horses do naturally. This teaching system has gained worldwide attention. In this photo, the Squeeze Game is being played.

learn only so much from a book, only so much from a video.

In a video, I'd try to explain in one hour the philosophy, the concept, the theory, the details and the skills necessary to execute the techniques. But it was almost an impossible task. And no matter what I did on video, someone would ask, "Yeah, but what about a horse that does it like this?"

Linda and I realized that it was impractical and inefficient to try to get it done in one medium. Then it occurred to us that a home-school program for horse owners might work, so we patterned the packages after that model. Both of my children were home-schooled, and I remember getting a packet of materials that taught us how to educate our kids. Professor Berry did the same thing years ago for horse owners. He advertised in all the horse publications and sold his horsemanship correspondence courses as a way for people to home-school themselves and their horses. I still have all his booklets.

I decided to do the same and create a natural horsemanship home school for horse people, following the steps in my invisible ladder, only we made it visible by putting Levels 1, 2 and 3

programs into Partnership, Harmony and Refinement packages respectively.

In developing the packages, we found out that people learn in different ways – some are auditory learners, some visual learners, some are kinesthetic learners (learn by moving or doing). Most people learn best in a combination of these ways. We devised the program packages so people could make best use of this fact. We put the philosophy on the audio tapes, theory in the book, and the concepts on video. We could actually give people the picture of what we were trying to tell them on the audio and in the books. In the theory book, we delved into all the "whys and wherefores" of what we were trying to impart to them.

We also came up with the idea of pocket guides, small booklets you can put in your pocket and take to the barn or corral. Each booklet has two lessons in it, and they're refreshers for all the material on the audio and videotapes.

This has been the simple brilliance behind our students' great success. Now that we've got our intellectual material in audio, video and print form, students are making progress 10 times faster than they were 12 years ago when I first started doing videos and had a book. This is the most exciting breakthrough for a person like me who's a share-a-holic. I want people to get it sometimes worse than they want to get it.

For Members Only

For years, I've wanted to have some way to keep in touch with my most dedicated students. Having them take a course once a year is great, but it's difficult to sustain any kind of lasting relationship that way.

We created the Savvy Club, a subscription-based group in which members receive something from Parelli monthly, either a magazine or DVD to help further their knowledge of natural horsemanship. While mostly educational, our Savvy Club material also offers viewers fun things to watch or read. Laughter and education have always gone hand in hand at Parelli Natural Horse-Man-Ship. It's been one of the secrets of my success as an effective teacher and communicator.

Benefits are also part of the club package and members receive free or discounted tickets to all our events and a significant discount on courses at our centers in Colorado and Florida. The club really took off, with over 7,600 members the first year.

Australia also has its own Savvy Club. We've used that country as a guinea pig, of sorts, for almost everything we've tried over the years, and we found out what works.

For example, we started our Parelli Savvy Club Tournament program in Australia. The tournament is similar to dog agility competitions in which the contestants must perform certain tests in a prescribed course. We held it at the 2003 Australasia Equitana and gave out $48,000 worth of prizes to the winners. The first place team of two people each won an all-expense-paid trip to the United States and a two-week course in Colorado, which was worth $27,000 per person.

There were also more traditional types of competitions at Equitana, but the largest purse the other events came up with was only $3,500. It was funny to see the big, fancy, well-bred horses and their well-turned-out riders competing for peanuts compared with our plainly dressed students on their average horses vying for far more money. Obviously, our tournament attracted a lot more attention.

An Idea Whose Time Had Come

Because of her extensive business and educational background, Linda brought several great perspectives to what I was doing in my clinics and horsemanship program.

In the world of cosmetics that Linda had come from, a company such as Ella Baché needed educated, informed beauticians selling their products in order to have beauty salons carry their products. Through her instructional programs, Linda made sure that was the case, so the company could grow and prosper.

As Linda saw it, I needed my own set of instructors so I wouldn't get burned out teaching the same thing over and over again. To explore the possibilities of an instructor program, I invited several of my best students, who also happened to be my close friends, to a meeting to discuss building such a structure.

They hated the idea! Maybe I didn't present it well; I don't know. But the whole thing flopped in America, so we decided to try Australia.

By this time, Linda's sister Vivian and Vivian's husband, Barry Black, had taken over the reins of Parelli Australia from Linda, since she'd moved to the States. They ran the business for nine years and continued Linda's great work with scheduling tours.

Try, Try Again

On this tour, we decided to try again to put together the ill-fated instructor program. We still had faith in the idea and, after all, my presence in that country was more limited than in the States. It only made sense to develop a set of instructors to carry on natural horsemanship in my absence.

About 30 top students showed up at Kate and Owen Gwen's beautiful, 5,000-acre property, where we had tents set up for our advanced clinic.

155

PHOTO BY COCO

Neil Pye is one of only five Five-Star Instructors within the Parelli instructor program.

Linda and I explained our ideas for an instructor program, and I'll be darned if the same thing didn't happen again. Many of the students seemed really excited and ready to join, but most of them bailed on us.

The only thing I could blame this second failed attempt on was people's fear of unionization or franchising or some such thing. Maybe no one wanted to work under someone else's banner. It was a mystery to us. It seemed like an idea whose time had come, and we had some exceptional students who could fill the bill.

But one good thing did come out of that meeting. Neil Pye stood up and gave his impression of what we were offering. I didn't know Neil all that well; he'd been in our program about a year. He became involved with horses late in life and found that our program made the most sense to him, after having a go at traditional lessons and training with little success. Neil had an interesting background in that he owned three Kentucky Fried Chicken franchises and other chain-type businesses, so our concept wasn't lost on him.

He stood up and said, "Ladies and gentlemen, you have no idea what kind of opportunity you're about to pass up."

He explained what it generally took to get into a big franchise, such as McDonalds or

Kentucky Fried Chicken – over $1 million in some cases.

After all the resistance we'd run into with this idea, I was flabbergasted that someone else, like Neil, would see the light. Neil's inspirational speech divided the room in half – 50 percent of them left and 50 percent stayed.

Our Australian instructor program grew from that meeting, and eventually our American program got off the ground, as well.

Raise the Bar

We've discovered there are five questions all instructor applicants should ask: What does it take to get in? What does it take to stay in? What does it take to advance? What do you get if you advance? And what does it take to be demoted or kicked out?

Over the years, we've developed unbelievably high standards our instructors must adhere to. I would say that 20 percent of them can't keep up with the standards every year. This is actually not a bad thing. It keeps our program's professionalism high.

I can compare our instructor program to the process necessary for becoming a doctor or lawyer. Medical and legal candidates must pass medical exams or the bar exam if they intend to practice those professions. And then

Certified instructors gather at the Parelli Center in Florida.

they have to keep up with continuing education to stay on the leading edge of new methods and discoveries.

For some reason, compared to other professional industries, the horse industry has incredibly low standards. Anyone can put up a shingle and charge for his or her services. I know; I've been there and done that. That's how I started, and I knew I didn't know what the heck I was doing.

I'm familiar with the horse-training industry from most every angle. I've been a customer; I've been a quasi-professional; I've had people mad at me; I've had people want their money back; I've had people's checks bounce. I've had every sorry thing happen while I was trying to earn a living with horses.

Business, not a Hobby

In order to be a professional, you have to have four things. You have to have competency, people skills, marketing savvy and business acumen. There was no place I could go to learn all that in the horse industry.

After taking Michael Gerber's business development course years earlier, I realized how little help a horse person had. I did know that there were a lot of people who made a

small fortune in the horse industry by starting with a large one, though.

Besides the business course, I helped further my personal and professional development by reading books, such as Ray Kroc's *Grinding It Out: the Making of McDonald's*. Kroc, the founder of the fast-food chain, defined a true business as a company that paid all its bills, all its employees, including the owners, and still made a profit. Anything else is just a hobby. A lot of people in the horse industry have fooled themselves into thinking they have a business, when it's only a hobby. What they've done is just create themselves a job.

After I took Gerber's course and read Kroc's book, I had a vision in my mind, for the first time, of what a horse professional should be. I decided that I would create my own real business in the horse industry, and I'd help others to become professionals, as well.

Our instructor program evolved over the years and most people have stuck with it. Some left, but in the end, the program survived.

Only graduates of the horsemanship program can become instructors. After they meet certain criteria, we certify them and stand behind their education and integrity. We've found that some instructors are better as people-people and some are more comfortable

PHOTO BY COCO

Dr. Stephanie Burns, a noted expert in the field of adult learning and communication, has been instrumental in revamping the educational materials for the Levels Programs.

as animal-people. However, our programs can accommodate a wide range of personality types and talents.

Instructors are qualified to teach Levels 1 through 3. They can specialize in their favorite areas or become masters of many.

Level 3 graduates can apply to become Parelli Professionals. Our motto is "Hard In, Easy Out," meaning we're looking for only a few good people, like the Marines.

Those who want to compete in the show world can qualify for certificates in five key competition areas – racing, jumping, dressage, reining or cow-horse events.

We also have certificates for instructors who want to be professionals in certain specialty areas, such as foals and yearlings, first-ride specialists, foundation training, driving and challenging horses.

We offer certificates for those professionals who handle horses on the ground, such as farriers, veterinarians, grooms, racehorse handlers and so on.

The Parelli Professionals Program has a star rating system from one to five, with One- and Two-Star instructors being interns, all the way to Five-Star instructors, who are our most qualified pros. It's a world-class, worldwide program for developing professionals in the equine world.

If a person is truly a professional and master of his or her trade, then someday he or she will be asked to perform in front of kings and queens. That's exactly what happened to me (See Chapter 25, "All the King's and Queen's Horses").

Learn to Learn

Over the years, I've learned to learn, and I want to help others do the same. But I can't help someone unless he or she wants to help themselves. I've learned not to go the extra mile for someone going the other direction. I've learned to feed people knowledge with a spoon and not a shovel, and to teach them at their level.

I've learned to deal with people who've never ridden a horse up to the likes of such great horsemen as David O'Connor and Craig Johnson. I've learned to oscillate between those different levels and to fill in information that's pertinent to the individual.

And so, after 20-plus years of learning, millions of miles of traveling, over 22,000 students who've ridden with me personally, thousands of horses that I've caught, clipped, loaded into a trailer, started, improved their behavior or performance problems, all this has added up to a diverse group of skills that allows me to share my horsemanship knowledge and experience with the world.

People's Perspectives on Pat

Fan and Friend

Like a lot of people, I didn't grow up with horses. I was raised in the suburbs of big cities, and the only time I got to see horses was on television Westerns.

It wasn't until I was an adult that I had the time and money to buy a horse. I bought one I thought I could look good on and ride off into the sunset. I thought it was going to be easy. I got myself in all sorts of trouble. I couldn't get the horse to go; I couldn't get him to slow. It seemed like he spent his every living, breathing moment in the pasture thinking up ways to get on my nerves.

I looked for help, but I'd ask one question of 10 people in the horse world and get 10 different answers. I was just about to give up and get out of horses. I was going to sell everything for a quarter of the price I paid for it just to be rid of the problems.

I'm not the smartest man in the world, but I figured I wasn't the dumbest either.

I told my neighbor I was going to quit, and he told me about a guy coming to town the following weekend. "He's a bit of a different duck," he said. "He's from the States, but I think you'll like him. His name is Pat Parelli, and he talks about life from the horse's point of view."

At that point, his wife joined the conversation. As neighborly as we were, she and I saw everything the opposite. If she saw things as up, I saw them as down. If she saw things as white, I saw them as black. We just didn't agree on anything.

She said, "Pat Parelli will teach you how to get killed by a horse."

I thought to myself, "I must go."

I audited the clinic and in the first 10 minutes Pat made more sense than anything I'd ever heard before. He pointed out things like the prey/predator barrier, and why the horse is just doing what Mother Nature intended.

He made me realize that the problems didn't lie with my horse; they were with me. To cause that to change, I had to change.

Of course, in Pat's usual, inimitable style, his use of stories and humor, he quickly captivated everyone's attention, including mine.

I'd been extremely frustrated in the horse industry and treated shabbily. To me, as an outsider, the horse industry was a hard thing to get involved in. I used to hear them say they wanted to grow their associations, but their actions made sure you felt alienated. No wonder they don't grow much.

When I saw and heard Pat, he was the antithesis of all that. I was enamored with his message and how he communicated it.

To make a long story short, I stayed at the clinic for two days and in that time I heard more logic, more sense than ever before, and, more importantly, I was presented a plan I could follow.

Fast forward 13 years – I became a good student, a fan, an instructor and a friend.

I got involved in the Parelli program in Australia and found myself at a point in my life where I wanted to follow my passion. I'd lost interest in my business, and what Pat offered really appealed to me. I knew he was building something big that would change the world. It's not often a person gets a chance to become involved in a transformational process.

I sold all my businesses and moved to America when Pat asked me to help him run his schools. I'm still a fan and still a friend.

Neil Pye
5-Star Parelli Instructor
Dean of the Parelli Centers

PHOTO BY COCO

Neil Pye discovered horses late in life, but eventually became a Parelli instructor and dean of the Parelli Centers.

21 NATURAL HORSEMANSHIP ON NATIONAL GEOGRAPHIC

"This approach-and-retreat stuff really works."

Arts & Entertainment television network wanted to produce a TV special that highlighted the many different facets of the horse industry, titled "In the Company of Horses." They were looking for whatever was new at the time – in racing, showing, recreation, etc. Everywhere they turned, they heard our name. "You've got to have Parelli," they were told repeatedly wherever they went.

The camera crews arrived in August, 1999 and shot a segment all about the ranch and our horsemanship programs. This was our first major exposure on national television, but there was more to come.

I can't be absolutely sure, but our appearance on that A&E television program probably helped when National Geographic Explorer came a-knocking in 2000. When one major media network does its due diligence and decides something is suitable for broadcasting, then other networks must think that what you have to offer is valid. Parelli Natural Horsemanship must have passed the test somehow because we had the opportunity to strut our stuff before a mainstream audience again.

PHOTO BY BRIAN ARMSTRONG

The National Geographic film crew got plenty of action out of the savvy Parelli team.

The Mustang Challenge

One of National Geographic Explorer's producers, Brian Armstrong, called and asked me if I'd accept their challenge, for a television special titled "America's Lost Mustangs."

Pat explaining a point for the A&E television crew filming the special, "In the Company of Horses."

The country west of Albuquerque was rough. The mustangs were found on top of the giant mesa pictured in this photo.

I immediately and emphatically answered, "Yes." Then I asked, "Ah, what is it?"

He explained the project was to capture a certain herd of mustangs in New Mexico in order to gather blood samples for DNA testing. The premise was to see if the mustangs traced back to horses brought to America by the early Spanish settlers. Scientists would look for Spanish Barb DNA markers in the mustangs' blood. Wild horses are typically a mixture of horses of early Spanish descent and domestic horses gone feral. In their testing, scientists have found most mustangs have around 13 to 23 percent Spanish Barb DNA markers. They discovered later that the band of mustangs we captured for the television special had as much as 80 percent Spanish Barb ancestry.

Through research, it was determined that where the legend of the lost horses had probably occurred was somewhere outside Albuquerque. The National Geographic Explorer crew had already attempted to capture the mustangs with men on motorcycles, but people and horses got hurt. They realized they needed another way.

The challenge they presented to us was to find the mustangs in the New Mexican desert, capture, halter-break, ride and gentle them so it was safe to draw blood without using chutes or other mechanical means.

I was told we had three days to accomplish that feat. That's all the filming time they could give it. I took a deep breath, but agreed to the project. However, I needed some help in the form of helicopters to find the horses in the million and a half acres they had to roam. The roundup was to take place on the Laguna Pueblo, about 40 or 50 miles west of Albuquerque.

Savvy Team

I put together my savvy team of wranglers: my wife Linda, my mentor Ronnie Willis and my top students Andy Booth, Bruce Logan, Wally Gegenschatz and Mikey Wanzenreid. I rode Cash, my good Quarter Horse mare, Linda rode her Thoroughbred gelding Siren, Wally rode a mule, and even Brian got on a horse.

It's interesting to note that Brian's sister is a Level 2 student of ours in Australia, and Brian and all the camera crew were Aussies.

Little did we know that we were all about to recreate the mountain riding scenes from "The Man from Snowy River."

The day before we got started, we had a major mishap. The little Bell helicopter we were to use to locate the herd crashed. Luckily, no one got hurt, but the cameraman was badly shaken up. That part of New Mexico is at an altitude of about 7,000 feet; we obviously needed more of a flying machine to handle the atmospheric conditions.

The next day a much more powerful Jet Ranger helicopter arrived – something we should've had in the first place. We flew for an hour and a half looking for the horses. We finally spotted them on top of a huge mesa, which was 1,000 feet from top to bottom and had a 30- or 40-foot rock face. We couldn't figure out how to push the horses down off the steep mesa. We flew around it, and even landed a few times to look for "soft spots" – areas that might allow us to drive the horses down. We found a few but they were ultra steep. I couldn't even stand up straight on them without falling over. Our horses wouldn't have been able to make it, either. But the mustangs had gotten up there somehow, so they must also have known the way down.

The only hope we had was a road that went to the top, but in order to take it we had to go 30 miles out of our way in the opposite direction of the box canyon where we wanted to head the horses. The next morning before dawn, we loaded our horses and drove the 30 miles to the mesa top.

We got there at dawn, saddled and then had to figure out in which direction the mustangs were on a mesa that was 12 miles around.

It was an honor for Pat to share the National Geographic Explorer experience with Ronnie Willis.

The Chase Was On

We picked a direction and trotted to within a quarter mile of the mesa's edge. The mustangs were nearby, and they must have felt our pressure. They rebounded and practically ran right over the top of us. The chase was on.

Of course, the camera crew wanted to shoot some footage, so they were flying right along with us. The scared but gutsy cameraman had strapped himself to the edge of the helicopter and leaned over to get his footage.

We ran after the mustangs full tilt for about six miles. While mesas are often called tabletops, they're not perfectly flat on top; there are arroyos and draws to jump over and through. We jumped, ducked and dodged the entire way. It was real western.

Linda had her hands full. Siren was an ex-racehorse who'd been on the track for five years. His blood was definitely up; he wanted to run 90 miles an hour.

Brian had given me a very expensive radio so I could communicate with the helicopter and other members of the crew. Well, it'd

Linda "cowgirled up" for the mustang gather.

fallen off somewhere in the first two miles of chase. There was no way to contact me.

With expert wrangling from my crack team of riders, we got around the mustangs and got them stopped within a relatively short time.

The camera crew wanted a close-up shot, of course, so the helicopter swooped down and, when it did, the horses naturally spooked. We'd just gotten them under control and off they went again in another blaze of blinding speed.

We ran probably another four or five miles to the other end of the mesa. The mustangs looked as though they thought about going over the edge, which is where we wanted them to go, but the helicopter, once more, got in the way. It was situated off the mesa's edge, and the mustangs obviously didn't want to go toward it.

We choused them with our flags as best we could for about 15 minutes, and Andy kept cracking his Australian stock whip. Finally, the lead mare dropped over the edge and they all followed.

We all looked over the precipitous edge and certainly had second thoughts, but realized there was no other choice. We had to follow.

We dove off the edge and doooowwnnnn we went. Even the mustangs couldn't navigate the difficult terrain any faster than a trot. We were right on their heels. My mare Cash was raised in similar New Mexican country, which is why I picked her for the roundup. She was six years old before she was ever started and she was eight then. I knew she'd have the bottom for this kind of work.

As we slid down the mesa, I looked behind me and saw Mikey and Wally, but no one else. Ronnie, Linda and Andy weren't in sight, but I couldn't turn around and go back. I found out later that because of the steep terrain, Linda's English saddle had gone over her horse's head. Ronnie managed to help her get squared away, and no one was hurt.

The three of us were still on the mustangs, which were about a half-mile ahead of us, but going in the right direction toward the box canyon corrals we had set up beforehand.

If the mustangs missed the canyon, it'd be almost impossible for us to steer them back again.

Out of Gas?

All of a sudden I hear a voice from out of nowhere. "Pat, Pat, Pat," it kept getting louder. There was the cameraman, all alone in the middle of the desert.

I asked, "Where's the helicopter?"

He said, "We were low on fuel. They dropped me off so I could film you coming, and they went back for more fuel."

What a time to run out of gas! We had the horses moving in the right direction toward the canyon, but we didn't want them to get there too quickly because we had no cameraman to film the capture. I told Mikey to head the horses off and drive them back toward us. We didn't want them turning and running the 12 miles around the mesa.

Mikey turned them and then he and Wally held that line so the mustangs couldn't get to the pens too soon. The horses took off in another direction. I saw which way they went and followed, at full tilt again. In the distance I could see dust being kicked up. The mustangs were going through a sandy wash.

Approach and Retreat

I managed to get around the herd and they stopped. When they did, the stallion took one look at me and snorted a warning. I backed off a little. The herd started to walk toward me and I backed off again. Every time the herd looked at me, I'd back off. Pretty quick, the horses realized I wasn't going to chase them and they grew more confident and curious.

Finally, after approaching and retreating several times, I was within 30 yards of the herd. I allowed my horse to graze; the mustangs also grazed. One after another, the mares laid down and rolled in the sand, with the stallion watching over them – a sure sign of confidence.

I started riding away, and they started following me. I thought to myself, "This approach and retreat stuff really works. It's too bad no one is here to witness this or a camera to document it. The only ones that will ever really know for sure that this really happened are this herd of horses and me."

PHOTO BY BRIAN ARMSTRONG

Pat gentles one of the mustangs.

PHOTO BY BRIAN ARMSTRONG

Pat (right) and Wally Gegenschatz play with the mustangs in the Priefert corrals.

I was all by myself and I didn't have a radio to tell anyone where I was.

Well, sure enough, here came the helicopter with the blades making their characteristic menacing sound.

Off go the mustangs and the chase is on once more. Luckily, by this time Linda, Andy and Ronnie had come in behind me, and Mikey and Wally were up ahead.

We all had only one last swoop left in us. We drove the mustangs around a corner, over some rocks and down the canyon right into the panel corrals.

We'd been galloping hard for three hours and our horses' stamina was amazing. I'd expect that kind of endurance from the wild horses, but not our saddle horses. They all had between 150 and 250 pounds or more on their backs and still were able to keep up with the mustangs. I was really impressed with our horses' staying power.

Tame in No Time

The camera crew was ready to roll and film us interacting with the horses. I told them to pick one, any one. They selected the lead mare's four-year-old filly, the wildest one in the bunch.

We drove her into the round corral and the first thing she did was crash into the Priefert panels. Fortunately, they were strong enough to hold her, but she bloodied her nose in the attempt. I thought, "Oh my God, here's my chance of a lifetime on national television, and why did this horse have to get a bloody nose!"

But the camera crew was there to film the story no matter what transpired, so we continued. I played with the filly and got some good things going with her, which the cameraman got down on film.

By this time, the film crew was exhausted, so they went back to start the editing process.

We stayed behind to gentle the horses. We had three days to make them tame enough to have a veterinarian draw blood.

To water the horses we brought in a 500-gallon Army tank. We put water buckets down next to us, about 20 feet away from the horses. They eventually overcame their fear enough to drink as we stood near them. By the next morning, they drank as we held the water buckets in our hands.

We played with all the horses and had a blast. The stallion bucked like crazy. Wally got on him, and the horse ejected him real high.

Before long, though, they all were fairly tame. They responded to the lead rope and to having their feet handled. We rode them bareback and with saddles. We taught them to accept the needle by pinching them on the jugular vein and having them tuck their chins.

Two Great Things

Two great things happened toward the end of filming. By this time, we had a passel of newspaper reporters on hand to witness the story.

The veterinarian showed up on the evening of the third day. He said to me, "Look me in

The veterinarian was able to easily draw blood from the mustangs Pat and his crew had gentled.

graze. We crawled off their backs and took off the halters. The horses didn't exit stage left, as you'd think wild horses would do immediately upon being set free. They stayed there with us, ate grass and showed no signs of fear or anxiety. Finally, as the sun was setting, they nonchalantly walked off into the New Mexican sunset. What an unforgettable sight that was!

This experience was one of the most fabulous I've ever had in my life with horses. I was really proud of my students and of Linda. And I was especially honored to have done something special like that with Ronnie. Then to have it captured on film forever happens only once in a lifetime.

National Geographic Explorer said it was the most requested show that they had in years.

the eye and tell me I'm not going to get hurt. I'm no movie star. I'm no stunt man. I don't want to risk myself."

I told him, "I promise you, sir, you'll be fine."

The vet drew blood on all the horses and when he was through, he turned to me and said, "I can't believe this. I was at a stable this morning and these wild horses were easier to handle than any of the domestic horses at the stable."

The second wonderful thing happened when it was time to release the mustangs. We rode them out of the pens bareback and with only halters and lead ropes. We rode out of the canyon to a place where the horses could

Enjoying a break from filming. From left: Andy Booth, Wally Gegenschatz, Pat, Ronnie Willis.

People's Perspectives on Pat
Fish or Cut Bait

I ran into Pat and Linda many years ago in Abilene, Texas, and invited them to come by the ranch. It happened to be at a time when we had the chuck wagon out in The Breaks, a rough part of our country where we were gathering cattle. They joined us in our gather.

Pat impressed me as what I call a "fish or cut bait" type of guy. That's a saying that means you're either fishing or getting ready to fish. By that saying I mean Pat doesn't sit around and waste time, which I really appreciate. He was always doing something – talking about horses, telling stories, tying knots, riding his unicycle to better his balance, lots of things.

He impressed us with his abilities and the cowboys even more with his horsemanship.

Bob Moorhouse
Vice president and manager, Pitchfork Land and Cattle Co.
AQHA Board of Directors

22 THAT WAS THEN AND THIS IS NOW

"We were able to get out of the office and onto our horses to do what we do best."

With the center and conferences in full gear and Linda and I becoming "horsehold" names, our business was growing exponentially, but it was about to get even bigger.

I got a phone call in the summer of 1997 from Mark Weiler. He explained that he had one of my instructors trailer-load his wife's horse, and he was impressed with the entire procedure and intrigued about our program. He wanted to visit me and present an idea about blueprinting a Parelli center.

A Good Fit

Mark was highly successful in his other business endeavors, and he's especially astute when it comes to building businesses. He did

The Big Rig transports the Parelli horses in style. Behind is Pat and Linda's motor home, pulling another horse trailer.

his due diligence on our little company, researched our competition as far as other horsemanship clinicians and their programs and realized he could offer us some ideas.

Timing, as they say, is everything, and Mark's timing was perfect. We'd just fired our business consultant because he didn't have the same principles we did. Even though he was into natural horsemanship, it wasn't a good fit.

We visited with Mark at length. His philosophy and approach to business matched our own. We recognized that he was the right one to advise us, and he agreed to become our business consultant.

Karen Scholl had been doing a phenomenal job as president, and our company was right on track. In 2001, however, she attended a 10-day Tony Robbins motivational business seminar, which must have inspired her to visualize her real dreams because when she returned, she informed us that she no longer felt she should be our president. Instead, she wanted to return to being one of our instructors and develop her own business. We understood and agreed to support her wishes.

Mark offered to fill in as temporary president for a year until we could find another one. However, after the year was up, he told us he loved everything about our people and business and wanted to stay involved. His excitement and enthusiasm, not to mention his business acumen, impressed us. We hired

Yvonne Wilcox, Linda's sister, heads up the Parelli multimedia department.

him full-time, and he's now the president of our corporation.

Mark took the company to even greater heights. Now, we've got approximately 50 employees, with full marketing, public relations and multimedia divisions. We're the largest FedEx account in the Four Corners area (Pagosa Springs is located near the juncture of Colorado, Utah, Arizona and New Mexico). We do over 40 percent of our business electronically over the Internet. We have our own tack, equipment, product and apparel lines. We've increased the ranch size from 130 acres to over 1,000 with yet another 1,000 leased acres. We have a touring division with

Mark Weiler, president of Pat's corporation, has taken the company to new heights.

two semi-trucks and a Prevost tour bus for Linda and me. Besides our extensive tour schedule, our big bash of the year is the annual Savvy Conference with over 2,000 attendees.

Linda's older sister, Yvonne Wilcox, moved from Australia to Pagosa Springs to take charge of our marketing and multimedia departments. She used to work for a graphic arts company, and we were lucky to use her considerable talents in our Australian branch, run by Linda's younger sister, Vivienne, and her husband, Barry Black. Yvonne helped create our brochures and printed materials. My original fear of nepotism crumbled after seeing what Linda's sisters could do for us. Yvonne later met and married Clint Wilcox, stepson to one of my instructors, Jim Walker. We asked them both to work for us, and it's been one of the best decisions we've ever made.

Our business team and all our employees are extremely talented and highly professional – just what we need to drive the empire we've built.

With Mark's help, we were able to get out of the office and onto our horses to do what we do best. In turn, Mark does what he does best, which is develop businesses.

Enchanted Forest

Mark had a farm in Ocala, Florida, where he'd wintered for many years. I'd never thought much about the state and had no idea how gorgeous the Ocala area was, nor that it was a horseman's mecca, with every kind of equine discipline calling it home – English, racing, western, all breeds.

We spent two winters with Mark and fell in love with the place, the weather and the horse community. Ocala has a beauty all its own. With the Spanish moss hanging from the live oak trees, emerald green pastures and miles of high-class board fences, it's like living and riding in an enchanted forest.

Every time I'd get off a horse, I'd get into a car and drive around looking at the incredible properties. I said to myself, "I've got to have a place here."

About a week after we left the second winter to return to Colorado, I got a phone call from Mark. "I think I've found the place for you," he said. He sent us a video, and we could tell that it was the right place. Mark negotiated a deal, and the next thing we knew we had a place in Ocala to build a winter

Pat and Linda's Florida winter home and school is green all year-round.

PHOTO BY COCO

Spanish moss hanging from the live oak trees gives the Ocala center the feeling of an enchanted forest.

Pat teaching a course at the Florida center.

haven for us and a center for our students. That was in 2002 and we've been holding our courses there every winter since. Our versions of a horseman's heaven on earth now exist in two places – Colorado and Florida.

Special People

Every once in a while, I run into someone from high school or college or from my horse-training career. They'd look at me and always ask, "I remember you when… How did you become this successful? I never saw it."

The interesting thing is that the people who've really helped me have told me that they saw "it" in me. My mom saw "it" in me first.

"It" simply means passion and the drive to succeed in whatever ignites that passion.

I now have a perspective on this and can see it in other people. I'll never forget the time when I met Linda. I knew she had "it" in her. She's one of those special people with dedication to whatever she's doing foremost in her mind and in her heart.

The first time I met Neil Pye, Dave Stuart, Dave Ellis or Mark Weiler, I saw that special spark in their eyes. I realized how really remarkable these people are. The people who surround me in my closest circles, and that includes my family, are extraordinary. Special people help make special things happen.

23 OTHER PEOPLE'S DREAMS

"If our dreams are close enough, but our realities are different, maybe there's a reason to go forward together."

Ronnie Willis (left) and Pat helped make each other's dreams come true.

I'm a very lucky man. I feel so blessed in what I do and in being able to make other people's dreams come true at the same time I'm making mine a reality. Here's how I brought two people's dreams together, continued living my own dream and made life better for horses at the same time.

The French Connection

William Kriegel, a Frenchman, moved to the United States in 1988 when the electric companies were deregulated. He leased a little creek in Idaho, put a small electric plant on it and started generating electricity. From that he built a multibillion-dollar business. However, at one time he was involved in 35 nuclear power plants around the world, including in China, Brazil, Australia, Singapore and Canada, so seeing the bigger picture is nothing new to William.

He now lives in New York, but his Quarter Horse farm in France is on 900 beautiful acres just 40 minutes outside of Paris. Besides stunning surroundings including lakes, creeks and a forest, Haras De La Cense also has a 500-year-old castle, indoor arena and incredible horse facilities.

Sylvia Furrer was still organizing my European tours and she arranged for us to lease Kriegel's French facility for a clinic. William decided not to charge us anything for the lease. I found out later that he'd had many horse-whisperer-types come through, and he'd always give everyone a chance. He just never found anyone to his liking.

Around 150 people attended our seminar, and William was there to watch. He was quite impressed with what he saw and invited us to his castle for supper that night. We talked and shared our dreams, which is one of my favorite things to do. You never know about other people's dreams. They might match yours. I like to say, "If our dreams are close enough, but our realities are different, maybe there's a reason to go forward together."

Pat starting a colt at La Cense France.

Ride into the Sunset

What we found out was that he had a passion for western horses, especially riding Quarter Horses out in the open. He was enamored of the Marlboro Man concept, the grand lope-across-the-field fantasy, the ride-off-into-the-sunset dream.

What he originally wanted to do was to buy horses he could bring over to France to sell in the recreational market. But all he'd managed to do was run into Americans who wanted to sell him expensive show horses. When he invited his family, friends or other wealthy people to ride, the arena-trained horses fell apart out in the forest. People were bucked off or run off with. He had a barn full of well-bred, champion horses that couldn't do diddly-squat outside a perfectly groomed arena. They were frightened of the trees and water on the trails.

William wanted to have horses trained in a more natural way and he wanted them unafraid of ordinary things in Mother Nature. I proposed that we work out a mutually beneficial deal. He would buy the horses; we'd use them in our schools for our students, and at the end of the season, we'd ship them to France for him to keep or sell.

William liked the idea and made the shift from buying performance horses to recreational mounts. The concept worked so well for both of us for two seasons that he decided to buy a ranch in America and do the same thing – raise and train well-bred American Quarter Horses for the recreational market.

La Cense Montana

I asked him how big a ranch he wanted, thinking 300 to 400 acres.

He said, "I want from 10,000 to 100,000 acres." He was serious about a full-fledged, working American ranch.

We looked at ranches near Pagosa Springs, but nothing came of it. While Linda and I were in Australia on a tour, he called and said he'd found his ranch in Dillon, Montana.

As soon as Linda and I returned to the States, we flew to Dillon to look it over. The 86,000-acre ranch comprises 120 square miles in the southwestern part of the state. It produced 17,000 tons of hay and had 3,000 Black Angus mother cows. With the existing hay and cow/calf operations in place, all he needed to complete his dream was a bona fide horse operation.

We helped him design the facility, which is called La Cense Montana. It needed a manager, one affiliated with our program. I'd already sent one of my top instructors, Andy Booth, to France to run William's facility there, which he still does.

The best person I could think of for the job was Ronnie Willis.

Reunion with Ronnie

I need to back up a bit and explain how Ronnie Willis re-entered my life.

Ronnie was a bit of an elusive character. He'd disappeared on me after our colt-starting clinic on my Clements ranch 14 years ago, and I never could locate him. It's as if he'd fallen off the map. I'd heard reports that he was doing all sorts of things in different parts of the West, but they were all rumors.

Then, someone mentioned that they'd seen him in Yuma, Arizona. I found his name through directory assistance, called and left messages with his wife a couple of times. But nothing. I think she was afraid to give him my phone number because she knew he'd want to get back into horses. She probably thought horses would be the death of him, but as it turned out, horses were the life of him.

Linda and I were in Del Mar, California, on our way to Scottsdale, Arizona, to do a clinic. I told her there were two ways to get there. We could go through Palm Springs or we could go through Yuma and try to find Ronnie. Linda had never met him. I gave it one more try and dialed his number and, low and behold, he answered the phone.

I said, "Ronnie Willis."

He said, "Pat Parelli. I was wondering when you were going to call. Where the heck have you been?"

I laughed and said, "Well, I'm a lot more visible than you are! You're the one playing hide-and-seek."

We talked for a while, and I asked if he cared for a visit.

"Oh, God, yes," he said.

Linda and I drove to Yuma, kept the horses at the fairgrounds and spent a few hours with Ronnie.

I wasn't sure he really wanted to see me, though. It occurred to me that he probably didn't want to be found and that maybe he was just being polite. So, I said, "Ronnie, before I go, I've got to show you something."

I showed him a video of my students and their horses, in particular Silke Vallentin, a German gal with a Friesian horse. Silke is handicapped and directs her big black partner from her wheelchair.

A big tear came to Ronnie's eyes. He couldn't believe what he saw.

"My friend," he said, "you've really done something here. I'm proud of you."

I told him we were on our way to Scottsdale for a clinic, and asked if he'd like to see our program for himself.

He agreed that it'd be nice, but he was very noncommittal. Again, I thought it was his way of being polite.

13, Not 3

Yuma is only about three-and-a-half hours from Scottsdale, but Ronnie was a no-show, as I sort of expected. I told Linda that I thought we'd seen the last of him.

From Scottsdale, we drove all night long to Albuquerque for our next seminar. We had clinics lined up mid-week and on the weekend; we were really hauling hard.

Albuquerque is at least a 13-hour drive from Yuma, maybe more. Just as we pulled up to the fairgrounds, the first person I saw was Ronnie, watching my students warm up their horses.

He'd driven 13 hours, instead of three, to see us. He explained that he couldn't get out of what he was doing the previous weekend, but "By God, I told you I was going to try to come, and this is the first clinic I could make."

I was blown away.

He watched our seminar, and Linda did a fabulous job that day. Things couldn't have been more perfect.

Ronnie was impressed with what he saw, with what Linda had done and how I'd matured with what he'd taught me. He saw how closely I'd kept to the philosophy and approach he'd shared with me 14 years before.

When people teach you something and you take it and change it, thinking that you're doing it for the better, it's insulting to the person doing the teaching. Ronnie could see that I'd kept the integrity of what he taught intact. I did his thing, my way.

After the seminar was over, I invited him to come to the ranch in Pagosa Springs. It wasn't all that much farther away.

He jumped in his "buggy," as he called it, a red Dodge pickup with a camper, and off to the Colorado mountains we went.

PHOTO BY COCO

Ronnie Willis (right) and Pat at a colt-starting in Pagosa Springs.

We gave Ronnie a tour of the ranch, and I asked him to come back to a colt-starting clinic the following May.

"You know," I winked at him, "I've not been very good at it since you left, and I'd really like for you to be there to help me," referring to our one and only colt-starting clinic in Clements all those long years ago.

He laughed and agreed.

The Cowboy Hat

The following spring Ronnie showed up for the clinic. We had 120 colts to start! He hadn't ridden in all those years, so I put him on one of my good mares. He was really in his element then. After about his sixth ride, I could see that he was addicted again. But strangely enough, he was riding around in a baseball cap.

I asked him why he'd given up riding. He explained that because of his diabetes, he didn't have the coordination he once had.

"I couldn't offer a horse what I should be able to offer him," he clarified.

I countered with this analogy: "Just because you're used to using a sharp knife, if it gets dull, you don't throw it away or put it in the drawer. It might not be the sharpest knife in the world, but there's a way you can use it."

He agreed that I had a point.

I knew things had changed when he got rid of the baseball cap and showed up one morning to ride in his high crowned cowboy hat. I never saw him in a baseball cap again. He was a horseman once more.

PHOTO BY COCO

When Ronnie (standing) took off his ball cap and put on his cowboy hat, Pat knew he'd decided to become a horseman again.

173

PHOTO BY COCO

The late Ronnie Willis helped develop and steward the PNH horsemanship program at La Cense Montana.

The Gift

I remember telling Ronnie that he'd helped a lot of my dreams come true.

He said, "Yes, and you've used it well."

"You gave me the gift," I said. "What in your life have you always dreamed of doing?"

Ronnie drew a deep breath. "I've always wanted to go to Australia."

"Consider it done," I remarked. "I'm going in November. Just bring $5 and a new shirt. You're on my ticket."

Six months later we were on a plane to Australia for 30 days. Fulfilling Ronnie's dream made me feel as though I'd had a chance to repay him for all he'd given me.

After finishing the colt-starting course, Ronnie started camping at the ranch regularly. We conducted another colt-starting the following year, and after that he headed up north to take over the reins of La Cense Montana.

Ronnie's wife, Gina, had seen her husband become healthier, now that he was on the back of a horse again. She'd always been concerned about his health and worried that horses would be his demise.

Ronnie once told me that he'd made Gina a promise. She'd followed him around, working on ranches, moving from one place to the next, to support his roving cowboy ways. After his

diabetic episode in Clements, Ronnie promised her he'd support her town-life from then on. They stayed put in one place and lived a non-horse lifestyle. When the La Cense opportunity brought them to Montana, however, the couple was content. They had a nice house, and Ronnie claimed this was the last job he'd ever have.

Another Graduation

To showcase the horses, facility and program, La Cense put on an open house in May 2003. They held a two-day seminar during the middle of the week, and still about 700 people showed up in the indoor arena.

In the trailer-loading portion of the clinic, I had an unusually scared and disrespectful horse. The mare took one look at the trailer and decided she was going to invent trailer-loading as a problem. It took a bit, but I finally got through to her.

After it was all over, Ronnie gave me the thumbs-up, put his hand on my neck and said, "Now you've made it."

I looked at him bewildered and said, "I thought I made it about five years ago."

He countered, "Nope, now you've made it."

I invited him to have a drink in our tour bus, but he said he couldn't. He was really tired and wanted to "adjust his lipstick." He was a diabetic and that meant he was going to give himself an insulin shot. I told him I'd see him in the morning.

He said, "Well, maybe. But there's one thing for sure. I'm going to dream about horses tonight."

And that's what he did. He laid down and graduated to Horseman's Heaven. Ronnie died that night.

Despite the fact that I spent most of the night at the hospital, the next morning I had to be ready for the people who showed up for the second day of the open-house clinic. Private grieving for one of my most cherished mentors had to be put aside, and I had to put on my public face. I continued with the clinic, which is something Ronnie would've wanted. I gave sort of a eulogy on Ronnie, told about his life and what he'd done for me. It was one of the hardest things I've ever had to do.

At the time of publication, the successful program Ronnie spearheaded at La Cense Montana is now in the capable hands of Steve Byrnes, one of our top students who'd worked under Ronnie.

People's Perspectives on Pat
Out of the Box

I remember when I first met Pat Parelli. My wife had been talking about him for months, and he was coming to Lexington (Kentucky) for a seminar. I thought I'd score some points with my wife if I went. I saw Pat interact with his horses and other people's, and realized that I needed to think more "out of the box" when it came to my own horses. Pat made me think from the horse's perspective. I have applied it ever since.

About a year later, we had trouble breaking a yearling colt at Winstar Farms, where I'm employed. The colt was literally a bucking bronco. Pat helped us in the short time he was there, and we named the colt after him – Pats Cat – and he's about as slow as Pat!

Elliott Walden
Thoroughbred trainer

Elliott Walden trained Victory Gallop, winner of the Belmont Stakes and Champion Older Horse

24 MAGIC MOMENTS

"She's the most versatile and talented horse I've ever ridden."

In 1999, Linda and I gave a seminar in Tasmania, an Australian island south of the mainland. The seminar took place in one of the island's largest towns, Launceston. As we do in all our seminars, we invited people to bring their most challenging horses for us to play with. I would pick the one I liked and spend some time with it.

Panic-aholic

Of the three horses brought to us for that seminar, one was a little black mare named Spider. They called her that because she reminded them of a black widow. I chose her because I liked her looks and she had the most interesting bio. It went: "My horse is perfect, except..." and it had a long litany of misbehaviors, such as hard to catch, runs away, bucks, won't trailer load. Everything was a panic problem. She did everything in a panic.

The facility we used was in a community park that had an arena behind a railroad track. There was a grandstand along the arena's long side, and there must have been 500 people watching.

As I played with Spider, she responded as if she were a hummingbird buzzing around on the end of a string. She was everywhere. I eventually got her saddled and ridden. Things were going along great, and I was able to ride her bridleless with Carrot Sticks.

Then the inevitable happened – the train came by, and it scared her so badly she ran off. There I was, being run away with on a horse with no bridle! She finally came to a sliding stop on the slick, wet grass (it had

Pat liked Magic so much that he left her owner with a blank check.

PHOTO BY COCO

Pat and Magic, thrilling the crowd at the 2003 Savvy Conference. The once panicky horse now does anything for Pat.

rained). The crowd roared and clapped. That scared her as well. She took off again and ran the opposite way. Between the train and the people, it must have looked as though I were riding a pinball – back and forth at a high rate of speed – bouncing off everything.

I lived through the whole experience and by the second day the black mare was doing fabulous, so much so that I rode her into a trailer with the Carrot Sticks, my head leaning backwards, my nose sticking outside the trailer. To back her out, I simply motioned with the Carrot Sticks.

Blank Check

Needless to say, I fell in love with her. Even though she did things in panic mode, I could feel her talent. Her owner said she'd been through four trainers – a horse-breaker, cutting horse trainer, reining horse trainer and one other professional predator. They all said the Quarter Horse mare was far too panicky to be a good horse. I offered to buy her, but the owner didn't want to sell her even though she was way too much horse for him. He wanted a solid trail-riding horse, and, at that time, she was anything but a fearless trail mount. Still, he didn't want to part with her.

I left him with a blank check. Four months later, he called my office personnel in Australia, who, in turn, contacted me to find out if it was all right for him to fill in the check. I said "yes," but first ask him how much. The amount wasn't out of line, so I agreed that he could write the check. That was in November 1999.

I left the mare in Australia and rode her every time Linda and I went there, which was at least twice a year. She made unbelievable progress. But I couldn't stand calling her Spider. Every time I rode her, it was a magical experience. I had to call her Magic.

At one time, we were at Kate and Owen Gwen's cattle ranch, where we held calf-branding schools to teach people how to rope and brand buckaroo-style. Australians didn't know how to do that. They simply choused cattle through a squeeze chute. I must have branded over 500 head of calves on Magic during the time she was there.

Pasture Piaffe

There was one special time I remember during one of the branding courses. I opened a gate for the class to enter a pasture, and

177

PHOTO BY COCO

Pat and Magic performing the piaffe in a Florida pasture.

they all filed through. By the time I got the gate closed, however, the clinic goers were about 100 yards ahead of me. I could feel Magic building up, getting antsy over being left behind. I tried something unique on her. I held her back with the reins, but let her move forward a little bit at the same time. This caused her to execute a rudimentary passage (a slow, rhythmical, cadenced trot, with a moment of suspension between the diagonal pair of legs). From then on I used the same cues that encouraged her to perform the maneuver, and, within three days, I had her doing both the passage and piaffe (a similar movement as the passage, but performed in one spot). What I did was take her nervous energy and put it to use.

She's just amazing. She's the most versatile and talented horse I've ever ridden. She's race-horse fast, has stamina like you can't believe, can jump four-and-one-half feet easily with me and a heavy, western saddle on her back, perform piaffe and passage, change leads every stride, rope steers, drag calves to the fire, work a cow like a cutting horse, slide to a stop and spin like a reining horse, anything I ask her to do. I've had dressage enthusiasts tell me she can perform as nice a piaffe as they've ever seen any horse do. She's just absolutely phenomenal!

I wish I had been able to own her as a young filly, without the challenges she came with. I tried to lease her mother, but never got it worked out. The lady who raised her came to Australasia Equitana, held in Melbourne. I told her I'd do anything to have a chance at another Magic – buy her mother, lease her, whatever. Her sire, Deck And Chrome, was still alive, and I wanted a full brother or sister. But, for some reason, we never completed a deal. I don't remember exactly why because the dam's owner agreed to the idea, but nothing ever came of it.

I rode Magic at the Australasia Equitana, in front of around 3,000 people. Some of her former trainers were there, sitting in the grandstand watching the horse they said was absolute junk. Little did they realize that she'd be one of the highlights of the event.

Piaffe for My Compadre

I eventually decided to bring Magic to the States. It was exciting for me to fly her over here and finally have her full-time. I've used her consistently in my demonstrations and courses. She keeps building upon her strengths and gets better with every ride.

I was especially happy when Magic could make the wish of master horseman Jack Brainard come true. Jack, in his 80s as of this printing, is well-known as a trainer of trainers. I'd heard about him through Ray Hunt and always wanted to meet him.

I was invited to participate in a horse whisperer contest in downtown Fort Worth, Texas, in 2002. I knew Jack lived north of town and one of my students, who takes lessons from him, had his phone number. I called him and told him I'd very much like to meet him.

When Pat found out that Jack Brainard had always wanted to ride a piaffe, he obliged him with a ride on Magic. This photo was taken at the 2003 Savvy Conference, where Jack gave a lead-change demonstration on Pat's horse, Cash.

179

Pat and Magic galloping across one of the Florida center pastures. Pat wishes he could find another Magic.

When we got together, I noticed his conversation ran a lot to dressage, which is a tad different for a guy who's known for his western performance background. He mentioned that he'd always wanted to perform a piaffe, and I told him I could make that possible. I had Magic in mind.

There were three clinicians at the contest: Craig Cameron, Josh Lyons and me. We each had a pen of two horses to pick from to start. They were supposed to be of similar ilk, but they really weren't. Of my two, one was sick or

at least he looked sick, with a frail body and weepy eyes. He looked like a 90-pound weakling. I didn't think it right to select that one, so the other one was my only choice. He was just the opposite – snorty and rank.

Josh Lyons won the contest. Even though Jack wasn't a judge, as one of the horse industry's senior statesmen, he was given the mike to give his impression of the day's events. He explained that everyone did a fantastic job, but he thought my horse was indeed the toughest, but a week later would be the most prepared. I was really honored that he spoke up like he did.

Not long after, I went to Craig Johnson's ranch in Gainesville, Texas, and happened to have Magic with me. I couldn't wait until Jack could come over and ride her. The look on his face when he figured out the buttons to push to get her to perform a piaffe was priceless. He didn't want to stop. Jack has a special place in my heart. The moment we met, I felt he was a compadre.

Get Out of Bed

Personality-wise, Magic is the opposite of Casper. She's very gregarious, loves to be with other horses and people, too. What I'd like to do someday is get a world-class horse, like her, but without any baggage. I'll probably breed Magic to Casper or another outstanding horse using embryo transfer. That's my dream – to find another Magic.

I don't like to get up early. As a matter of fact, I like to get up at the crack of noon if I get the chance. But Magic's a horse even I'd get out of bed early to ride.

People's Perspectives on Pat

Man of Vision

I wasn't acquainted with Pat during his early years, and I regret that I didn't have a chance to observe him. I do know that he had great mentors, and that he studied his lessons. He's certainly not a stranger to hard work and perseverance, which are the keystones to his success. Best of all, he is a man of vision, and he saw the need for a type of horsemanship so badly needed but completely lacking in present-day horse culture.

His program is superior and is based first of all on safety, which is the prerequisite of any horse-rider combination. His ground-work school beats them all, and I doubt if anyone could devise a better system. He progresses his students through a series of Levels that give them confidence and a sense of accomplishment, and they're ready and willing to continue their quest for more knowledge and skill.

It is a well-known fact that no one has helped more beginning horsemen and women than Pat Parelli. His students number in the thousands and all are grateful for him. When we talk about accomplishments in the horse industry, Pat Parelli stands alone.

I am so happy that our trails crossed, and I look forward to seeing more of him.

Jack Brainard
AQHA Champion trainer
AQHA, NRHA, NCHA and
multibreed association judge
Author, Western Training, Theory & Practice

PHOTO BY COCO

Pat (right) and Jack Brainard, known as a "trainer of trainers."

25 ALL THE KING'S AND QUEEN'S HORSES

"If you master your trade, you'll be sought after by kings and queens."

I've always been interested in all breeds of horses, but have been particularly fascinated with Spanish horses – Andalusians and Lusitanos. The more I found out about them, the more I really liked them. They're often referred to as the "Horse of Kings," because European royalty favored riding the extremely elegant and showy animals, with their noble bearing, high-stepping action and long, flowing manes and tails. They're the horses who perform in the bullfighting ring, and they're equally adept at dressage.

PHOTO BY COCO

Pat on Nova, one of his Andalusian-Thoroughbred crosses.

Spanish Horses

Linda and I got a chance to go to Lisbon and see the Portuguese Riding School, and also visit the farm of Luis Valenca, a nephew of the legendary classical riding master Nuno Oliveira. We were extremely impressed with Luis' beautiful facility, riding school and the evening demonstrations he'd put on for spectators. Riders dress in royal blue costumes and put his fabulous horses through their paces.

Luis educated us on Spanish and Portuguese horses and classical horsemanship. He explained how Lusitanos from Portugal and Andalusians from Spain used to be the same breed of horse, but a civil war closed the stud books in those countries, and there are now two separate breed registries.

Spanish horses have been bred for centuries to excel as war mounts and to handle cattle. Their conformation makes it easy for them to move in a collected manner and to perform high-level maneuvers, such as the piaffe and passage. However, they're also famous for being able to perform the Spanish Walk, where the horse's front legs reach high and forward in a spectacular march. We witnessed Luis do some phenomenal things with his horses. For example, he performed the Spanish Walk backward and did some beautiful in-hand work, such as having a horse canter and perform lead changes next to him, as he walked. And even more amazingly, Luis cantered a horse backward and performed lead changes at the same time. The capacity of his horses was unbelievable.

"Rank" Doesn't Describe It

Luis was a friend of Freddie Knie, and he'd heard I was pretty good with problem horses, so he had me look at one of his. He had an Andalusian-Thoroughbred cross that was extremely impulsive and had even jumped out of Luis' indoor arena and landed in the grandstand, bucking.

They brought the horse to the bullfighting ring for me to play with. I started with the

Pat taming a troubled Lusitano horse in Portugal.

Catching Game at liberty. The scared, but extremely athletic, horse tried to leap over the wall. In doing so, he turned his body sideways like a track-meet high-jumper, but didn't quite make it and fell back in. He wasn't hurt. I must say that he was one of the toughest horses I've ever had to deal with.

I played with the horse for three hours; he was exceptionally rank. Actually, "tough" and "rank" don't even come close to describing that horse. If you'd gotten on him, he wouldn't have thrown you off, he would've thrown you away.

I used all the tools in my arsenal to get through to the troubled horse. After a good long while, I finally broke through his barriers enough to saddle and mount him, but he wouldn't move forward. At first he didn't want to stand still for me to mount; then, when he did, he bucked when I tried to untrack him (cause a horse to move out of his tracks by bending or moving forward). I asked Linda to walk around the bull pen and let him follow her. It worked beautifully, and the horse became more and more confident as the

The Royal Mews is the stable at Buckingham Palace that also houses official state vehicles, including the Gold State Coach used for coronations.

PHOTO BY HAMISH MITCHELL, COURTESY OF PARELLI UK

evening wore on. He was a handful, but I got him under control and moving forward. A few months later, Luis told me that they were able to ride him and things were going well.

Designed by Nature

Spanish horses are designed by nature to do what they do well, similar to a Border Collie's natural talent for herding cattle and sheep. A Border Collie knows how to run wide around a herd or flock, stop on command, crawl on his belly and nip errant animals. That's natural for the breed. Same thing for a cutting horse: He knows how to lock onto a cow, dare it to move and then control it. Spanish horses have the ability to collect themselves naturally. Their bodies are like accordions. They can compress and expand (or extend) at will, and can be taught to do so on command. It's not all training; it's their natural talent coming through.

The entire Portuguese experience encouraged me to seek out horses designed for certain activities and try to develop them to their fullest. Like a cutting horse, they either have it in them or they don't. We now have several horses of Andalusian descent in our program and are having loads of fun playing with them.

Her Majesty, The Queen

Our presence in foreign countries is handled through distributorships, run by our top instructors. Dave Stuart, Charlotte Dennis and Richard Marriott operate our British distributorship and have their own Savvy Center outside Devon, England, where they teach students, including a fair number of Level 3 graduates. Whenever there's a horse expo or fair, we're geared up to send a crack team to demonstrate natural horsemanship.

Queen Elizabeth happens to be a real animal- and horse-lover who rides quite a bit herself. The royal family has hundreds of horses for all sorts of ceremonial activities in addition to horses for their personal pleasure. The Queen's Troop, for example, is stationed at Buckingham Palace, and its function is to provide horses and carriages for parades and state ceremonies.

At an equine fair in 2003, troop members saw our UK students perform and were curious about our methods and how they might apply to the troop's horse program. They contacted Dave and inquired if Linda and I would ever come to England. As it turned out, we

PHOTO BY HAMISH MITCHELL, COURTESY OF PARELLI UK

From left: Pat's mom Doris Parelli, Pat and Linda in front of one of the royal coaches.

were scheduled to be there that September. They were very interested in attending the two-day clinic, and we gave them VIP tickets.

After the clinic, they invited us to dinner, where they mentioned they'd like us to demonstrate for The Queen and, of course, we agreed.

A couple of weeks later we got a phone call saying that our presentation might be on, but nothing was etched in stone. They were in the midst of planning fun things for The Queen's birthday, and they thought we'd make a nice addition to the day's events.

In preparation for a presentation before The Queen, we sketched out our demonstration to include a variety of people and horses. The whole thing was taking shape, but we knew it was one of those on-again-off-again deals. Nevertheless, we were prepared if it became a reality.

My Mom or No Go

When I told my mom what was potentially on the horizon for us, she reminded me that I once told her that if there ever was any place she'd like to go with us, she could. Well, this was it. I said I'd see what I could do.

Getting a royal invitation isn't easy to do. Anyone who is granted an audience with The Queen has to be checked out by Scotland Yard for security reasons.

The event was a couple of weeks away when I called my contact in England, and told him I wanted my mom included in our entourage. I was told the limit of people had been reached, so, no, she couldn't come. I told them that if my mom couldn't come, I wouldn't come.

Lo and behold, the next day they found room for my mom. Evidently somebody else didn't get to go, and my mom took their place. She, too, had to be cleared by Scotland Yard.

We were told that we had to keep our audience with The Queen a secret for security reasons. We couldn't tell anyone what we were about to do or they'd cancel our demonstration. I guess they were worried about bombs in suitcases, that sort of thing.

We arrived at Buckingham Palace with our UK team and had to undergo another extensive security check, complete with mirrors on sticks to see if we were hiding anything under the car. We were met by the head organizer of The Queen's activities, who gave us a tour and also informed us of the proper etiquette we were to exercise in The Queen's presence.

Neil Pye (left) and Dave Stuart in front of the Australian ceremonial carriage. Dave, who runs the Savvy Center in England, took part in the troubled horse demonstration.

In the riding hall, which was at least a couple of hundred years old, there were around 100 people, 50 of them from the King's Troop (soldiers) and the rest were dignitaries.

Before this whole thing happened, however, I called Will Farish, the United States Ambassador to the Court of St. James and owner of the famed Lane's End Thoroughbred Farms in Versailles, Kentucky, and Hempstead, Texas. I'd met Will when I helped him with his troubled colt, Parade Ground, some time before. We became fast friends, and he invited us to the Kentucky Derby, where we had the privilege of sitting in his box on the finish line.

I let Will know that we were coming and that I'd like for him to be present at the demonstration. He was a friend of The Queen and sat next to her. Linda and my mom were in the next row.

Horses Are Like Husbands

After our team was introduced, Neil Pye narrated the demonstrations. From her wheelchair, Silke Vallentin had her horse, Biko, performing at liberty, and the rest of the UK team played with their horses, as well.

Then came time to play with some of the troop's problem horses. We made two small round corrals out of tape and situated them in the middle of the hall.

Pat helps a King's Troop rider.

PHOTO BY HAMISH MITCHELL. COURTESY OF PARELLI UK

UK students Ingela Sainsbury (left) and Charlotte Dennis get ready for the Queen's demonstration. The Queen and the audience were in the foreground of this picture in a small mezzanine. Photographing The Queen isn't allowed.

They brought out a spooky Irish draft horse that was at least 1,400 to 1,500 pounds – a big fellow. I played the Seven Games with him, and it didn't take but a few minutes for him to make a change.

Dave Stuart was in the arena behind me, playing with a four-year-old gelding that had a reputation for bucking everyone off. Before long, Dave stood on the bronc's back.

Then, I got a horse that was afraid of manhole covers. I got him to walk over plastic and on top of pedestals.

Our audience was treated to the horses making significant changes right in front of their eyes. Linda said The Queen leaned forward, mesmerized.

Of course, to spice things up a bit, I threw in some of my more humorous lines. The Queen almost fell back in her chair when I said, "Horses are just like husbands; they never do what you want, they just do what you tell them." She laughed and clapped. We were told later she never does that.

Once I got on a roll and had The Queen laughing, everyone joined in; we all had a blast at Buckingham Palace. How many cowboys can say that?

The Queen was slotted to watch the demo for 30 minutes and then move on to other appointments. Instead, she stayed an hour and 15 minutes.

At the end, I said, "Your Majesty, I know your time is short." She was startled and realized that I was right. I'll bet she would've stayed there another hour if I hadn't brought it up.

Master Your Trade

Queen Elizabeth really loves horses. She knew the names of every one of the horses in the stables. She's the head of the humane society in Britain.

After our presentation was over, we got to meet her and shake hands. I introduced her to Linda and my mom.

She said something to the effect: "If only I could've known this (natural horsemanship) back when I was younger, I could've used it."

One funny thing: Linda and I gave The Queen our *Keepin' It Natural* book as a small gift. I wanted to sign it for her, but I've got terrible handwriting and can't spell. I wanted to put, "For Her Majesty," but I didn't know how to spell "majesty." I whispered to Linda for help, and she whispered back the correct spelling.

I gave the book to Linda to sign and just as she was about to do it, The Queen looked

Silke Vallentin and her Friesian gelding, Biko, were part of the presentation to Her Majesty, The Queen. However, this photo of the German girl and her horse was taken during their demonstration at the 2001 Savvy Conference in Pagosa Springs.

over her shoulder, saw my poor penmanship and said, "Oh dear, is that how you write?"

Linda was mortified. She has extraordinary handwriting and is a world-class speller, but she took a little heat for me that day.

When The Queen was about to leave, she bowed to us and told us she was honored that we were there.

Later that night I did another demonstration just for the troop and the rest of the dignitaries on a horse that normally had to be sedated to be clipped. I cured him of that in short order.

Afterward, there was a little party for us with drinks and some food. There was talk about us going to Windsor Castle someday, which is where The Queen's family horses are stabled. Of course, we were amenable to that idea.

That was an extraordinary encounter for me, Linda, my mom and our UK team.

As a kid in Bible study, I remember a passage that read something like: "If you master your trade, you'll be sought after by kings and queens."

After this experience, I thought, "Wow, it's true!"

People's Perspectives on Pat

The Hannibal Lector of Horses

I got involved with Pat because I was trying to improve the way we did things at the racetrack. In the process, we introduced Pat to other areas of racing, such as some of the breeding farms.

We had a particular incident at Lane's End Farm in Versailles, Kentucky. The manager, Mike Kline, said they had a stallion, Parade Ground, who was savaging everyone. They kept a halter with a bit attached and a long rope on him at all times. When anyone approached, he'd either rear, strike, kick or bite. Parade Ground was the Hannibal Lector of racehorses. They captured him by grabbing his rope with a long stick, cinching it down on a post and then putting two lead ropes on his halter. One of the handlers would have a club to keep the stallion off them, if needed. The stallion was impossible to deal with and had become quite a danger to the farm.

I asked Mike to let Pat have a look. Pat spent about three hours in the stallion's stall. During the course of that session, he transformed the horse from a monster to a workable animal. Pat was able to open the stall door, invite the horse out and ask him to return to his stall with no more than one long rope lead on him. The change that came over the horse that day was dramatic.

The next day, Pat took the stallion out of the barn with the rope lead, and led him to the round pen, which happened to be close to the breeding shed.

The muzzle was still on at this point. As Pat played with the horse, Parade Ground was paying attention to the activity going on in the breeding shed. Someone asked if they should stop the breeding. Pat said "No, the horse needs to have manners in all circumstances."

Pat roped one of the stallion's front legs and started controlling him with it. The horse would lead forward with light pressure. After a time, Pat roped one of the hind legs and did the same thing, only he led the horse backward.

Pat spent about an hour and a half with Parade Ground that day. He taught him not to rear and to withstand the approach of a human. Pat took off the muzzle, and the horse didn't savage him.

Now the clincher: Pat had to lead the horse out of the round pen and back to the stallion barn. This walk of about 400 yards required that they walk down a blacktop road and past a bronze statue of AP Indy, the farm's main stallion. By coincidence they had a maintenance crew steam-cleaning the statue with a pressure hose, which shrieked loud, hissing noises, spraying water everywhere. Also, there was a row of plant barrels along the way with plastic over the plants to protect them from the cool weather. They were about to be planted. Needless to say, the plastic bags flopping in the breeze added to the noisy symphony on Pat and Parade Ground's walk.

Between the road and the potted plants there was a grass path about three to four feet wide. Pat had Parade Ground on a 22-foot rope. He asked the horse to stay on the grass, but parallel to his shoulder, 22 feet away. The horse was not to walk on the blacktop; he was to stay on the grass next to the flapping plastic bags.

When Pat and Parade Ground got to the statue, the guys asked if they should stop. Pat said, "No, keep spraying away." The stallion wanted to balk and step off the grass path. From 22 feet away, Pat directed the horse back onto the path. The horse made it past the statue, in a calm manner and on a loose lead.

I don't know if I've ever seen quite that level of horsemanship from anyone. It was fantastic. Pat later said the horse was one of the 10 most difficult he's ever had to deal with.

Bob Duncan
Official Starter for New York Racing Association (retired)
Consultant to NYRA

26 THE FUTURE OF TRAINING

"We found that philosophically we were on the same page."

The future of training is in the hands of progressive horsemen and women, such as left to right: David O'Connor, Karen O'Connor, Pat and Linda, Craig Johnson, Lyn Johnson.

I remember an interesting conversation I had with Bob Avila and the late Bruce Gilchrist, who had been one of Troy Henry's apprentices. Both Bob and Bruce already were top-notch showmen in the western performance-horse industry by the mid-1970s.

We were at Nick Arismendi's Triple A Ranch for a cutting in Lockeford, California. I visited with the two of them, and they asked me if I'd seen the new movie titled, "The Man From Snowy River," which I hadn't. "It reminded us of you," they said, "and how you want to be a horseman, not a show-horse trainer."

King of the Back-yarders

In our conversation, Bob explained that his goal was to become the king of the western performance-horse world, which he did later in his life. He's won several NRCHA snaffle bit futurities, AQHA world championships and the NRHA Futurity.

I said, "Not me, I want to be the king of the back-yarders."

Bob gave me a funny look

"Yep, that's me," I explained. "I want to

PHOTO BY COCO

Craig Johnson (left) and Pat put on the first reining super course in 2003 at the Pagosa Springs center.

help people who want to be helped, no matter what their breed of horse, no matter if they wear a cowboy hat or jodhpurs."

I did start out wanting to be a big name in the reined cow horse and cutting world, but changed my mind due to Troy Henry's advice about showing horses.

Even though I have a performance-horse background and it's never left me, I built my business based on regular people getting extraordinary results.

Linda, too, has a performance-horse background, and both of us have always had an ear cocked in that direction, thinking that it'd be great to make inroads into the show world

someday. Our wishes have come true, and here are some of the people who made it happen.

Scooch Mountain

Craig Johnson is an NRHA Futurity and Derby winner, AQHA and APHA world champion and one of the NRHA's top money-earning riders. He first heard about me from his father, Burdette Johnson, who came to one of my clinics in Ohio many years before. Burdette told him he needed to check me out.

Craig called and we instantly hit it off on the phone. I invited him out to the ranch to

PHOTO BY COCO

The Parellis and the Johnsons, from left: Craig, Lyn, Linda and Pat.

PHOTO BY COCO

Art and Letitia Glenn have developed the Parelli Collection, a line of Parelli equipment and logo-wear apparel.

Mountain Horse Expo in Denver, Colorado. And better yet, we've entered into a mutually beneficial arrangement where we exchange some of our students and horses. I put the foundation on his, and he puts the finish on mine. I'm also now in partnership with him on his champion Quarter Horse stallion, Sailing Smart.

Reputation-maker

Art and Letitia Glenn are partners in our Parelli Collection, a product line that is mainly apparel, but includes other innovative products as well. They used to own O'Farrell's hat company and every year they would exhibit at the Western & English Sales Association Denver International Western/English Apparel & Equipment Market for equestrian retailers.

One year they shared their booth with Jim Hill, owner of J.B. Hill Boot Company. Dr. Hill is a veterinarian and he used to own the great racehorse Seattle Slew.

We visited with both the Glenns and the Hills at the market and later went out to dinner with them. Naturally, the subject turned to horses. Dr. Hill came to ride with us that summer and still comes every year. We've become great friends.

Jim knew Bob Duncan, the head starter for racetracks in New York State. A racehorse has to get a starting ticket from Bob in order to race. Bob came to our school to learn more about ground-handling skills, which are crucial on the track. He learned the Seven Games and uses them to teach horses to load into the starting gate.

I told Bob that if he ever heard of a reputation-maker, let me know. He asked what that was, and I explained that it would be a horse that had huge potential or one that used to run and wouldn't anymore, something like that.

He turned us on to two difficult horses. One was Civilization, a very well-bred colt by Gone West, and out of Toussaud, who was the 2002 Kentucky Broodmare of the Year. She also foaled Empire Maker, who was second in the Kentucky Derby and won the Belmont Stakes, Florida Derby and Wood Memorial. Civilization was Hall of Fame trainer Bobby Frankel's Kentucky Derby prospect. Needless to say, there were high hopes for this colt.

ride. He cancelled a couple of warm-up futurities he was preparing for and came to Pagosa Springs instead. We had a grand time. Craig got to see the school in operation, ride with some of my top students and gather cattle on a nearby ranch.

On the ranch, I boasted to Craig that I could do a 70-foot slide stop from a standstill.

He said, "What?"

I said jokingly, "I'll bet you a new pickup. Just watch."

We were near a steep ledge on a mountainside, and I stepped off of it onto slippery shale. I held my horse into a frame, and she slid on her hind end all the way down. Craig followed on his champion reining horse. He's been bragging ever since about how he and Pat Parelli slid 70 feet from a standstill.

We like to call that mountain "Scooch Mountain" because a horse has to "scooch" all the way down it.

Craig is a very progressive person, but, at the same time, very fundamentally correct in his foundation training. We found that philosophically we were on the same page. We have similar concepts about stops, turns, lead changes, spins, everything.

Craig has co-taught courses with us and co-presented at our Savvy Conferences at the Pagosa Springs center and at the Rocky

PHOTO BY COCO

Pat played The Seven Games with this Thoroughbred racehorse who wouldn't "train," in other words, run. They're on the track at Belmont Park in New York.

Bobby called me one day and said he had a couple of colts who wouldn't "train," which means the horses wouldn't go forward.

Linda and I went to Hollywood Park in California to play with the two horses, Civilization and a French colt, on two mornings. The French horse had already won $180,000, but he'd quit running.

Civilization was a challenging horse, to be sure, but mostly he just wasn't broke. He'd barely make it around the track at a walk. He'd come off the farm too early in my estimation.

We played the Seven Games with both colts, and then taught the exercise boys what to do. Both horses started to train and eventually ran races.

We became really good friends with Bobby Frankel after that. He invited us to come to the Eclipse Awards (racing's high honors) with him twice.

Breaking Tradition

The word in the Thoroughbred industry spread quickly, and I got invited to do a seminar for the Thoroughbred Breeders Association at Belmont, New York. Jim Hill and Bobby Frankel introduced me to an audience of some of the country's elite racehorse trainers.

For the seminar, I was given another horse who wouldn't train. His pattern was to trot out about a quarter of a mile, stop, rear and refuse to go forward. I had the exercise boy get on him and try to make him go. He kicked the horse, spanked him, did whatever he could, but to no avail.

I brought out four plastic barrels, laid them end-to-end on the track and played the Seven Games with the horse for about an hour and a half. My idea was to give the horse some go-forward cues and to play the Squeeze Game with him to encourage his confidence in tight places. I rearranged the space between the barrels so he learned to negotiate through them and also jump over them. The horse wouldn't go over the barrels to save his life, but he finally learned to move forward on cue. I can only imagine what the racehorse trainers, who are deeply tied to tradition, were thinking: "Yeah, yeah, what does this have to do with the price of tea in China or racing?"

I then had one of my top students, Mikey Wanzenreid, a former European steeplechase jockey, mount the once-reluctant racehorse. He smooched to the horse, who took off like a jackrabbit and ran down the track.

The trainers couldn't believe that an hour-and-a-half's fiddling around on the ground would make a recalcitrant racehorse run. But

193

PHOTO BY BRANT GAMMA

David O'Connor has had an illustrious competitive career. He's shown here on Giltedge winning the Rolex, Kentucky, Three-day Event.

what I did was get the horse's respect and impulsion system up, and off he went.

Something to Learn

I first met Olympic Gold Medalist David O'Connor in 2001 when we were both giving clinics at Canterbury Farms in Gainesville, Florida. He gave a clinic to three-day eventers, and I did my seminar at night. He attended my demo, and afterward we struck up a conversation that lasted most of the night.

David told me about Gene Lewis, an Idaho cowboy who 10 years before had taught him how to jump horses on a line. Gene had been a hunter/jumper trainer in California and a friend of Ray Hunt's for years. It made perfect sense to David to have horses learn to jump on their own first, without weight on their back and a human getting in their way. David and I found we had a lot in common when it came to our approach to horsemanship.

The next year he arranged to have us invited to give a demonstration at the USET's winter training grounds in Ocala, Florida. My old friend, Captain Mark Phillips, was there as he was now the three-day-event team's chef d'équipe and coach.

Both the long and short list of Olympic three-day event riders were on hand to train.

Basically, everyone who's anyone in that sport was there. Linda and I took our team of 13 top riders for our demonstration.

When we arrived, someone on the course was riding a runaway. The horse flew by the jumps, totally out of control. It took the rider 15 minutes to get the horse stopped. This was supposed to be an Olympic-caliber horse.

For our demonstration, our team started by jumping their horses on-line. Then they turned the horses loose in the huge field, and they went over the jumps and through the ponds at liberty. Next, the riders mounted and jumped the same obstacles bareback and bridleless! This must have been an astounding sight to the three-day eventers.

When it was all over, we went over to talk to the group and Captain Mark Phillips said something to the effect: "Boys and girls, we're having trouble getting our horses stopped and under control with everything in their mouths but the trailer hitch. And you just saw some cowboys and cowgirls riding around here bareback and bridleless, jumping our jumps. Maybe we have something to learn here."

That evening we put on a barbecue and a seminar where people were able to ask questions. Some brought horses they were having problems with. One was a horse that wouldn't change leads. I played with the horse that night

PHOTO BY COCO

The Parellis and the O'Connors co-instructed an eventing course at the Pagosa Springs center. From left: Karen, Pat, Linda, David.

and the next morning. In those two sessions, I got him to perform a series of drop-to-the-trot lead changes, followed by flying lead changes.

A Couple of Collaborators

At the barbecue, I asked David if he had any horses he'd like for us to play with and he did. The next morning we went to the O'Connors' winter training facility in Ocala, and David brought out a horse named Tigger, who wasn't confident, always skeptical of things and a little impulsive. I played with the horse on line over jumps, and when he made some good changes, I got on and jumped him bareback. Afterward, I showed David how to play the Seven Games, and he got it immediately. Tigger was potentially one of David's Olympic horses, but he had to have two colic surgeries that sidelined him a long time. He did recover, though, and went on to become a good horse.

I asked the O'Connors if they'd be interested in an apprentice-trade program and they agreed. I sent one of our best students to their camp, and they sent one to ours.

We sent a Level 3 graduate from England named Charlotte Dennis, who already was an eventer before I met her. She was also the girl-friend of Dave Stuart, one of my Five-Star instructors in England.

I remember calling and asking David how things were working out with Charlotte. He said, "I didn't know people with her kind of skills existed. Most of the people I get come out of college equine programs and are young kids who've ridden, but if a horse gives them any kind of grief, they don't know what to do. They're lost on a horse that's hard to bridle or clip."

He said within two weeks, Charlotte was able to trailer-load some horses his regular students had difficulty with, and she put first rides on others.

David was so impressed with her, he exclaimed, "They should give gold medals to people like this."

Since then, David, Karen, Linda and I have collaborated on several things. We've co-taught two weeklong programs at our center in Pagosa Springs. We've also co-presented seminars at the Rolex three-day eventing competition in Lexington, Kentucky, and the Rocky Mountain Horse Expo in Denver.

At the latter event, 3,000 people showed up to watch our "The Future of Training" demonstration. Besides our usual seminar in which we offer natural horsemanship theories and

PHOTO BY COCO

Pat (right) talks with co-presenter Craig Johnson at the 2003 Rocky Mountain Horse Expo in Denver, Colorado.

the O'Connors jumped their horses over a single, upright barrel with only a savvy string around their horses' necks. That brought the house down. I got Magic over two barrels, with 250 pounds of cowboy and tack on her back. I was so proud of her.

The next night we had Craig Johnson on our demo team and put on sliding stop contests. I surprised David, who was sitting in the audience watching, by having him come down into the arena and participate in the contest. I gave him a cowboy hat and chinks and mounted him on my stallion Liberty Major. He ended up winning the sliding contest among the three of us.

Light Hands

In addition to the United States, Linda and I have found progressive horsemen in Europe.

One is Michel Henriquet, a French architect in his 80s, who was a student of the famed horseman Nuno Oliveira and his clinic host for 35 years. Michel is a legendary dressage trainer and rider himself, and his wife, Katherine, has represented France at the Olympics and the world championships in dressage competition.

Another brilliant horseman is Colonel Christian Carde, head rider of the Cadre Noir (French Riding School). He and Michel are friends and both came to a seminar I gave at William Kriegel's horse facility outside Paris. Michel later invited us to come to his dressage school, about 40 minutes away.

Katherine had a horse that was her Olympic hopeful, a Trakehner stallion named Isgaard. She was pleased with the horse's development, but said that it would take five more years to get him rebalanced and off his front end. She asked if I'd ride him.

I saw her tiny dressage saddle and knew I couldn't ride in that. So I peeled the saddle off and jumped on the stallion bareback. The first thing I noticed was that he "purged" or leaned into the bit, which, of course, caused his weight to fall forward. I didn't allow him to do that. I kept backing him up every time he'd lean, which broke his pattern. He responded rather quickly and found his own self-carriage.

techniques, we put on fun competitions between the O'Connors and the Parellis that the crowd really got into.

We were an eclectic sight for the audience, that's for sure. I was in my cowboy hat and chinks, riding my 14-2"-hand Quarter Horse mare Magic. Linda was on her big warmblood gelding Remmer, and the O'Connors were on their Olympic horses, Custom Made and Giltedge.

We set up some jumps and had a striding contest to see who could do the most strides in between the jumps. We started with six, then went to seven, eight, nine and so on. Magic, catty little Quarter Horse that she is, ended up doing 17 strides.

During another portion of the demo, we brought out four barrels and put them upright in a row. Everyone made it over the four. In every round, we took down one barrel. Then,

Within 30 minutes, I pulled the bridle off and rode him around with the savvy string around his neck. Michel and Katherine were extremely impressed that the stallion had shifted his weight instantly, even in the piaffe, instead of taking five more years to learn how.

Michel and Colonel Carde have organized a new dressage association whose name translates to "lightness in hand" or "riding with light hands." I'm honored to say that Michel and Colonel Carde have asked me to be on the honorary board of directors for their new association.

Look to the Future

Our inroads into the performance-horse world have been gratifying and they're ongoing. There's much work to be done before natural training methods are considered standard practices in the competitive arena. To us, training in the future will be done naturally, enhancing the horse's natural talents, maintaining the horse's dignity and preserving the horse's longevity. More attention will be given to foundation and fundamentals, and the fancy stuff will follow.

With such progressive and high-profile people as Bob Duncan, Bobby Frankel, John Hill, David and Karen O'Connor, Craig Johnson, Michel Henriquet and Colonel Carde, we've got a good start in making the world a better place for performance horses.

People's Perspectives on Pat

Shout it from the Mountaintop

When my father, Burdette Johnson, returned from attending a Pat Parelli clinic, he called me and told me I really needed to see this guy. He was the "real deal." My father has been a professional in the horse business as a breeder, showman and judge, all his life. For him to say something like that really got my attention.

So I did one better; I called Pat and went to Pagosa Springs for three days to ride with him. We had a blast and, yes, dad was right. Pat is the real deal.

A few weeks later, Pat flew to Texas to ride with me. That was three years ago, and we've been teaching each other great things ever since.

We found our worlds weren't that far apart. Natural horsemanship is something the horse has been waiting a long time for us to find.

Pat's and Linda's knowledge and creativity open up a universe of possibilities for anyone seeking to better their horsemanship. Each opportunity I've had to spend time with them has given me the chance to see the horse without blinders and the rider without limitations.

For example, there was the time on a Colorado mountaintop when Pat challenged me to ride down it. Now scooching down the side of mountain on a world champion reining horse isn't something many would consider normal. My horse really had to use his hindquarters to get the job done. We weren't spinning and stopping in a perfectly groomed arena. We were sliding down a mountain!

Such experiences have shed a light on the sense of purpose created when the process becomes more important than the product.

Pat not only has a broad view of the horse world, but also, and more importantly, a broad view of the world of the horse – a necessity for anyone whose goal is the next level.

Craig Johnson
NRHA Futurity and Derby champion AQHA and APHA world champion USET gold, silver and bronze medalist

PHOTO BY COCO

Craig Johnson is one of the nation's top reiners.

27 MY VISION FOR THE FUTURE

*"If I don't see you in the future,
I'll see you in the pasture."*

My vision for the future of horsemanship is pretty clear. The seeds of natural horsemanship have been sown, and I predict good things on the horizon.

Horse People Today

Today, for the first time, more than 80 percent of all horse owners in the world are recreational riders. In the past, horses were mainly used in the military, in agriculture and for transportation, and they were owned mostly by the aristocracy or at least people of wealth and means.

That 80 percent is the largest group with the smallest voice, because they don't set any records, they don't have any champions, they're not in the limelight in any way. Only a small percentage own horses strictly for competition.

The other interesting thing is that more than 70 percent of all horse owners are

PHOTO BY COCO

Pat (third from left) and students ride the pasture at the Parelli Center in Pagosa Springs.

PHOTO BY COCO

The Parellis and the Johnsons are now partners on Sailing Smart, the Quarter Horse stallion Craig campaigned to an AQHA world championship in reining and a gold medal in USET reining competition. Under Craig's guidance, the stallion has had a long and successful career in the show pen.

female. This is the first time in history that this has been the case; in the past horses have been in male-dominated sports or activities.

Love, Language and Leadership

What that tells me is that most horse people today are more apt to be principle-oriented and less apt to be goal-oriented.

Therefore, the people who are the majority will have a louder voice due to the accumulated efforts of all the natural horsemanship clinicians, and they'll question the way things have always been done.

These people are saying, "Whatever result you get, if it's not done with the horse's dignity being put first, if the process wasn't done through love, language and leadership, in equal doses, we're not interested."

As a matter of fact, I think there'll be a time when all the cruel things that happen in the horse industry, such as harsh and unnatural breaking procedures, inhumane devices used for behavior problems or so-called performance enhancers to get horses to run faster, jump higher, step higher, etc., will be universally frowned upon.

The ingredients of love, language and leadership, on the other hand, result in a strong bond between horse and human, with the horse willingly doing what's asked of him. This is the approach and philosophy that the silent majority will demand.

I find this all relates to the premise I started with and my first public statement on horsemanship: "Horsemanship can be obtained naturally through communication, understanding and psychology versus mechanics, fear and intimidation."

Cake, Icing and Candles

I think we'll see this attitude enter the competitive world. People will have a better understanding of the difference between cake, icing and candles.

"Cake" means the foundation training or the first 300 to 1,000 hours that a horse is ridden. During this time a horse acquires the basics, the broad-based knowledge he needs to be successful in his riding career.

"Icing" would be the specific training the horse receives according to his respective talents. It could be racing, jumping, dressage, reining, cutting, roping, barrel racing, whatever.

199

Often the "icing" is drilled into the horse without sufficient foundation training. Less icing would be needed if the horse had enough scope and depth in the basics. The reason: The more foundation the horse has, the more flexible his mind is and the better learner he is.

Foundation training that focuses on the horse becoming a good learner encourages him to synchronize his whole life around his human partner's wishes, just as he did with his dam's wishes. The horse recognizes the human as the alpha member of his herd. When this happens and the horse is given the icing or specific training, he has the advantage of already being a great learner. Instead of being close-minded or hard-headed as some young horses appear to be when undergoing specific training that's too stressful, he becomes a malleable, flexible, learning, exuberant animal.

Then, the TSTL formula comes into play: talent, skills, try and luck. Talent is the innate characteristics God gives the horse. Skills are what he learns from his mother, herd, environment and humans. Try is the amount of exuberance the horse puts into what's being asked of him. And, the horse is lucky if he's owned by a person who understands that the cake is more important than the icing.

"Candles" refer to competition. You can have the most talented, trained, skilled and exuberant horse and still make a technical mistake on the day of the contest. But in the end, you're going to be a winner because your horse is going to feel like a winner. He's going to try for you and win for you more often because you gave him the chance to learn and understand his job.

Unfortunately, we're living in an era of the disposable horse that's retired by the time he's four or five years old, and sometimes sooner. The major cause of equine attrition in the show world is high-stress training techniques designed to produce young equine athletes capable of winning at the major events. If a horse doesn't hold up – mentally or physically – under high-performance training methods, he's sent home to his owner and another one takes his place in the trainer's barn.

With a change in philosophical thinking regarding horsemanship and training techniques, we'll see horses that'll get better and better as they grow older. They'll stay competitive until they're 12 and 15 years old and more.

Changing Standards

I predict that horse-show industry standards will change. My viewpoint right now is that if you compare the equine industry to most any other industry rated on standards of integrity and professionalism, it would rank among the lowest.

There are lots of people who're very good with horses. They're intuitive and natural in how they handle horses. But there are plenty who aren't. Anyone can hang out a shingle and declare himself or herself a professional horse trainer. And the consumer (typical horse owner) has no way of knowing whether a horse trainer uses mechanics, fear and intimidation to get results or communication, understanding and psychology. Most everyone talks a good line, but the reality is that where knowledge ends, violence begins.

What I think will happen, without getting PETA (People for the Ethical Treatment of Animals) involved, is that we're going to have industry standards that the consumer can count on.

My Solution

I've always believed that if you're not part of the solution, you're part of the problem. So, I'm going to offer what I view as the solution.

The answer is to have education and certification available to people who've passed horsemanship proficiency tests in the four savvys (classifications): on-line, liberty, freestyle and finesse.

Of course, top riding skills are a must. The rider should be able to teach any horse to use the partnership side of his brain while being ridden, not act like a prey animal, not change gaits or direction, watch where he's going and put effort into what he's doing. And the person should be competent to deal with behavior problems in horses.

There will be people who are foal and yearling experts, or colt-starters or first-ride specialists, or foundation specialists who are excellent at putting the first 300 to 1,000 hours on a horse. The latter will be able to give horses the depth and scope necessary to be either rock-solid horses for the general public or rock-solid performance horses that are mentally, emotionally and physically fit enough to withstand the pressures of competition and still have longevity.

Equine Sports Psychology

I predict we'll see people in competition in the big five – racing, jumping, dressage, reining and cow-horse events – who'll know not only how to use equine psychology, which is what our program's first four horsemanship levels are about, but also can use equine sports psychology, which is what our Levels 5 and 6 are about.

I believe that we'll see more and more true champions. These are people who are not only winners of competitions, but their horses think they're champions. The public thinks they're champions because they always put everything in a win-win situation where principles are placed before goals.

There are key people coming to the forefront who are using these techniques and philosophies in the competitive world. Some of the better-known trainers and competitors are Bobby Frankel in the racing industry, David and Karen O'Connor in the jumping/eventing industry, Michel Henriquet and Colonel Carde in the dressage industry and Craig Johnson in the reining industry. These people are performance-oriented and getting top results based on lightness. Lightness, to me, is the true test of performance.

It's like today's vehicles. For example, a modern pickup truck drives almost like a sports car. You press on the gas, and it'll rock you back in your seat. Push on the brakes, and you'd better have your seat belt on or a mouth guard because this thing is going to stop. It turns and stops with just ounces of pressure. It maintains a great level of self-maintenance. It doesn't require a tune-up every 5,000 miles. Vehicles today last much longer than they did before.

So, I compare the progress we as consumers have demanded of our vehicles with the same progress in the horse industry. Riders will demand horses that love to be with people and know how to be partners with people.

Sportsmanship Versus Horsemanship

I believe that my mission statement is already coming true, and that is to help raise the level of horsemanship worldwide. I feel as though I've already made a significant difference to some extent. I'm pleased, but I'm not satisfied. More work needs to be done.

For example, the genetic makeup of horses has been improved over the last 30 years due to our progressive breeding techniques and standards. We have the best horses the world has ever raised living today. Even some of our mediocre horses are better than some of our champions 20 or 30 years ago. We have fabulous horses, fantastic surfaces for them to ride and compete on and great breakthroughs in nutrition and horsekeeping.

Everything has improved except horsemanship. Horsemanship has gone away; sportsmanship has replaced it. Sportsmanship has become an artificial means of measuring success. What I mean is that most champions, most people who are very, very good at the sports they're champions in, couldn't do the job you asked them to do in a real-life situation.

For example, most ropers can catch a calf or steer only if it comes out of the chute straight. They probably wouldn't be able to catch and doctor an animal out in the pasture.

It's the same for competition cutting horses. Most couldn't gather cattle and handle a rogue steer if that was needed. They're not in a perfectly groomed arena where all the help is doing part of the cutter's job by containing the herd.

Most jockeys in the racehorse industry have never ridden a saddle horse, and most racehorse trainers have never ridden a horse.

Most stadium jumpers would be afraid to leap over the arena fence to jump out of the stadium or to use that jumping skill to ride cross-country.

Dressage developed as high-level equine training for the purposes of warfare and bull-fighting. Most dressage riders will never go to war on their horses and would never dream of challenging a bull in the arena.

Reining, often called "western dressage," originally developed as a contest to show off the skills of a well-reined ranch horse. Most competitive reining horses would be hopeless on a cow, much less a bull.

Principles, Purpose and Time

I'm really excited to see some other types of competitions developing, such as the ranch horse versatility contest, which is an event based on practicality and real-life situations and not exaggeration and show-offmanship.

Too often, we have a lack of principles, purpose and time in our competitive endeavors. There will always be a place for competition in the horse world. What I'm championing is putting the principles before the goals. I'd like to see sportsmanship accomplished from the horse's point of view. The rider can have the goals if he allows the horse to be in charge of the principles and timelines.

Principles are the framework, the ABC's of true learning. They're the basics or foundation the horse is given.

Purpose (or goals) gives everything a meaning. There's no reason in the world to learn mathematics if you don't have a practical application for it.

The same thing applies to horsemanship. If we're truly interested in the horse's dignity, we must remember that the purpose of what we ask him to do gives it a meaning. And if there is no meaning to the purpose, then the horse will ask what is the meaning of his life. If there is no answer, then there is no dignity.

I pity the poor performance horse that gets ridden in circle after circle after perfect circle, never knowing why he's doing it, other than to please his rider.

I'd rather be a bucking horse working eight seconds a weekend for about 12 rodeos a year and know that my job is to get a rider off, than to be a performance horse going through many hours of grueling training and not being able to fathom the reason.

As for time, some horses are faster learners than others, and some horses have better teachers who offer things to them more effectively. Each horse needs time to learn, according to his timetable.

Principles, purpose and time are the ingredients in the learning formula and regardless of how effective and efficient you are with horses, as long as you put principles first, the goal second and allow timelines to come naturally, you'll get where you want to go with a horse. It'll be a win-win situation for both of you.

Wave of the Future

My prediction is that horse owners will strive to become knowledgeable about equine psychology. All natural horsemanship is based on the true etiology of the horse, the study of their social behavior and what's natural to them.

Equine sports psychology is going to be the wave of the future. Human athletes are running faster and jumping higher with more heart and desire because they now work on their mental and emotional fitness as well as physical fitness. It will be the same with horses and horsemanship.

We're going to see early training principles come to the forefront, such as foal imprinting and weanling and yearling education. During a horse's most elastic and malleable period of his life he's going to learn mentally and emotionally how to become a great partner with a human being.

We've all heard the stories about the Bedouin Arabians raising their foals in their tents. Humans were part of the horses' herd, and the herd was part of the human family. This blood-is-thicker-than-water feeling that horses get comes from their identification as herd members.

Early education will mentally and emotionally prepare horses without physically taxing their growing bodies.

There's a huge waste of mental and emotional potential in young horses, especially in performance areas.

The Future is Youth

I think children are the future of horsemanship. Like young horses, children learn at a much more highly accelerated rate than adults. Their minds are impressionable and when they learn equine psychology right from the get-go, they'll be light years ahead in their horsemanship.

They won't ever get a chance to learn the five lies that everyone else has been taught about horses: 1. Catch the horse anyway you can. 2. Saddle him up and get on. 3. Kick him to go. 4. Pull him to stop 5. Use the reins to turn.

Instead, they'll be raised with the concept that you teach the horse to catch you. They'll know to check out the horse mentally and emotionally before they ever step foot in the stirrup. They'll find out what side of the corral the horse woke up on by first playing the Seven Games with him in the corral. They'll know you don't kick the horse to go, but use steady pressure by squeezing. If the horse doesn't go, then they'll know to use rhythmic pressure. They'll know you don't use your legs to get a horse to go; you use your legs if he doesn't go. They'll know you don't use your reins to stop or turn a horse; you use them if he doesn't stop or turn. And you use your reins for precision.

When the younger generation understands and uses these concepts, the face of horsemanship will change forever. These children won't know any other way. They'll already be on the true path of natural horsemanship.

Natural Horsekeeping

I predict a more holistic approach to horsekeeping will become commonplace. For example, equine nutrition will more closely mimic the horse's natural diet. Parasite control will be accomplished without the use of poisons. Equine dentistry, which gives horses a natural arcade in their mouths, will be a routine practice. Natural hoof trimming is already a growing farrier practice. Saddles, saddle pads and saddle-fitting will ascend new plateaus.

Old wives' tales, myths and bovine fecal matter will be a thing of the past.

PHOTO BY COCO

Pat sees the future of horsemanship in youth, who won't grow up believing in the "five lies."

The Revolution

What it all boils down to is that there's a revolution in horsemanship going on at this time. I believe the future is bright and imminent.

Remember, there are only two kinds of people in this world. Horse lovers and the other kind. But there are seven kinds of horse lovers and they all start with the letter "N" — natural ones, normal ones, nuts, nuisances, nerds, the nervous and the (k)nockers, the ones who take the frustrations out on the horse, the ones who don't have enough knowledge. The latter try to knock people who put their hearts in their hands and try to touch their horses with them. They try to knock that passion for horses out of their heads. The knockers will become the minority.

In the end, natural horsemanship won't have to be called "natural horsemanship" anymore. There will be only one kind of horsemanship – true horsemanship.

Horsemanship is natural. It's supposed to be. It's a natural phenomenon between the ultimate prey animal and the ultimate predator. The dichotomy in that relationship is the ultimate challenge. But natural horsemen and women are up to the task.

So, here's to the future of horsemanship. If I don't see you in the future, I'll see you in the pasture.

PAT PARELLI'S 45 P'S

I've repeated this statement thousands of times over the years, and it still embraces my philosophy. It's come to be known as my "45 P's."

"Pat Parelli proudly presents his provocative and progressive program and the proclamation that prior and proper preparation prevents p...-poor performance particularly if polite and passive persistence is practiced in the proper position, but that perspective takes patience from process to product, from principle to purpose. The promise that Pat plans to prove is that practice does not make perfect. Only perfect practice makes perfect. And isn't it peculiar that these poor prey animals perceive us people as predators and not partners."

I can also promise that my program will keep getting better and better and better. There will be more stories about its evolution.

PROFILE: KATHY SWAN

Kathy Swan considers herself one of the lucky ones to be able to combine her passions for reading, writing and riding into her life's work.

A lifelong horsewoman, Kathy has explored many trails. She's earned local, regional and national awards in both American Quarter Horse Association and American Paint Horse Association competition, in a variety of English and western classes. She's also competed successfully in North American Trail Ride Conference (NATRC) competitions and in hunter trials. Breeding Quarter Horses and Paints had been a serious hobby of hers for years, but she's also owned Arabians, Thoroughbreds and Andalusians. Today, she's an avid trail rider and enjoys exploring the West horseback.

Kathy has won awards for both her writing and her photography. She has a broad background in the equine publication industry: news editor at the *Quarter Horse News*, editor of *Horseman* and *Horse & Rider* magazines and associate editor at *Western Horseman*. Currently, she's the editor of the *Western Horseman* book division and executive editor of Cowboy Publishing's trade magazine division.

Other titles by the writer include *Ride Smart* by Craig Cameron, one of *Western Horseman's* 2004 releases, and two best sellers under her former name (Kadash) : *Reining, the Art of Performance in Horses* by Bob Loomis, published by EquiMedia, and *Natural Horse-Man-Ship* by Pat Parelli, published by *Western Horseman*.

Kathy lives in Scottsdale, Arizona, with her husband Rick and their well-loved horses, cats and dogs.

PHOTO BY COCO

Books Published by WESTERN HORSEMAN®

ARABIAN LEGENDS by Marian K. Carpenter
280 pages and 319 photographs. Abu Farwa, *Aladdinn, *Ansata Ibn Halima, *Bask, Bay-Abi, Bay El Bey, Bint Sahara, Fadjur, Ferzon, Indraff, Khemosabi, *Morafic, *Muscat, *Naborr, *Padron, *Raffles, *Raseyn, *Sakr, Samtyr, *Sanacht, *Serafix, Skorage, *Witez II, Xenophonn.

BACON & BEANS by Stella Hughes
144 pages and 200-plus recipes. Try the best in western chow.

CALF ROPING by Roy Cooper
144 pages and 280 photographs. Complete coverage of roping and tying.

CUTTING by Leon Harrel
144 pages and 200 photographs. Complete guide to this popular sport.

FIRST HORSE by Fran Devereux Smith
176 pages, 160 black-and-white photos, numerous illustrations. Step-by-step information for the first-time horse owner and/or novice rider.

HELPFUL HINTS FOR HORSEMEN
128 pages and 325 photographs and illustrations. *WH* readers and editors provide tips on every facet of life with horses and offer solutions to common problems horse owners share. Chapters include: Equine Health Care; Saddles; Bits and Bridles; Gear; Knots; Trailers/Hauling Horses; Trail Riding/Backcountry Camping; Barn Equipment; Watering Systems; Pasture, Corral and Arena Equipment; Fencing and Gates; Odds and Ends.

IMPRINT TRAINING by Robert M. Miller, D.V.M.
144 pages and 250 photographs. Learn to "program" newborn foals.

LEGENDS 1 by Diane Ciarloni
168 pages and 214 photographs. Barbra B, Bert, Chicaro Bill, Cowboy P-12, Depth Charge (TB), Doc Bar, Go Man Go, Hard Twist, Hollywood Gold, Joe Hancock, Joe Reed P-3, Joe Reed II, King P-234, King Fritz, Leo, Peppy, Plaudit, Poco Bueno, Poco Tivio, Queenie, Quick M Silver, Shue Fly, Star Duster, Three Bars (TB), Top Deck (TB) and Wimpy P-1.

LEGENDS 2 by Jim Goodhue, Frank Holmes, Phil Livingston, Diane Ciarloni
192 pages and 224 photographs. Clabber, Driftwood, Easy Jet, Grey Badger II, Jessie James, Jet Deck, Joe Bailey P-4 (Gonzales), Joe Bailey (Weatherford), King's Pistol, Lena's Bar, Lightning Bar, Lucky Blanton, Midnight, Midnight Jr, Moon Deck, My Texas Dandy, Oklahoma Star, Oklahoma Star Jr., Peter McCue, Rocket Bar (TB), Skipper W, Sugar Bars and Traveler.

LEGENDS 3 by Jim Goodhue, Frank Holmes, Diane Ciarloni, Kim Guenther, Larry Thornton, Betsy Lynch
208 pages and 196 photographs. Flying Bob, Hollywood Jac 86, Jackstraw (TB), Maddon's Bright Eyes, Mr Gun Smoke, Old Sorrel, Piggin String (TB), Poco Lena, Poco Pine, Poco Dell, Question Mark, Quo Vadis, Royal King, Showdown, Steel Dust and Two Eyed Jack.

LEGENDS 4
216 pages and 216 photographs. Several authors chronicle the great Quarter Horses Zantanon, Ed Echols, Zan Parr Bar, Blondy's Dude, Diamonds Sparkle, Woven Web/Miss Princess, Miss Bank, Rebel Cause, Tonto Bars Hank, Harlan, Lady Bug's Moon, Dash For Cash, Vandy, Impressive, Fillinic, Zippo Pine Bar and Doc O' Lena.

LEGENDS 5 by Frank Holmes, Ty Wyant, Alan Gold, Sally Harrison
248 pages, including about 300 photographs. The stories of Little Joe, Joe Moore, Monita, Bill Cody, Joe Cody, Topsail Cody, Pretty Buck, Pat Star Jr., Skipa Star, Hank H, Chubby, Bartender, Leo San, Custus Rastus (TB), Jaguar, Jackie Bee, Chicado V and Mr Bar None.

LEGENDS 6 by Frank Holmes, Patricia Campbell, Sally Harrison, GloryAnn Kurtz, Cheryl Magoteaux, Heidi Nyland, Bev Pechan, Juli S. Thorson
236 pages, including about 270 photographs. The stories of Paul A, Croton Oil, Okie Leo Flit Bar, Billietta, Coy's Bonanza, Major Bonanza, Doc Quixote, Doc's Prescription, Jewels Leo Bar, Colonel Freckles, Freckles Playboy, Peppy San, Mr San Peppy, Great Pine, The Invester, Speedy Glow, Conclusive, Dynamic Deluxe and Caseys Charm

NATURAL HORSE-MAN-SHIP by Pat Parelli
224 pages and 275 photographs. Parelli's six keys to a natural horse-human relationship.

PROBLEM-SOLVING, Volume 1 by Marty Marten
248 pages and over 250 photos and illustrations. Develop a willing partnership between horse and human — trailer-loading, hard-to-catch, barn-sour, spooking, water-crossing, herd-bound and pull-back problems.

PROBLEM-SOLVING, Volume 2 by Marty Marten
A continuation of Volume 1. Ten chapters with illustrations and photos.

RAISE YOUR HAND IF YOU LOVE HORSES by Pat Parelli w. Kathy Swan
224 pages and over 200 black and white and color photos. The autobiography of the world's foremost proponent of natural horsemanship. Chapters contain hundreds of Pat Parelli stories, from the clinician's earliest remembrances to the fabulous experiences and opportunities he has enjoyed in the last decade. As a bonus, there are anecdotes in which Pat's friends tell stories about him.

RANCH HORSEMANSHIP by Curt Pate w. Fran Devereux Smith
220 pages and over 250 full color photos and illustrations. Learn how almost any rider at almost any level of expertise can adapt ranch-horse-training techniques to help his mount become a safer more enjoyable ride. Curt's ideas help prepare rider and horse for whatever they might encounter in the round pen, arena, pasture and beyond.

REINING, Completely Revised by Al Dunning
216 pages and over 300 photographs. Complete how-to training for this exciting event.

RIDE SMART, by Craig Cameron w. Kathy Swan
224 pages and over 250 black and white and color photos. Under one title, Craig Cameron combines a look at horses as a species and how to develop a positive, partnering relationship with them, along with good, solid horsemanship skills that suit both novice and experienced riders. Topics include ground-handling techniques, hobble-breaking methods, colt-starting, high performance maneuvers and trailer-loading. Interesting sidebars, such as trouble-shooting tips and personal anecdotes about Cameron's life, complement the main text.

RODEO LEGENDS by Gavin Ehringer
Photos and life stories fill 216 pages. Included are: Joe Alexander, Jake Barnes & Clay O'Brien Cooper, Joe Beaver, Leo Camarillo, Roy Cooper, Tom Ferguson, Bruce Ford, Marvin Garrett, Don Gay, Tuff Hedeman, Charmayne James, Bill Linderman, Larry Mahan, Ty Murray, Dean Oliver, Jim Shoulders, Casey Tibbs, Harry Tompkins and Fred Whitfield.

ROOFS AND RAILS by Gavin Ehringer
144 pages, 128 black-and-white photographs plus drawings, charts and floor plans. How to plan and build your ideal horse facility.

STARTING COLTS by Mike Kevil
168 pages and 400 photographs. Step-by-step process in starting colts.

THE HANK WIESCAMP STORY by Frank Holmes
208 pages and over 260 photographs. The biography of the legendary breeder of Quarter Horses, Appaloosas and Paints.

TEAM PENNING by Phil Livingston
144 pages and 200 photographs. How to compete in this popular family sport.

TEAM ROPING WITH JAKE AND CLAY by Fran Devereux Smith
224 pages and over 200 photographs and illustrations. Learn about fast times from champions Jake Barnes and Clay O'Brien Cooper. Solid information about handling a rope, roping dummies and heading and heeling for practice and in competition. Also sound advice about rope horses, roping steers, gear and horsemanship.

WELL-SHOD by Don Baskins
160 pages, 300 black-and-white photos and illustrations. A horse-shoeing guide for owners and farriers. Easy-to-read, step-by-step how to trim and shoe a horse for a variety of uses. Special attention is paid to corrective shoeing for horses with various foot and leg problems.

WESTERN TRAINING by Jack Brainard
With Peter Phinny. 136 pages. Stresses the foundation for western training.

WIN WITH BOB AVILA by Juli S. Thorson
Hardbound, 128 full-color pages. Learn the traits that separate horse-world achievers from also-rans. World champion horseman Bob Avila shares his philosophies on succeeding as a competitor, breeder and trainer.

Western Horseman, established in 1936, is the world's leading horse publication. For subscription information: 800-877-5278.
To order other *Western Horseman* books: 800-874-6774 • *Western Horseman*, Box 7980, Colorado Springs, CO 80933-7980.
Web site: **www.westernhorseman.com**.